BARBICAN ART GALLERIES IN ASSOCIATION WITH PHILIP WILSON PUBLISHERS, LONDON

THE WILDE YEARS

OSCAR WILDE & THE ART OF HIS TIME

EDITED AND WITH TEXT BY

TOMOKO SATO
LIONEL LAMBOURNE

INCLUDING ESSAYS BY

MERLIN HOLLAND

MICHAEL BARKER · JONATHAN FRYER · DECLAN KIBERD

Barbican Centre

This catalogue was first published in Great Britain
by Barbican Art Galleries in association with
Philip Wilson Publishers Limited, 143–149 Great Portland Street, London W1W 6QN
on the occasion of the exhibition
THE WILDE YEARS: OSCAR WILDE AND THE ART OF HIS TIME
BARBICAN GALLERY, BARBICAN CENTRE, LONDON
5 OCTOBER 2000 – 14 JANUARY 2001

British Library Cataloguing in Publication Data:
A catalogue record of this book is available
from the British Library
ISBN 0 85667 535 0 (paperback)
ISBN 0 85667 526 1 (hardback)

Printed in and bound in Italy by Società Editoriale Lloyd, Srl, Trieste
House editor: Michael Ellis

Frontispiece: *Oscar Wilde*, 1882
Photograph by Napoleon Sarony, Courtesy Merlin Holland, London

The exhibition was organised by Barbican Art Galleries:

EXHIBITION CURATORS: TOMOKO SATO AND LIONEL LAMBOURNE

EXHIBITION ADVISOR: MERLIN HOLLAND

EXHIBITION ORGANISER: LOUISE VAUGHAN

RESEARCH ADVISORS: JANE ROBERTS AND MICHAEL BARKER

CURATORIAL ASSISTANT: SOPHIE PERSSON

BOOK DESIGNED BY JONATHAN BARNBROOK, JASON BEARD AND MANUELA WYSS AT BARNBROOK
EXHIBITION DESIGNED BY JOE EWART AND NIALL SWEENEY FOR SOCIETY

THE WILDE YEARS: OSCAR WILDE & THE ART OF HIS TIME

is a sequel to the exhibition, *Diaghilev: Creator of the Ballets Russes*, which Barbican Art Gallery presented in 1996. The chief aim of such projects is to offer alternative thinking about the interpretation of the art and culture of our century by examining the ideas and the work of great creative personalities whose influences stretched across many disciplines of art.

Oscar Wilde, in exile in Paris, met Sergei Diaghilev in 1898. Both men had much in common – dynamic, charismatic personalities and multi-faceted work and achievements. Celebrated for his wit and flamboyant lifestyle, Wilde was a central figure in the fashionable societies of *fin-de-siècle* London and Paris. He was a great entertainer with virtuoso 'conversational' skill. He declared: 'The man who can dominate a London dinner table can dominate the world.' As the author of four successful society comedies including *An Ideal Husband* (1895) as well as controversial works such as the novel *The Picture of Dorian Gray* (1891) and the play *Salomé* (1893). Wilde is widely acknowledged today as a major figure of Anglo-Irish literature and the theatre. Much less known is the unique position he occupied in the visual arts and culture of the turn of the century.

Taught by two aesthetic champions of his time, John Ruskin and Walter Pater at Oxford, Wilde became a leading advocate of the Aesthetic Movement during the early 1880s. Often portrayed in an 'aesthetic' costume with a sunflower or a lily in his hand, Wilde was one of the most caricatured personalities in *Punch* and other popular magazines of that period. He was a dandy, a leader of popular fashion as well as a presenter of art who promoted the credo of 'Art for Art's Sake' and the ideas of 'The House Beautiful' amongst the general public on the both sides of the North Atlantic. Creative talents of the two artistic capitals of Europe, Paris and London, figured conspicuously in his intimate circles: the artists Aubrey Beardsley, Max Beerbohm, Jacques-Emile Blanche, Charles Conder, Charles Ricketts, William Rothenstein, John Singer Sargent and James McNeill Whistler; the writers André Gide, Stéphane Mallarmé, George Bernard Shaw and William Butler Yeats; and the actresses Sarah Bernhardt, Lillie Langtry and Ellen Terry. Through their interactions, new ideas and works were born to form a legend of the *fin de siècle.*

As Wilde defined himself in a famous passage of *De Profundis*, Wilde was 'a man who stood in symbolic relations to the art and culture of my age' and with his actions and work he 'awoke the imagination of my century so that it created myth and legend around me.' *The Wilde Years* attempts to show these 'symbolic relations' between Oscar Wilde and the art and culture of his time and how these relations contributed to the thinking of the twentieth century. In the exhibition Wilde plays a symbolic part as a central, catalytic, creative force linking the artistic movements of the closing decades of the nineteenth century. In terms of display, this kind of exhibition is a great challenge because Wilde himself was not a practising visual artist. Yet, through his lesser known works as an art critic, journalist and progressive thinker, we can see how Wilde formed his aesthetic theories; how he viewed and influenced his contemporary artists; and what were the central issues for him. Based on these criteria, the exhibition features paintings and other objects produced by the artists who had particular associations with Wilde.

Wilde died in Paris, in poverty, on 30 November 1900. At the time he was an outcast, scorned by society, with a criminal record for 'indecent acts'. Only five years before, Wilde had been at the height of his career accompanied by the phenomenal box-office success of his plays, *An Ideal Husband* and *The Importance of Being Earnest*, both on West-End stages. His conviction for homosexual activities and subsequent imprisonment abruptly terminated his career.

On the centenary of Oscar Wilde's death, *The Wilde Years* is a timely opportunity for the re-evaluation of his achievements. Especially, as we stand in the last year of the twentieth century, Wilde has a particular contemporary relevance for us. Wilde's radical attitude as a critic and his showmanship as a presenter of contemporary art finds a strong resonance in today's media-orientated art world. Wilde has also been identified as an iconic figure in the Gay Rights movement. Understanding Wilde's experience and his own views of his sexual orientation might give an another dimension to the direction of the recent debates about Section 28. Additionally, his Irish background, the influence of Irish oral traditions on his literary style and his political stance have been the subject of increasing scholarly attention recently.

Furthermore, both his dramatic works and his life itself have been a source of inspiration for film-makers, theatre directors, actors, writers and artists in recent decades, as evident in productions such as Steven Berkoff's *Salomé*; the recent film *Wilde* starring Stephen Fry; Corin Redgrave's one-person play *De Profundis*; the latest film version of *The Ideal Husband* as well as Peter Ackroyd's fiction *The Last Testament of Oscar Wilde* and Maggi Hambling's controversial sculpture. Finally, the imposing full-size wax sculpture (6 foot 3 inches) at Madame Tussaud affirms Wilde's status today as a popular cult figure. With this exhibition, we hope also to present Oscar Wilde as a modern man who stood as a bridge between Victorian moral values and those we share today.

In organising this exhibition we have been supported by a number of individuals and institutional colleagues. Our special thanks go to Merlin Holland, grandson of Oscar Wilde and Advisor to our project, whose in-depth knowledge and balanced view of Wilde were essential to the making of this re-appraisal. We are particularly indebted to Lionel Lambourne, Co-curator of the exhibition, whose expert knowledge about Victorian art and culture added great depths to our presentation.

We would also like to thank Michael Barker, Jonathan Fryer and Declan Kiberd who contributed to this book with stimulating articles, as well as Jane Roberts, who was a valuable link with French lenders.

Finally, we are very grateful for all the lenders to this exhibition and Resource: The Council for Museums, Archives and Libraries. Without their generosity and organisational support, we could not have materialised *The Wilde Years*.

TOMOKO SATO   JOHN HOOLE
CURATOR   DIRECTOR

BARBICAN ART GALLERIES

7

The title of this book, and accompanying exhibition, '*The Wilde Years*' is a pun on 'the wild years' with which the nineteenth century drew to a close, a time of radical changes and happenings. Indeed, the period that Oscar Wilde essentially belonged to – the 1880s and the 1890s – experienced striking developments in politics, economics, social and moral thinking as well as in artistic and cultural modes. It was the time when the British Empire reached its peak with the proclamation of Queen Victoria as Empress of India in 1877. Yet it also saw new political and social ideas which began to shake the traditional values of the Victorian establishment. In response to the increasing awareness of the working and living conditions of the underprivileged classes, there was a rapid spread of socialist ideas: a radical Marxist party, the Social Democratic Federation, was formed in 1881 and the more gentrified Fabian Society was founded in 1884. Also, it was during this period that the terms 'feminism' and 'homosexuality' first came into use, as New Women and male aesthetes redefined the conventional notions of gender roles.[1] The novelist George Gissing described this period as 'sexual anarchy', meaning the breakdown of the governing principles of sexual identity and behaviour.[2]

In art, alongside the tradition of Pre-Raphaelitism, there was the development of the Aesthetic Movement, which embraced not only 'High Art' but also decorative arts and popular culture. It was not about a single style of painting or design but about attitudes, individual aesthetic tastes and lifestyles. One of the most significant aspects of this movement was its underlying doctrine 'Art for Art's sake' and its implication: the assertion of the subjectivity of the artist and the independence of art from nature and social functions. As the French Symbolist poet Baudelaire believed – a belief also vigorously held by Whistler – beauty was not an inherent property of the object, but what the artist chose to bring to it. It was a time when the seeds of the concept of the '-isms' of modern art were sown, ideas and ideals which Wilde, a master of paradox, summed up in the last aphorism in 'The Preface' to *The Picture of Dorian Gray*: 'All art is quite useless'.

As Holbrook Jackson pointed out, it was also around this time that a new kind of art came into vogue: 'the art of shocking'.[3] It was primarily a desire to astonish the 'middle class', the authorities, or anyone that was considered to be unimaginative, uncreative and unchallenging. It was a process of 'individual' expression, and the ultimate purpose of such behaviour was to gain the attention of the public. In this new art, along with the actual art products, the artist's lifestyle and personality as *perceived* by the general public became the important components of his art. To be fashionable, to pose as a decadent dandy, to be different, to be outrageous – they were all necessary tactics to draw public attention and project the desired image. Wilde was one of the first to practice this art, and he put this process thus; asked about his 'walking down Piccadilly with a poppy or a lily in his mediaeval hand', the image perpetuated by Gilbert and Sullivan's *Patience*, Wilde said: 'To have done it was nothing, but to make people think one had done it was a triumph.'[4] This statement anticipates a key aspect of the publicity tactics employed by the media industry of our own time.

As we will see, the *Wilde Years* were the age of new ideas and the transition from the Victorian world to the twentieth century. This transition prepared all the modern values – social, political, ethical, cultural and artistic – that we share today. Through this book and the accompanying exhibition, we hope to portray the art and culture of this age and how they related to Oscar Wilde who believed: 'It is personalities, not principles, that move the age'.[5]

TOMOKO SATO   LIONEL LAMBOURNE

Notes

1   Elaine Shawalter, *Sexual Anarchy: Gender and Culture at the Fin de Siècle* (New York, 1990), p.3

2   Ibid

3   Holbrook Jackson, *The Eighteen Nineties: A Review of Art and Ideas at the Close of the Nineteenth Century* (2nd edition: Hassocks, Dublin 1976): Chapter VIII

4   *New York World*, 8 January 1882, quoted in Richard Ellman, *Oscar Wilde*, London, 1987

5   Quoted in Jackson, ditto, p.86

· Lenders to the EXHIBITION

BARBICAN ART GALLERIES WOULD LIKE TO THANK ALL THOSE LENDERS
LISTED BELOW, AND THOSE WHO WISH TO REMAIN ANONYMOUS.

Belgium

Musée Félicien Rops, Province de Namur

France

Musée Carnavalet, Paris

Musée des Arts Décoratifs, Paris

Musée Gustave Moreau, Paris

Musée Rodin, Paris

Republic of Ireland

Hugh Lane Municipal Gallery of Modern Art, Dublin

Italy

Gabinetto Disegni e Stampe degli Uffizi, Firenze

Japan

Suntory Museum, Osaka

Switzerland

Musée Cantonal des Beaux-Arts, Lausanne

United Kingdom

Aberdeen Art Gallery and Museums

Victor and Gretha Arwas, London

Visitors of the Ashmolean Museum, Oxford

Balliol College, University of Oxford

Birmingham Museums and Art Gallery

Bristol Museums and Art Gallery

Board of Trustees of the British Museum, London

Stephen Calloway, Brighton

Cheltenham Art Gallery and Museum

Tish Collins, London

Sheila Colman (The Lord Alfred Douglas Literary Estate), Lancing

The De Morgan Foundation, London

The Syndics of the Fitzwilliam Museum, Cambridge

Paul Grinke, London

Guidhall Art Gallery (Corporation of London)

Catherine Haill, London

Merlin Holland, London

Richard Hollis, London

Collection Barry Humphries, London

The Jersey Heritage Trust

Lionel Lambourne, London

Leeds City Art Galleries

The Maas Gallery, London

Manchester City Art Galleries

The Warden & Fellows of Merton College, University.of Oxford

Collection Andrew McIntosh Patrick Esq., London

William Morris Gallery (London Borough of Waltham Forest)

Mucha Trust, London

Board of Trustees of the National Portrait Gallery, London

Nottingham Castle Museum and Art Gallery

A Pope Family Trust, St Helier, Jersey

Julia Rosenthal, Oxford

The Royal Photographic Society, Bath

Ruskin Foundation (Ruskin Library, University of Lancaster)

Sheffield Galleries & Museums Trust

Sotheby's, London

Southampton City Art Gallery

Board of Trustees of the Tate Gallery, London

Tullie House Museum and Art Gallery, Carlisle

Board of Trustees of the Victoria and Albert Museum, London

The University of Wales, Aberystwyth

Walker Art Gallery, Liverpool (Board of Trustees of the National Museums and Galleries on Merseyside)

Trustees of the Watts Gallery, Compton, Guildford

Wightwick Manor, Staffordshire (The National Trust)

Simon Wilson, London

United States of America

Paul Jeromack and Robert Tuggle, New York

Mark Samuels Lasner, Washington, D.C.

The Toledo Museum of Art

Mr and Mrs Michael W. Wilsey, San Francisco

9

FROM Madonna Lily TO ✠

GREEN CARNATION

MERLIN HOLLAND

'In matters of grave importance, style, not sincerity is the vital thing'

(*The Importance of Being Earnest*, Act III)

Fig.1
Oscar Wilde, 1889
Photograph
by Downey
Courtesy
Mary Evans
Picture Library,
London

OSCAR WILDE:
PROFESSOR OF AESTHETICS OR THE FIRST DOCTOR OF

SPIN? Gifted and influential populariser of a new artistic creed or just a brilliant self-publicist, who, in the words of James McNeill Whistler (one-time friend and later arch-enemy) 'dines at our tables and picks from our platters the plums for the pudding he peddles in the provinces'?[1] A hundred years after his death the questions are still not easy to answer. His detractors maintain that he was merely a passing socio-cultural phenomenon who concealed nothing behind a mask of sparkling superficiality. By contrast, those who have taken the trouble to look behind the mask have discovered a modern thinker, bridging two centuries. In Wilde, they find an astute critic and commentator, a writer at odds with the stuffiness of his age and a man whose 'over-the-topness in knocking the bottom out of things', in Seamus Heaney's words, amused but finally enraged his tight-laced Victorian contemporaries.[2] The reality, as in most things Wildean, lies somewhere in between the views of his detractors and those of his admirers.

From an early age Wilde's learning in all things cultural was undoubtedly prodigious. His father, Sir William, was by profession a doctor, and by inclination a Victorian polymath whose interests ranged across the whole field of Celtic studies. As a teenager Wilde would accompany his father on archaeological field trips around Ireland, measuring, describing and even drawing artefacts and buildings. They were skills, together with his classical education, that he would later attempt to put to good use when he came down from Oxford, by applying for an archaeological studentship at Athens.[3] In the event he failed to get it, partly, one suspects, because a reputation for lacking in the requisite conformity had probably preceded him.

At Portora School, Enniskillen, apart from regularly scooping the classical awards, he twice won prizes for drawing, once at fifteen and once shortly before he left at seventeen. There still exists a tolerably good watercolour, painted later in 1876 from above the Wilde's country house on Lough Corrib for his girlfriend Florrie Balcombe. It survives as evidence of his artistic ability, though it is clear that he managed to transform the rolling hills of County Mayo into the foothills of the Alps; artistic exaggeration for effect was already alive and flourishing in the twenty-two-year-old Wilde.[4]

In 1871, at the age of seventeen, he won a scholarship to Trinity College Dublin, where he came under the influence of John Pentland Mahaffy, the Professor of Ancient History. Mahaffy, like his father was another polymath, and there was undoubtedly a strong paternal/filial element in their relationship. He had lived in Greece and saturated himself with Greek thought and Greek feeling, deliberately taking the artistic standpoint towards everything – a standpoint with which Wilde was becoming more and more in sympathy. Mahaffy's tutelage in classical culture, and Greek art and aesthetics in particular, was a debt which Wilde would still acknowledge nearly twenty years later at the height of his theatrical successes: 'My dear Mahaffy, I am so pleased you liked the play, and thank you for your charming letter, all the more flattering to me as it comes not merely from a man of high and distinguished culture, but from one to whom I owe so much personally, from my first and my best teacher, from the scholar who showed me how to love Greek things.'[5]

While at Trinity, the College offered a course in aesthetics which Mahaffy most probably would have encouraged Wilde to attend, particularly as in 1872 Mahaffy had published his first volume of commentary on Kant's *Critique of Judgement* entitled *The Aesthetic and the Analytic*. In the commentary, he defended the Kantian argument that there can be no strict mathematical definition of beauty in nature, art, poetry or music and that beauty was relative to taste. But, even if Wilde had not started on a formal study of Kant while he was in Dublin, he certainly did at Oxford three years later as his surviving college notebooks reveal.[6] More significantly,

Cat.189
George Frederic Watts
The Genius of Greek Poetry, c.1878

Mahaffy was also one of the most gifted conversationalists of his age and believed passionately in the educational value of informal verbal exchange in the development of his pupils' character and ideas. It would, therefore, be surprising if aesthetics had not been a subject of discussion between them and it would undoubtedly have been raised on the two vacation trips which they later made together to Italy and Greece in 1875 and 1877.

In 1874, without taking a degree, but with the coveted Berkeley Gold Medal for Greek in his pocket, Wilde left Trinity and went to up to Magdalen College, Oxford on a well-deserved scholarship. There, as a young man of decidedly artistic tastes and already confident in his youthful intellect, he found himself in the same close community as the two scholars he most wanted to meet – John Ruskin and Walter Pater.

Ruskin was the Slade Professor of Fine Art at the University when Wilde arrived and had already started to move away from the pure art history and criticism of his younger days to concentrate more on the social aspects of contemporary art and his somewhat idealised view of the craftsman finding fulfilment through doing work with a valid purpose. Wilde, having attended Ruskin's lectures on Florentine art in his first term, was soon persuaded to take part in his new mentor's practical beautification of the countryside, and found himself rising at dawn to help pave the Hinksey Marsh Road (Cat.152). The road to Hinksey, as Richard Ellmann so aptly puts it, was for Wilde the road to Ruskin and the reward was less in the toil than in the pleasure of breakfasting with Ruskin afterwards.[7] The enthusiasm, however, soon waned, the road sank back into the marsh but the friendship flourished. When Wilde sent him a copy of *The Happy Prince* (Cat.57) in 1888 he accompanied it with a note: 'The dearest memories of my Oxford days are my walks and talks with you and from you I learned nothing but what was good … There is in you something of prophet, of priest, and of poet.'[8]

Pater was less uplifting for the soul but dangerously attractive to the senses. Wilde had read his *Studies in the History of the Renaissance* (Cat.115) soon after his arrival in Oxford and found himself disturbingly attuned to its philosophies especially those in the 'Conclusion' in which Pater had written that 'Not the fruit of experience but experience itself is the end,' and continued: 'To burn always with this hard gem-like flame, to maintain this ecstasy, is success in life.' He also declared that enrichment of our given lifespan consisted of 'getting as many pulsations as possible into the given time,' and of having 'the desire for beauty, the love of art for its own sake.' Writing from prison, Wilde would refer to it as 'that book which has had such a strange influence over my life.'[9] There were echoes of Dorian Gray's total surrender to the poisoned perfection of the novel Lord Henry gives him in which 'The life of the senses was described in the terms of mystical philosophy.' There was a sense even of these two great figures of

12

Cat.85
Edward Kaiser,
after Giotto
*St. Francis
preaching to
the Birds*, 1877

his Oxford days, Ruskin and Pater, competing for the soul of the young 'Dorian Wilde', a struggle between two forces which would remain largely unresolved until the end of his life.

Each appealed to a different Wilde; Ruskin to the intellectual, the noble, the high minded; Pater, more insidiously, to the sensual, the decadent, the mystical. The excitement of new teachings, however, did not lead Oscar to abandon old friends and he still found time for Mahaffy, with whom he travelled to Italy in the summer of 1875. They visited Florence, Venice, Padua, Verona and Milan, where he decreed the cathedral 'an awful failure' but admired Bernardino's *Madonna* at the Brera Gallery and a seventh-century Irish manuscript at the Ambrosian Library. 'Venice,' he wrote to his mother, 'in beauty of architecture and colour is beyond description.' Ruskin's teaching had fired him with the desire to experience the Renaissance for himself, and his old tutor from Trinity had provided the opportunity. And if his letters home with their illustrations and rather precise descriptions smack a little too much of the West of Ireland field trips, there are the germs of later Wilde as he sat in the piazza San Marco watching the moon over the Giudecca reflected in the water. 'The scene was so romantic that it seemed to be an artistic "scene" from an opera,' he wrote to his

... BEAUTY IS THE ONLY THING THAT TIME CANNOT HARM ...

mother, presaging the argument of 'Life Imitating Art', which he would develop in 'The Decay of Lying' in 1889.[10]

Indirectly, Mahaffy also gave him the opportunity to meet the reclusive Walter Pater, to whom Wilde had still not been introduced by the end of his third year at Magdalen. Mahaffy led a second classical tour, this time to Greece, in the spring vacation of 1877, and as a result of an unscheduled week in Rome on his return Wilde was late back to Oxford, fined and rusticated for the rest of the academic year. Turning adversity to advantage, instead of going directly to Dublin he contrived to get himself invited to the opening of the Grosvenor Gallery in London and reviewed the exhibition for the *Dublin University Magazine* as his first piece of published prose. It was his début as an art critic and the subject was a controversial one.[11]

The Grosvenor Gallery was the inspiration of Sir Coutts Lindsay, himself an artist, who felt that the entrenched favouritism of the Royal Academy was beginning to stifle innovation in modern British Art. Many otherwise distinguished artists unwilling to subject themselves to the cliquish disfavour of the Academy's 'Hanging Committee' (in particular, Edward Burne-Jones) were hardly seen at all, and Lindsay's new gallery exhibited on the principle of invitation rather than submission and narrow-minded selection. It was a revolutionary idea with some revolutionary paintings (notably by James McNeill Whistler) and Wilde, after his brush with the college authorities, would have been in a suitably defiant mood to champion innovation against the Established Order.

13

Fig.2
Horace Harral
'The Grosvenor Gallery,
New Bond Street —
The Entrance'
From *The Graphic*,
19 May, 1877

14

The review was part laudatory, part critical, and in places couched in outspokenly sensual language, almost to the point that one could read a homoerotic flavour into the descriptions. Eros in Spencer Stanhope's *Love and the Maiden* is praised:

'His boyish beauty is of that peculiar type unknown in Northern Europe, but common in the Greek Islands, where boys can still be found as beautiful as the Charmides of Plato. Guido's *San Sebastian* in the Palazzo Rosso at Genoa is one of those boys and Perugino once drew a Greek Ganymede for his native town, but the painter who most shows the influence of this type is Corregio, whose lily-bearer in the Cathedral at Parma, and whose wild-eyed, open-mouthed St Johns in the 'Incoronata Madonna' of St Giovanni Evangelista, are the best examples in art of the bloom and vitality and radiance of this adolescent beauty.'

G.F. Watts' *Love and Death* (Cat.188) moves him to similar musings about the terror-filled eyes and quivering lips of 'Love, a beautiful boy with lithe brown limbs and rainbow-coloured wings, all shrinking like a crumpled leaf'. He compares the painting, 'in intensity of strength and in marvel of conception,' with the ceiling of the Sistine Chapel, an excess of enthusiasm which earned him a sharp smack on the wrist from *The Court Circular*, which said that the comparison was rather too much for the reader's nerves. The concept of love and beauty clouded by the presence of fear and death was a theme that was to run strongly through his fiction twelve years later.

Reading between the lines of the review, it is clear that there are several hidden agendas at work. Besides being a genuine, if somewhat gushing, expression of his views on contemporary artists, it was undoubtedly a double exercise in self-promotion and ingratiation. The twenty-two-year-old Wilde airs his learning and his continental travel in the manner of a long-established reviewer. He criticises Alma-Tadema for his inaccurate colouring of the Parthenon frieze, saying it is 'un-Greek' and that the artist seems more at home in the Greco-Roman art of the Empire and later Republic than he is in the art of the Periclean age. Wilde also contrives to drag in the fact that he had recently been in Italy by making reference, when discussing Whistler, to the latter's peacock ceiling. He mentions, quite incidentally, that another rather splendid one in mosaic had been done in Ravenna a thousand years before. The footnote, for that is what it is, finishes up, 'Mr Whistler was unaware of the existence of this ceiling at the time he did his own,' further implying that the two were personally acquainted.

He praises Burne-Jones and Holman Hunt (Cat.91), saying that they were the greatest masters of colour that England had produced with the single exception of Turner, which would have doubly pleased his mentor, Ruskin; he quotes Walter Pater on the subject of colour in the same paragraph, showing familiarity with Pater's essay on Botticelli; he makes a further appeal to Ruskin remarking that for all its mining districts and factories and vile deification of machinery, England has still produced some great masters of art; and he tops out the edifice almost sycophantically by referring to: '… that revival of culture and love of beauty which in great part

Cat.43
Edward Coley
Burne-Jones
*The Sleeping
Princess*, 1872–4

16

Cat.91
William Holman Hunt
The Afterglow in Egypt, 1854—63

Fig.3
James McNeill Whistler
*Nocturne in Black and Gold:
The Falling Rocket*, c.1875
The Detroit Institute of Arts,
Gift of Dexter M. Ferry, Jr.

17

'Worth looking at for about as long as one looks at a
real rocket, that is, for something less than a quarter
of a minute.' Oscar Wilde in his review of the first
Grosvenor Gallery exhibition, 1877

owes its birth to Mr Ruskin, and which Mr Swinburne and Mr Pater, and Mr Symonds and Mr Morris, and many others are fostering and keeping alive each in his own peculiar fashion.'

He also manages, with a considerable degree of skill, to side with Ruskin over Whistler's *Nocturne in Black and Gold* (Fig.3) – which Ruskin had famously described in his 18 June 1877 *Fors Clavigera* letter as 'flinging a pot of paint in the public's face', while still praising Whistler as 'an artist of great power when he likes'. Unlike Ruskin, who was broken by the ensuing libel suit for his remarks, Wilde trod carefully, knowing the expediency of *not* saying all that he may have felt.

As soon as the review was published, Wilde calculatingly sent a copy of it to Walter Pater, who replied with effusive praise and invited Wilde to call as soon as he was back in Oxford: 'The article shows that you possess some beautiful, and for your age, quite exceptionally cultivated tastes: and a considerable knowledge too of many beautiful things. I hope you will write a great deal in time to come.' [12] Pater had recognised in Wilde precisely the effect that Wilde had wanted to create, namely that the mode of expression as an art form was as important as the criticism itself. By hitching his wagon openly to the still rather nebulous Aesthetic Movement, Wilde had aligned himself with the new worshippers of beauty and their creed of Art for Art's Sake, realising that he could benefit from the increasing controversy which it was generating. A certain notoriety had already attended his widely reported remark at Oxford about how hard he was finding it to live up to his blue china, but Wilde aspired to higher things than notoriety in the provinces, and the Aesthetic Movement gave him the perfect vehicle for a temporary ride in the right direction.

When Wilde came down from Oxford he went to London and set up house with an artist friend, Frank Miles. Once more it was a calculated move since Miles was already established as a Society portrait painter of sorts and was able to effect valuable introductions, especially to Professional Beauties (P.B.s) such as

Lillie Langtry (Cats 116, 191), enabling Wilde to short-circuit the necessity of making the arduous social climb on his own. He attended one of Whistler's famous Sunday breakfasts and made himself sufficiently agreeable to be a regular guest. Ruskin and Pater were forced to yield temporarily to the new charms of the artist in person, and for a time Wilde found himself in the position of disciple to a very different master. Ruskin had preached the need for Art to be true to Nature; Whistler, by contrast, now insisted that the artist was in every way superior to Nature. Pater had seduced Wilde's mind with aesthetic theories and the sensual as well as the intellectual appreciation of art; Whistler abominated all aesthetes and their theorising. How, therefore, was Wilde to reconcile all that he had absorbed in the last eight years from his various mentors with the iconoclasm of his new teacher? Quite simply, he didn't. The fact that they all revered Art with a capital 'A' was common ground enough. He started to go his own way, taking with him the articles of baggage which most suited him, styled himself 'Professor of Aesthetics' and proclaimed that the secret of life is art to anyone who would listen. Lillie Langtry did, and Wilde became her adviser in matters cultural and sartorial. It was a mutually convenient relationship between two desperately ambitious individuals – she to improve her mind, he to improve his social connections.

In the spring of 1879, he once again reviewed the Grosvenor Gallery exhibition at which, as he said, 'we are enabled to see the highest development of the modern artistic spirit as well as what one might call its specially accentuated tendencies,' doubtless intended as a rather tongue-in-cheek reference to Whistler. On the one hand, he enthuses over Burne-Jones's *Annunciation* (Cat.44) and four pictures representing the legend of Pygmalion as 'works of the very highest importance in our aesthetic development'; on the other, he talks of 'Mr Whistler's wonderful and eccentric genius which is better appreciated in France than in England', and encourages his readers to appreciate *Harmony in Green and Gold*

18

Cat.116
Edward Poynter
Portrait of Lillie Langtry, 1878

'as an extremely good example of what ships lying at anchor on a summer evening are from the "Impressionist point of view"'. The praise was qualified but it was praise nonetheless. If he was setting himself up as an arbiter of the beautiful, Whistler, as the *enfant terrible* of the English art scene, needed to be considered rather than simply dismissed.[13]

Embracing the new, however, did not mean breaking with the old and part of the wait for recognition entailed hedging his bets and making sure that Society, for whatever reason, was constantly aware of his name. 'There goes that bloody fool Oscar Wilde,' someone remarked as he passed in the street. 'It's extraordinary how soon one gets known in London,' said Wilde to his companion. But recognition, albeit of a somewhat backhanded sort, came at the end of 1881 when he was invited by Richard D'Oyly Carte (Cat.173) to tour America to show the audiences of *Patience* one of the originals on which its satire was based. The relentless caricatures of *Punch*, in which he had appeared loosely as the aesthete Jellaby Postlethwaite, and the largely acid reception which had greeted publication of his collected poems in the middle of the year, ensured that he was the perfect candidate. The groundwork of three years had paid off: the money was good; the opening from national to international notoriety was timely; and the only risk was that of ridicule from the bluff, bustling New World. Wilde picked up the gauntlet, packed his velveteens, donned his fur coat and sailed.

The gospel that he took with him was only partly written by the time he arrived – in more senses than just the script. He had been billed as the spokesman for the Aesthetic Movement which, even before he left England, had aggravated those who were 'doing' rather than merely talking. Rossetti had rather tetchily accused Burne-Jones of 'taking up with the young man posing as the leader of the new aesthetic movement' and Wilde had yet to tie up the threads of what was still rather an amorphous artistic creed. He had somehow to show coherence and direction among the poets, painters, designers, architects and craftsmen of Britain. And he had to explain that their aim, apart from the quest after beauty for its own sake, had the added goal of eliminating ugliness in the everyday things of life, instead transforming them into graceful objects or materials for all to enjoy.

On his arrival in New York on 2 January 1882, he told reporters that aestheticism was a search for the beautiful, a science through which men look for the correlation that exists between painting, sculpture and poetry, which were simply different forms of the same truth, and, more exactly, it was a search for the secret of life.[14] It was all good heady stuff but sounded a little too close to the airy-fairy young men of *Patience* for down-to-earth America, and in the next week before his first appearance at Chickering Hall he attempted to give more formal structure to the vagueness. The lecture, which was to have been the main lecture of the tour, was 'The English Renaissance of Art'.[15] It was part homage, part plagiarism, part evangelism and spanned a good two thousand years of Western European Art and Literature. It was over-ambitious, over-long (nearly two hours) and it over-estimated the cultural background of his listeners. Whether it was his monotonous delivery, as reported, or the subject matter or both, even in New York the boredom was ill-concealed. The synthesis, too, between the Whistler/Rossetti school of creative art and the more down-to-earth applications of the decorative arts movement as championed by Morris and Ruskin lacked a certain cohesion. There were borrowings in Wilde's address from Ruskin, Morris and Pater, some almost verbatim, but in a sense it was of little concern.[16] What interested practical America was not what Wilde or anybody else had to say about the history of European thought, Hellenism and the birth of the Aesthetic Movement in the French Revolution, but rather what the New World should do about its own arts and crafts and how the Apostle of Beauty would advise Americans to decorate their homes.

Within a month the lecture had undergone a radical transformation to become 'The Decorative Arts' – shorter, simpler and altogether more appealing. Wilde fine-tuned the talk, adding appropriate anecdotes as he travelled around the country, and it became the main lecture for his American tour from mid-February onwards.[17] Once again, Wilde compromised to suit his marketplace. He may have been in America as the self-appointed spokesman for the Aesthetic Movement, but he was also there to further his own career. The changes were beneficial to lecturer and audience alike, showing a more creative Wilde, thrown back to a greater degree on his own ideas and experience.

His second lecture of the tour, 'The House Beautiful', was reserved for towns in which he had two engagements and frequently was given to predominantly female audiences. It reads in places like a Conran manifesto from the 1970s, advocating plain rather than heavy cut glass, the simple beauty of natural wood and, if you cannot afford the finest and most expensive in Persian rugs, put down elegant rush matting. Alongside the message of beauty and simplicity, there were elements of pure Ruskin: 'Nor will your art improve until you seek your workmen and educate them to higher views of their relation to art, and reveal to them the possibilities of their callings … all art must begin with the handicraftsman, and you must reinstate him into his rightful position, and thus make labour, which is always honourable, noble also.'[18]

The American tour, however, represented a watershed in the development of Wilde's views on art. Until then he had largely absorbed the ideas of others like a sponge, vaguely transforming them to suit his manifesto of the moment. But from this point he began to express himself with the confidence of one who has developed theories of his own. They were not strikingly original theories, but they were delivered with conviction by a man who was ambitious and to an audience that was receptive. And if reaching

The name of Dante Gabriel Rossetti is heard for the first time in the Western States of America. Time: 1882. Lecturer: Mr. Oscar Wilde.

Cat. 31
Max Beerbohm
*The Name of Dante
Gabriel Rossetti is
heard for the first
time in the Western
States of America,* 1916

21

Cat.108
William Morris
Foliage Tapestry,
c.1887

'Lord Bless us how nice it will be when I can get back
to my little patterns and dyeing, and the dear warp and
weft at Hammersmith'. William Morris, 1881

an audience meant taking the more popular approach of 'The Decorative Arts' rather than the intellectual theorising of 'The English Renaissance', then so be it.

On his return to England, after a few months in Paris, Wilde was pleased to find that his Transatlantic cultural antics had been widely reported in the British press, of which he immediately took advantage by arranging a series of similar lectures on home territory. One of the first was to the art students of the Royal Academy.[19] Back among the scalpel-wielding critics and those who felt he had usurped the power of his position, he could not allow himself the sort of outrageous statements that he had made in America, such as: 'Let me tell you how it first came to me at all to create an artistic movement in England, a movement to show the rich what beautiful things they might enjoy and the poor what beautiful things they might create.' Had he done so, he would have been howled out of the lecture hall.[20] Instead, to the art students he stated that he was not going to deal in abstract definitions or philosophies or histories of art but rather 'what makes an artist and what does an artist make.' The direct relevance of art to modern life had become his message.

Confident now that he had found the pulpit from which to preach, there was more than just a touch of the outrageous starting to creep into Wilde's pontification. His public at home, as it had been in America, was more interested in the present than in the past, so he added three new lectures to his repertoire – 'Personal Impressions of America', 'Dress' and 'The Value of Art in Modern Life' – which reflected his changing view of what would continue to make him badly-needed money and keep him in the public eye. In the first of these new talks he speaks somewhat slightingly of the American attitude to beauty, but also, a very long way now from Ruskin's criticisms of the industrial age and its 'vile deification of machinery', he enthuses quite unexpectedly over a feature of modern America:

'I have always wished to believe that the line of strength and the line of beauty are one. That wish was realised when I contemplated American machinery. It was not until I had seen the waterworks at Chicago that I understood the wonders of machinery; the rise and fall of the steel rods, the symmetrical motion of the great wheels is the most beautifully rhythmic thing I have ever seen.'[21]

Over the next five years Wilde's message remained broadly consistent: the application of a theory of beauty to any aspects of modern life where it was at all appropriate. In the autumn of 1884 he wrote to *The Pall Mall Gazette* criticising the tight-laced corset which had been defended by a reader as necessary for making her narrow waist from which to hang petticoats. 'The mistake,' he explained, 'lies in not suspending all apparel from the shoulders. The body is left free and unconfined for respiration and motion, there is more health, and consequently more beauty,' and in passing advocated a return to the broad brimmed hat and cloak of the

23

seventeenth century for men as being both more practical and aesthetic than the 'chimney-pot' hats and overcoats of the 1880s.[22]

In February 1885, Wilde's occasional sparring partner James McNeill Whistler, threw down a gauntlet in the form of his 'Ten O'Clock Lecture' in which he expounded his theories of art (Cat.193). In part, it was a thinly veiled attack on Wilde, whom he felt had appropriated many of his own ideas, in particular for his lecture to the art students.[23] Wilde reviewed it good-naturedly the following day, agreed with much that Whistler had said, in particular about Art for Art's Sake, the need to look *at* pictures rather than *through* them from some social or moral point of view, and the fallibility of Nature as a model. He took gentle exception, though, to the view that only painters were qualified to judge paintings, and that art had been debased by the dilettantes and the amateurs of the Aesthetic Movement, and those who had pressed it into practical service with the Arts and Crafts.[24] His review was followed by a brief skirmish between the two in the pages of *The World* with Wilde, in so many words, telling Whistler to stick to painting and leave the lecturing to him. There was as much mileage to be had out of a public dispute as there was out of giving public lectures.[25]

A year later, Wilde made another of his attempts to secure gainful employment (he had already made several, unsuccessfully, to

Cat.114
Bernard Partridge
*Portrait of James
McNeill Whistler,*
c.1890

**'What has Oscar in common with Art? except that
he dines at our tables and picks from our platters
the plums for the pudding he peddles in the
provinces. Oscar – the aimiable, irresponsible,
esurient Oscar – with no more sense of a picture
than of the fit of a coat, has the courage of the
opinions – of others!'. J.A.M Whistler, 1889**

become an Inspector of Schools) this time applying for the Secretaryship of the Beaumont Trust. The trust was a philanthropic body which was to open the People's Palace in the East End of London, providing higher education in the subjects of Art, Literature and Science to a section of the population that would otherwise have been denied it. In the letter of application, Wilde says sweepingly, 'since taking my degree, I have devoted myself partly to literature and partly to the spreading of art-knowledge and art-appreciation among the people.'[26] In the event he was not selected, and at this time one senses in Wilde an unexpressed concern at the lack of progress in his life. He had embraced the nebulous profession of what would probably be called today a 'style guru' and so had nothing to sell but a few ideas, and these ideas were now beginning to have a feeling of *déjà vu* about them.

The editorship of a magazine called *The Lady's World* came his way in 1887 and gave him a mouthpiece through which to talk to the newly emerging 'Modern Woman' on matters of literature, art and style generally. He even managed to persuade the publishers to change the title to *The Woman's World* before taking up the editor's chair, but the novelty of the work soon wore off. Then, with his last aesthetic gasp, he reviewed the closing lectures of the Arts and Crafts Exhibition in November 1888 – Morris on Tapestry (Cat.108), Symonds on Sculpture, Walker on Printing and Illustration and the legendary Cobden-Sanderson on Bookbinding – after which he simply felt it was time to move on.[27]

England, Wilde felt, was now ripe for shocking, so in January the following year he published an essay, the very title of which was guaranteed to get up the Victorian establishment's nose – 'The Decay of Lying'. It was essentially a plea for a return to artistic imagination in literature and the arts rather than the current vogue for realism. He criticises novels 'which are so life-like that no one can possibly believe in their probability' and further develops the 'Art for Art's Sake' theme even beyond the Whistlerian fallibility of Nature to suggest that far from Art imitating Life it is Life which imitates Art no less in literature than in painting:

'Nature is no great mother who has borne us. She is our creation. It is in our brain that she quickens to life. Things are because we see them, and what we see, and how we see it, depends on the Arts that have influenced us. At present, people see fogs, not because there are fogs, but because poets and painters have taught them the mysterious loveliness of such effects. There may have been fogs for centuries in London. I dare say they were. But no one saw them, and so we do not know anything about them. They did not exist till Art had invented them. Nobody of any real culture, for instance, ever talks nowadays about the beauty of a sunset. Sunsets are quite old-fashioned. They belong to the time when Turner was the last note in art. To admire them is a distinct sign of provincialism of temperament.'[28]

Wilde now had a new mission – to turn the established order upside down, and if there were a few eyebrows raised over the views in 'The Decay of Lying' it was nothing compared with the outcry which was raised over the application of those views eighteen months later when he published *The Picture of Dorian Gray*. It appeared to almost universal press condemnation. Phrases such as: 'a poisonous book, the atmosphere of which is heavy with the mephitic odours of moral and spiritual putrefaction,' abounded to Wilde's delight and gave him the opportunity to engage in a lengthy public debate about the question of Art and Morality. 'I am quite incapable of understanding how any work can be criticised from a moral standpoint. The sphere of art and the sphere of ethics are absolutely distinct and separate,' wrote Wilde, and continued, 'Good people, belonging as they do to the normal, and so, commonplace type are artistically uninteresting. Bad people are, from the point of view of art, fascinating studies. They represent colour, variety, strangeness. Good people exasperate one's reason; bad people stir one's imagination.'[29] It was an intolerably subversive point of view and Wilde found added pleasure in the idea that he was casting himself in the role of two of his favourite French authors, Baudelaire and Flaubert, both of whom had been charged with outraging public morality with their work.

From this moment on there was no holding Wilde back. Shortly after the appearance of *Dorian Gray* he published 'The Critic as Artist', in which he argued that, in his highest manifestation, the critic once freed from his subordinate role will become more creative than the artist himself. 'He will represent the flawless type. In him the culture of the century will see itself realised. You must not ask of him to have any other aim than the perfecting of himself.'[30] Whistler's reaction to the heresy seems to be unrecorded.

Then, with the banning of *Salomé* (Cat.95) from the stage in 1892 and its publication in English with Aubrey Beardsley's illustrations (Cat.15) in 1894, Wilde's reputation, which had been balanced on a razor's edge, finally went from that of flamboyant critic with revolutionary ideas on modern art and literature to that of purveyor of immorality and decadence which threatened the very foundations of Society itself. He had pushed his views on art to the limits of what the British could stand, and, to make his point, had published two works of fiction which were seen as an offence to public decency. The following year *Dorian Gray* would be cited in his libel case against the Marquis of Queensberry as 'an immoral and obscene work designed to describe the relations intimacies and passions of certain persons of sodomitical and unnatural habits tastes and practices' and 'was calculated to subvert morality and to encourage unnatural vice.'[31]

Oscar Wilde's wish that he had expressed so long before at Oxford – 'that if he couldn't be famous he would be notorious'[32] – finally came true, but the price of asking art to metamorphose from the Renaissance purity of the Madonna lily to the monstrous

Fig.4
Oscar Wilde
From *The Sketch*,
19 January, 1895
Courtesy Mary Evans
Picture Library, London

unnatural green carnation of the *fin de siècle*, which will ever be associated with him, was ultimately and indirectly the cost of his life.

The pursuit of Art to Oscar Wilde was the pursuit of life itself.
Occasionally it was his master, more often he tried to make it his
slave. He undoubtedly used it as a means of self-advancement, and
later as a vehicle for rebellion, but there was also a genuine, almost
a passionate belief in its life-enriching quality which he found
words to describe and which has left us with some of his most
intriguing and paradoxical writing. That he had a philosophy of
art is clear, but whether that philosophy was consistent is open
to interpretation. Perhaps he would have persuaded us that it was,
but with Wilde appearances are not what they seem. As he summed
up at the end of his essay 'The Truth of Masks':

'Not that I agree with everything that I have said in this essay.
There is much with which I entirely disagree. The essay simply
represents an artistic standpoint, and in aesthetic criticism attitude
is everything. For in art there is no such thing as a universal truth.
A Truth in art is that whose contradictory is also true. And just
as it is only in art-criticism, and through it, that we can apprehend
the Platonic theory of ideas, so it is only in art-criticism, and
through it, that we can realise Hegel's system of contraries. The
truths of metaphysics are the truths of masks.'[33]

Notes

1 James Whistler, *The Gentle Art of Making Enemies* (1882), p.164.

2 Seamus Heaney address at the unveiling of Wilde's memorial window in Poets' Corner, Westminster Abbey, 14 February 1995.

3 Letter to Professor A. H. Sayce, 8 December 1879, in *The Complete Letters of Oscar Wilde* (2000).

4 Reproduced in Merlin Holland, *The Wilde Album*, (1997).

5 Letter to J. P. Mahaffy ?April 1893, in *Letters.*

6 *Oscar Wilde's Oxford Notebooks*, ed. Michael Helfand and Philip Smith (1989).

7 Richard Ellmann, *Oscar Wilde* (1987), p.48.

8 Letter to John Ruskin June 1888 in *Letters.*

9 Letter (known as *De Profundis*) to Lord Alfred Douglas January – March 1897 in *Letters.*

10 Letters to Lady Wilde, 23 and 24 June 1875, in *Letters.*

11 In the *Dublin University Magazine*, July 1877. It was reprinted in *Miscellanies*, vol. 14 of the 1908 *Collected Works*, pp.5–23.

12 Quoted by Wilde in his letter to William Ward, 19 July 1877, in *Letters.*

13 *Saunders' Irish Daily News*, 5 May 1879, reprinted in *Miscellanies.*

14 *New York World*, 3 January 1982.

15 Published in Miscellanies, pp.242–77.

16 See Ernst Bendz, *The Influence of Pater and Matthew Arnold in the Prose Writings of Oscar Wilde* (1914), pp.30–31.

17 *Complete Works of Oscar Wilde* , London, 1999, pp.926–7.

18 *Complete Works*, p.913.

19 Published in *Miscellanies*, pp.309–21

20 *Buffalo Courier*, 9 February 1882.

21 *Complete Works*, p.938.

22 Letter to *The Pall Mall Gazette*, 14 October 1884, reprinted in *Letters*

23 Whistler, *The Gentle Art*, pp.131–59.

24 Mr Whistler's Ten O'Clock' in *Miscellanies*, p.63.

25 Whistler, *The Gentle Art*, pp.161–3.

26 Letter to the Secretary of the Beaumont Trust, 22 February 1886, in *Letters.*

27 These reviews appeared in *The Pall Mall Gazette* throughout November and were reprinted in *Miscellanies*, pp.93–105.

28 *Complete Works*, p.1086.

29 Letter to the *St James's Gazette*, 26 June 1890, reprinted in *Letters*

30 *Complete Works*, p.1149.

31 *The Trials of Oscar Wilde*, ed. H. Montgomery Hyde (1948), p.344.

32 David Hunter Blair, 'Oscar Wilde as I Knew Him' in *The Dublin Review*, July 1938, pp.90–105.

33 *Complete Works*, p.1173.

Cat.19
Aubrey Beardsley
Salome;
The Woman in the Moon, 1894
From *A Portfolio,* published in 1906

27

OSCAR WILDE AND POPULAR CULTURE

LIONEL LAMBOURNE

For many young people, the year after taking a degree and leaving University is a disturbing time in which life may lack clear goals. The Academic process gives way to the mundane but challenging task of finding an occupation and making a reputation for oneself. Often it is the particularly brilliant students who find this task most difficult, and many never recover from the glamour of winning a First Class Degree. Even Oscar Wilde, who graduated aged twenty four from Oxford with a First in Greats and the Newdigate Prize for his poem *Ravenna*, toyed with the idea of becoming, like Matthew Arnold, an inspector of schools, before abandoning such worthy academic leanings. With apparently effortless ease, by publishing poems and reviewing art exhibitions, he became a leading figure in the Aesthetic Movement, then closely identified with the fashionable Grosvenor Gallery. There, Wilde became a prominent figure at private views, learning to charm society with his conversation and astonish it with his long hair, velvet jackets, knee breeches and striking button-holes of orchids.

Paradoxically, Wilde's aesthetic lifestyle was also to be inextricably linked with the popular culture of his era. He became a universally recognised figure, thanks to a never ceasing series of lampoons on the stage, in comic journals and in popular songs, and the use of his likeness in advertising. His popular image was achieved by means of photo shoots and press interviews, which, though common journalistic practices today, were novel methods at the time. Whatever Wilde did had the magic quality of providing 'good copy' for the papers and magazines, never failing to add spice to a dull week.

This particularly applied to the weekly issues of the comic journal *Punch*. For its writers and cartoonists, the then fashionable Aesthetic Movement, with its exaggerated hyperbole of language and the bizarre costumes worn by its adherents, provided an ideal target. What on earth, asked the editors on behalf of their philistine readership, did the word aestheticism mean?

How did it come to be applied to 'the worship of the lily and the peacock's feather'?

To make fun of these targets before Wilde's advent on the scene, the cartoonist George Du Maurier (pp.102–3) of *Punch* created a series of caricatures not of individuals but of types. He invented an aesthetic family, the Cimabue Browns, and their friends the dilettantes, Mr and Mrs Ponsonby De Tomkins. They all deeply

Fig.5
George Du Maurier
The Six-Mark Teapot
From *Punch*,
30 October, 1880

admire, with an affected use of language, the painter Reginald Maudle (painter of maudlin and sentimental love agonies) and the poet Jellaby Postlethwaite, whose works possess thinly veiled 'coded' references to the poetry of Algernon Swinburne, the criticism of Walter Pater, and the paintings of Rossetti, Simeon Solomon, Whistler and Walter Crane.

Amongst the funniest aesthetic cartoons are those that appeared in *Punch* between 1874 and October 1880 ridiculing the craze for collecting blue and white china. One of the most famous was the first to be inspired by a remark credited to Wilde as an undergraduate at Oxford: 'I find it harder and harder every day to live up to my blue china'. Just why these flippant words should have so scandalised the university is a mystery, but it provoked criticism from the pulpit of St Mary's, Oxford, where Dean Burgess denounced a time when:

'… a young man says not in polished banter, but in sober earnestness, that he finds it difficult to live up to the level of his blue china, there has crept into these cloistered shades a form of heathenism which it is our bounden duty to fight against and to crush out, if possible.'

From such promising early notoriety reputations are made, and soon the aphorism became widely celebrated by Du Maurier's cartoon *The Six-Mark Teapot* which appeared in *Punch*, 30 October 1880. The cartoon depicts an affected newly married couple. The Aesthetic Bridegroom speaks:

'It is quite consummate is it not?
The Intense Bride replies:
'It is, indeed! Oh, Algernon, let us live up to it!' (Fig.5)

Life imitating art in this way may well have given Du Maurier pause for thought. Had he, like an aesthetic Doctor Frankenstein, created a monster from his figures of fun, Maudle and Postlethwaite, which had taken the form of Oscar Wilde?

Other much publicised incidents were Wilde's presentation of bunches of lilies to the great actress Sarah Bernhardt (Cats 38, 47) and the fashionable beauty Lillie Langtry (Cats 116, 191), who was busy conquering London with her looks, just as Oscar was with his wit. These events prompted several cartoons by Du Maurier in *Punch*, notably *An Aesthetic Midday Meal*, 17 July 1880, in which Postlethwaite contemplates a lily in a glass of water in lieu of lunch. Again, the cartoon was prompted by a report of Wilde, about which he later remarked: 'To have done it was nothing, but to make people think one had done it was a triumph'.

Again and again, over the next fifteen years *Punch* would turn to Oscar Wilde for copy. The *Punch* review of 23 July 1881 criticised Wilde's first volume of poems as 'Swinburne and Water' but praised the book's appearance: 'the cover is consummate, the paper is distinctly precious, the binding beautiful and the type is utterly too'. *Punch* was not alone in singling out Wilde as a satiric subject, for comic dramatists also used Wilde extensively as a comic butt. On 20 November 1880, *Where's the Cat?* opened in London with a character based on Wilde, followed by the even more successful *The Colonel* in February 1881, which was to run for over a year. But both these shows were eclipsed by the triumphant opening, in April 1881, of Gilbert and Sullivan's operetta *Patience*.

Bunthorne, the central character of *Patience*, is based on an amalgam of Wilde's personality with characteristics from Walter Crane and Whistler, while in the character of Grosvenor, Rossetti's soulfulness, Swinburne's sensuality and Ruskin's Gothicising were all parodied. But the public closely identified the character Bunthorne with Wilde's charismatic personality.

In Act I Bunthorne sings:

'Though the philistines may jostle, you will rank as an apostle
   in the high aesthetic band,
If you walk down Piccadilly with a poppy or a lily in your
   mediaeval hand.'

Wilde's later life can, with hindsight, be seen as one long jostle with the philistines, but for the moment he could enjoy the glamour of being the leader of what Queen Victoria trenchantly described as:

'the foolish aesthetic people who dress in such an absurd manner, with loose garments, large puffed sleeves, great hats and carrying peacock's feathers, sunflowers and lilies'.

Although he had a popular hit on his hands, the impresario Richard D'Oyly Carte (Cat.173) was perturbed by a review that noted how many of the jokes had passed over the heads of even the worldly first night London audience. Carte sensed that the theme of aestheticism needed explanation to the American public when *Patience* opened in New York on 22 September 1881, five months after its London première.

The idea of a lecture tour of America by the new laureate of aesthetic values was put forward by D'Oyly Carte, who also had business interests in running such events, popular since the exciting readings given by Charles Dickens in 1867–8. Oscar Wilde, still in his mid-twenties, was a new star worth promoting, and his tour would also help *Patience* to succeed in America. Colonel Morse, the

People are going "Wilde,"
(not Oscar)
over our Æsthetic designs in
WALL PAPERS.

HEGAN BROS.,
348 Fourth Avenue,
LOUISVILLE, KY.

"Conceive me, if you can,
A matter-of-fact young man,
An alphabetical, arithmetical,
Every-day young man!"
PATIENCE.

Cat.200d
'Aesthetic' advertisement:
'People are going "Wilde"
over our Aesthetic designs
in WALL PAPERS',
early 1880s

'Aesthetic' advertisements:

Left and right:
Cat.200k and l
'Use Garland Stoves & Ranges',
early 1880s

Centre:
Cat.200j
'Strike me with a Sun Flower',
early1880s

Below:
Cat.200e
'Warner Bros. Coraline Corsets,
The Latest Aesthetic Craze',
early 1880s

32

Fig.6
Oscar Wilde
Photograph by
Napoleon Sarony, 1882
Courtesy Merlin Holland,
London

American representative of Richard D'Oyly Carte, made the initial approach to Wilde, reporting back: 'Wilde is slightly sensitive, but I don't think appallingly so … I told him he must not mind my using a little bunkum to push him in America.'

Wilde himself was aware of the need for 'a little bunkum' and began to plan what to *wear*. This proved a problem, for Wilde's initial foray to a furrier from which he emerged wearing 'a befrogged and wonderfully befurred green overcoat' and a Polish cap, was observed by a vigilant Whistler, who screeched in a letter (published in *The World*), 'OSCAR, – How dare you! What means

this unseemly carnival in my Chelsea! Restore these things to Nathans … [the theatrical costumier]'.

Undeterred, Wilde sailed for New York on Christmas Eve, arriving on 2 January 1882 to a rapturous social reception, before embarking on the gruelling schedule of 140 lectures in 260 days from 'sea to shining sea' with additional visits to Canada.

Before Wilde left New York, Morse arranged an appointment for him at the studio of Napoleon Sarony (1821–96), a specialist in the photography of theatrical personalities. The photographer, himself a flamboyant personality, had found fame with his portrait

of the famed actress Ada Isaac Menken as Mazeppa, clad in a flesh-coloured body stocking, an image which made the pulses of mid-Victorian gentlemen race. Sarony was reputed to have posed and photographed thousands of actors and actresses, and was praised by the *New York Times* as being 'a master of composition, without a rival in the arrangement of subjects and settings'. Wilde looks every inch a star in the series, completely relaxed and at ease in the studio, clearly enjoying posing in what became one of the most famous early photo shoots. The set of around twenty-seven images retain an arresting immediacy, for looking at them we know Oscar Wilde in a way that cannot be paralleled by any other famous figure before this date. Many of the photographs show him wearing his new fur coat, to which he became as devoted as a child with a security blanket. Years later he tried to find it when in Reading Gaol writing of it: 'it was all over America with me, it was at all my first nights, it knows me perfectly, and I want it'.

Wilde's likeness lent itself to the process of advertising campaigns and was used to sell soap, hosiery, sewing machines, aesthetic corsets, cigars, a bosom beautifier and even stoves, as this little jingle reveals:

'Aesthetic stoves are all the style
Some very tame, some very "Wilde".'

Colonel Morse, like Colonel Parker, who shaped the career of Elvis Presley in more recent times, devised a series of engagements that led to Wilde crossing and recrossing America with the velocity of a twentieth-century pop star. His journeys took him from New York to San Francisco, and from McDonald's Opera House, Montgomery, Alabama to Leadville, Colorado, in the Rocky Mountains. There, in Colorado, Wilde enjoyed his famous encounter with the miners:

'I spoke to them of the early Florentines, and they slept as though no crime had ever stained the ravines of their mountain home.'

Because they mined for silver he read them passages from the autobiography of Benvenuto Cellini, the great Renaissance metal worker:

'I was reproved by my hearers for not having brought him with me. I explained that he had been dead for some little time which elicited the enquiry, "Who shot him?"

In a corner of the Casino, Wilde found a pianist, 'sitting at a piano over which was this notice "Please don't shoot the pianist; he is doing his best", I was struck with this recognition of the fact that bad art merits the penalty of death, and I felt that in this remote city, where the aesthetic applications of the revolver were clearly established in the case of music, my apostolic task would be much simplified, as indeed it was.' [1]

Back in England, after spending the profits from the tour in Paris, Wilde must have relished his role as the central figure in Frith's famous picture of *The Private View of the Royal Academy, 1881* (Cat.84), which was one of the main talking points of the Academy show in 1883.

In this detail of Frith's painting, Oscar Wilde wearing a lily is surrounded by a circle of admirers including Ellen Terry and Sir Henry Irving depicted just over Wilde's left shoulder. To their right is the bearded figure of the caricaturist George Du Maurier, the Punch satirist of the Aesthetic Movement, and the moustached figure of the journalist George Augustus Sala wearing a red tie and a white waistcoat. In the complete composition (p.34), on the extreme right can be seen the top-hatted figure of Millais, and on the extreme left the novelist Anthony Trollope. Behind a group of Aesthetic Ladies is the poet Robert Browning. Gladstone is seen in the centre of the picture with his back to Lord Leighton, the President of the Royal Academy who bends his head to talk to some seated ladies. Nearby is the 'society beauty' Lillie Langtry.

36

Right:
Cat.46
Jules Chéret
*La Danse du Feu, La Loïe
Fuller Folies Bergère*,1893

Below:
Fig.7
Phil May
Britons in Paris,1891
from the *Phil May Album*

The Morris advertising column so admired by Oscar
Wilde was invented in 1860 by Gabriel Morris as a
means of displaying playbills, and became a feature of
Baron Haussmann's 'grand boulevards'. The interiors
were used by street sweepers to store their equipment.

In his pompous but amusing memoirs written in 1888, Frith recalled his desire to record 'for posterity the aesthetic craze as regards dress. I wished to hit the folly of listening to self-elected critics in matters of taste, whether in dress or art. I therefore planned a group, consisting of a well-known apostle of the beautiful, with a herd of eager worshippers surrounding him. He is supposed to be expounding his theories to willing ears, taking some picture on the Academy walls for his text.'

Frith then lists exhaustively the names of other sitters 'celebrities of all kinds, statesmen, poets, judges, philosophers, musicians, painters, actors, and others'. He continues:

'I received the kindest assistance from all these eminent persons, many of whom came to me at great sacrifice of time and engagements … Pictures composed of groups of well known people are always very popular at the Academy, and *The Private View* was no exception to that rule, a guard being again found necessary to control the crowds of visitors … the sixth painting by me that has received this special compliment.'

Wilde must surely have relished the cartoon by Harry Furniss that appeared in *Punch* on 12 May 1983 satirising Frith's painting as a Salvation Army Sunday meeting to which 'A number of celebrities have brought their hymn books … and are joining heart and soul in a hymn, which is being led by the aesthete Mr Oscar Wilde.'

It would be fascinating to know what Wilde's views were on being painted by Frith, the most popular artist of the day. He would surely have been flattered at being featured at the centre of the high society of the good and the great to which Wilde so passionately wished to belong. As an aesthete, however, Wilde shunned Frith's works, and his only surviving comment on the artist came years later in 1890 in *The Critic as Artist*, in which one character remarks about Frith: 'it seems that a lady once gravely asked the remorseful Academican … if his celebrated picture of "A Spring-Day at Whitely's" or "Waiting for the Last Omnibus", or some subject of that kind, was all painted by hand? … To which the response comes "And was it?"'.

Short of funds once again, Wilde began a new series of lectures right across the British Isles in 1883–4, making just as many appearances as in the USA but for far less money – 'ten to twenty-five guineas per night is all they will pay'. His lecture themes included not only *The House Beautiful* and *Dress* but also *Personal Impressions of America.*

Marriage, with its new responsibilities, led to Wilde abandoning the constant travelling involved with lecturing and, instead, he tried the world of journalism. In 1887, he become the editor of a year-old shilling monthly magazine entitled *The Lady's World*, a title which he democratically changed to *The Woman's World*. For two years he coped with the problems of spring bonnets and tea gowns, while his own dress became less aesthetic but just as elegant. Nevertheless,

Wilde always retained his sympathy for the larger-than-life personalities of the American world of showmanship. Walter Crane in 1887 recalled Oscar Wilde pronouncing a eulogy of 'Buffalo Bill' (Colonel William Cody, 1845–1917):

'who was rather a lion of the season when he and his cowboys first appeared on the wild prairies of Earl's Court … Wilde took us to visit the Colonel in his tent after one of the performances, greatly to the delight of our two boys, who examined his rifles and trophies with keen interest, and afterwards endeavoured to improvise a sort of 'Wild West' of their own …'.

In early December 1891, Wilde wrote from Paris praising: 'the charming kiosks that decorate Paris (Fig.7); institutions, by the way, that I think we should introduce into London. The kiosk is a delightful object, and when illuminated at night from within, as lovely as a fantastic Chinese lantern, especially when the transparent advertisements are from the clever pencil of M.Chéret.' [2] A fine example of Chéret's work is provided by a full-colour poster of Loïe Fuller performing her famous *Fire Dance* on a sheet of glass illuminated from below (Cat.46). Loïe Fuller (1862–1928) was the most innovative and original dancer of her time. Her impact on the visual and literary arts was profound. In 1896 she cashed in on the interest aroused by the first production of Wilde's *Salomé* on 11 February 1896. Loïe Fuller devised her own spectacular balletic version of the theme, captured in George de Feure's March 1895 poster (Cat.61). Not unnaturally, Wilde seems to have deeply disliked this production.

Wilde once quoted with approbation an epigram by the novelist Ouida: 'When Society is aware that you think it a flock of geese, it revenges itself by hissing loudly behind your back.' During the 1890s, the hissing began to take the form of an increasing output of reportage – very much akin to the knowing innuendoes of today's *Private Eye* – which began to be published in such journals as *Pick-Me-Up*, in which on 22 September 1894 a caricature of Wilde by Max Beerbohm appeared.

Years later, Beerbohm regretted that, 'when it was published, I hardly realised what a cruel thing it was: I only realised that after Oscar's tragedy and downfall.' Before making the drawing, Beerbohm made these verbal notes: 'luxury – gold-tipped matches – hair curled – Assyrian – wax statue – huge rings – fat white hands – not soignée – malmaison – catlike tread – heavy shoulders – enormous dowager – or schoolboy-way of laughing with hands over mouth – stroking chin – looking up sideways – jollity overdone – But real vitality – Effeminate, but vitality of twenty men. Magnetism – authority – Deeper than repute or wit – Hypnotic.'

This vivid picture of a man indiscriminatingly eager for adulation or notoriety, who enjoyed the central spotlight playing on him, slowly changed throughout the tragic events of 1895, when Wilde's name was seldom out of the headlines. Any account of Wilde and popular culture must come to terms with the crude

38

'I walked, with other souls in pain,
Within another ring,
And was wondering if the man had done
A great or little thing,
When a voice behind me whispered low,
"That fellow's got to swing"

Like ape or clown, in monstrous garb
With crooked arrows starred,
Silently we went round and round,
The slippery asphalt yard;
Silently we went round and round,
And no man spoke a word.'

In these moving verses, the once vainglorious Oscar Wilde, High Priest of 'Cultchah', abandoned all affectation and used a most direct form of language to create a poem which played its part in the long process of penal reform – a process that led to the Prison Act of 1898 and, eventually, to the abolition of capital punishment in 1964. Ten years earlier in 1954, a plaque had been erected on Wilde's house in Tite Street, and in 1995 a memorial window was unveiled in Poet's Corner in Westminster Abbey.

At last, Oscar Wilde had found his permanent niche in popular esteem.

woodcuts of the hostile witnesses Charles Parker, William Parker, or Alfred Wood, which illustrated sensational tabloids such as the *Illustrated Police Budget*. This journal also showed such scenes as *The arrest of Wilde in the Cadogan Hotel*, *The Closing Scene at the Old Bailey* (Fig.8) and the indignity of Wilde undergoing a prison haircut after his final trial and conviction.

These popular images convey the grubby immediacy of the trials with brutal directness but, ironically, it is Frith's work to which we turn for an image that reminds us most vividly of Wilde's years in prison. In his Hogarthian series *The Race for Wealth*, 1880, Frith wished to illustrate '… the common passion for speculation, and the destruction that so often attends the indulgence of it.' His fraudulent financier is based on the career of the entrepreneur Baron Albert Grant.[3] In the fifth painting of the series, *Retribution* (Cat.83), the confidence trickster is portrayed at exercise in the yard of Millbank Prison, site of what was to become the Tate Gallery! With his usual thoroughness, Frith obtained the permission of the Prison Governor to paint the scene. The subject inevitably recalls Wilde's own experience while exercising in the prison yard when a fellow convict whispered to him, 'I am sorry for you: it is harder for the likes of you than it is for the likes of us'.

Wilde's most traumatic prison experience took place in Reading Gaol on 7 July 1896 when a Trooper in the Royal Horse Guards, Charles Thomas Wooldridge, was hanged for the murder of his wife, whose throat he had cut. The poem which commemorates this event was written in Dieppe between May and July 1897. Of its creation, Wilde wrote 'I, of course, feel that the poem is too autobiographical … it was wrung out of me, a cry of pain, the cry of Marsyas, not the song of Apollo.' *The Ballad of Reading Gaol* was Wilde's swan song, his last great literary message to posterity. To convey this message, he adopted the popular ballad form, so often used in the broadsheets to describe the 'last dying words and confessions' of notorious criminals.[4]

Notes

1   Wilde letter to Mrs Bernard Beere, *Letters of Oscar Wilde*, ed Rupert Hart-Davis, pp. 111–12, London (1962).

2   Wilde letter to the editor of the *Speaker* magazine, *Letters of Oscar Wilde* ibid, p. 300, London (1962).

3   Grant's career also inspired Anthony Trollope's novel *The Way We Live Now* (1875).

4   Ironically, two broadside style ballads of this type had appeared in London after the trials symptomatic of prejudiced, homophobic rejoicing at Wilde's comeuppance. The ballads made fun not only of Wilde's defence of 'the love that dare not speak its name' but also his plight at being made to 'climb the golden stairs of the treadmill' on a diet of prison skilly.

Fig.8
Closing Scene at the Old Bailey –
Trial of Oscar Wilde
From *The Illustrated Police News,* 4 May, 1895
Courtesy The British Library, London

✦ ANARCHIST ATTITUDES ✦

Oscar Wilde

◆ ◆ ◆ ◆ ◆ ◆ ◆ ◆ ◆ ◆

DECLAN KIBERD

The Wilde family were social anthropologists by nature. If Sir William did his research among the duns of Aran, his famous son studied a rather different set of pre-historic ruins, the English upper class. Oscar Wilde anatomised his host society with its own favoured instrument, the 'Higher Criticism'. He employed figures drawn from the upper class as *dramatis personae* in his attempt to imagine a Utopian community, much as John Millington Synge would use the peasants of the Aran Islands a few years later. Synge is rightly praised for exposing himself to poverty and physical hardship, but Wilde was also a broker in risk, attempting to sketch the lineaments of an ideal society out of such unpromising materials. Both men were in flight from the chloroformed world of Protestant Dublin's professional class. And, in the course of their paths through Utopia, they discovered surprising affinities between the Irish peasantry and English aristocracy: a love of leisure, a

heightened sensitivity to the promises of language, a belief in beauty above utility and a sense that there is always plenty of time.

The drawing-room figures of Wilde's dramas are really the vagrants and rogues of nineteenth-century Irish writing brought indoors and civilised: and the play is the zone where the values of the old Gaelic and modern English aristocracies meet. What is under attack in both literatures is the imaginative narrowness of the new middle class. For the exponents of 'lying', wickedness is just another myth concocted by puritans to account for the curious attractiveness of others. The language of that middle class was mainly utilitarian; only the outcast and the aristocrat seemed attuned to the heightened promises of a poetic language.

If medieval tyrants had the rack, the puritan bullies of the nineteenth century employed the press to enforce conformity. By documenting its collective follies with such clarity in print, that middle class made Wilde's work so much easier: 'by giving us the opinions of the uneducated, it keeps us in touch with the ignorance of the community'.[1] His own witticisms are often no more than 'the inversion of the language of the press', a way of annoying the newly-literate public.[2] His counter-aphorisms ('all bad art springs from genuine feeling') are mockeries of English sincerity made in an oral style which wars on the decorum of the merely writerly.

One example of this false decorum was the manner in which fairy tales had been transformed within a couple of generations, from a subversive, underground, largely oral lore directed at adults, to sentimental, overground, printed narratives aimed at the moral improvement of Victorian children. Wilde's fairy tales are intended, perhaps mainly, for adults, but for children too. He had heard some of them from poor women — patients of his father in the Dublin surgery: unable to pay in cash, they offered a good story instead.[3] What the tales have in common is a strong sense of the subversive nature of the story of Jesus, especially when taken literally by children. The equation of the Irishman with the child in Victorian

Fig.9
A scene from
The Importance of Being Earnest (1909):
George Alexander
as Jack Worthing,
Stella Patrick Campbell
as Lady Gwendolen,
Helen Rouse as
Lady Bracknell
Courtesy Mary Evans
Picture Library, London

Cat.29
Max Beerbohm
*Mr W.B.Yeats, presenting
Mr George Moore to the
Queen of the Fairies*, 1904

41

thinking was based on the fear of the inner child within many adult males. It was this which had led to a ferocious disciplining of their offspring.

Nobody in Ireland has ever accused Wilde of plagiarising stories like 'The Happy Prince' (Cats 57, 113), 'The Selfish Giant' or 'The Fisherman and His Soul' in the way that English critics have routinely accused him of pilfering plots and devices. And for good reason. A moral code which enjoins that possessions be given Christlike to the poor is hardly in a position to issue such a rebuke. For Wilde, ideas and plots were made to do the rounds. As a believer in oral culture, Wilde thought of art as the individual enunciation of a collectively owned set of narratives.[4] He cheerfully offered his own plots to others in the knowledge that he had no originary claim on any of them: and, as a student of Proudhon, supported the contention that all property is theft.

His own quips and paradoxes have become part of the folklore of modernity, being repeated in conversation or printed on calendars without attribution. By a somewhat similar process, his children's stories – first tested on his own young sons – have re-entered the Irish tradition, through the astonishingly similar childhood parables of Patrick Pearse. Pearse's story, 'Íosagán' has obvious roots in 'The Selfish Giant', with its idea of a Christ-child bearing redemptive messages to a fallen adult world. Indeed, it would not be fanciful to suggest that the prevailing mentality which lay behind the Easter Rising of 1916 – that he who loses life will save it by a Christlike combination of goodness and social rebellion – is traceable to this thinking of the 1890s. Pearse was

hardly the only rebel who had been moved by the tales of Oscar Wilde, which saw in Jesus a conflation of artist and rebel, scapegoat and scapegrace.[5]

For all their differences of temperament, Wilde and Pearse shared something very fundamental with artists such as Synge and Joyce: a conviction that the modern world was a conspiracy against the individual. Wilde put it best:

'Most people are other people. Their thoughts are someone else's opinions, their life a mimicry, their passions a quotation. Christ was not merely the supreme Individualist, but he was the first in History.'[6]

The possibilities opened up by Jesus were now being destroyed by public opinion. A frustration with that process explains the strange blend of cultural traditionalism and social radicalism in Irish modernism. Because they were committed to the expressive freedom of the individual, the Irish artists drew upon more ancient traditions in their war upon the mass-produced philistines of the new bourgeoisie. Yeats (Cats 29, 93) loved old tales of kings and queens, and even Joyce spoke of a desire to enter 'the fair courts of life'.[7] They were all examples of the radical dandy – so radical, in fact, that they could not countenance conventional Victorian ideas of Progress. They succinctly revealed their dilemma as 'that of the revolutionary whose manners and way of life are attached to the old regime, whose ideals and loyalties belong to the new, and who by a kind of courageous exhibitionism is impelled to tell the truth about both'.[8]

The radical dandies donned the mask of the bohemian, deploying their witticisms as a wedge against national chauvinism, racial prejudice and, ultimately, the very forces of the literary market itself. Wilde always said that he would favour the social system most hospitable to art: but soon he despaired of the aristocracy. In his eyes, the dandies of the 1890s were the only real aristocrats left and, like the *filí* (Gaelic professional poets) faced with the collapse of their bardic patrons, had no choice but to sell their wares (with appropriate irony) on the open market.[9]

Just like the *filí*, Wilde soon began to denounce a pusillanimous aristocracy, no longer committed to a defence of artistic standards. He lashed them hard.

It was inevitable that such a complex set of impulses would lead the more intrepid artists towards anarchism. Yeats said that, although no gentleman could be a socialist, he might be an anarchist.[10] The young Joyce immersed himself in the writings of Italian and Russian anarchists.[11] Synge attended the lectures of Sebastian Fauré in Paris, his initial ambivalence ('très interèssant, mais fou')[12] giving way to an enthusiasm discernible in every section of *The Aran Islands*. But Wilde's involvement was arguably the deepest of all.

Anarchism attracted him because of its denial of the state. For most of the nineteenth century, after the Act of Union, the Irish had been compelled by the power of the British State to live like an underground movement in their own country: and well Wilde knew it, for his own mother had had many brushes with the despised law. The shock tactics used by anarchists in exposing the conflicted nature of authority appealed greatly to a dandy like Wilde, who

Fig.10
A.J. Finberg
John Burns, MP for Battersea, addressing an open-air audience, 1897
Courtesy Wandsworth Museum, London
(Wandsworth Council)

42

Cat.148
William Rothenstein
*Portrait of George
Bernard Shaw*, 1897

orthodox socialists and Friedrich Engels pooh-poohed a socialism which 'has actually donned evening dress and lounges lazily on drawing-room *caseuses*'.[15] That sentence is a perfect description of Wilde's tactic of bringing the shaughraun-figure into a high-society setting. But it also shows that Engels utterly misunderstood Wilde's underlying motive.

Such debates on the far left interested only a minority. The main effect of the publication of 'The Soul of Man' was 'to create feeling against Wilde among the influential and moneyed classes'.[16] They took some consolation from the flippant tone, but smarter readers knew from the outset that this was one of the dandy's techniques: 'the pleasure of astonishing and the proud satisfaction of never being astonished'.[17] Wilde was Exhibit A, the living proof of a system which would encourage every person to become an artist: and he was never more serious than when he was most flippant, for he knew that there was something of heroism in being sufficiently master of oneself to be always witty. For him, the great evil of Victorian society was its remorseless specialisation of realms. Under its dispensation, a few privileged souls were allowed to develop their individuality to an extreme degree, as poets, artists, scientists or governors, while everyone else suffered as wage-slaves, living a life just short of starvation. Now, the problem of slavery was being addressed in a mass culture by the foolish remedy of amusing the slaves. The old Roman palliative of bread and circuses had found a modern counterpart in the Society of the Spectacle.

The real remedy was to hand. Machines could be the new slaves, freeing persons to perfect themselves as individual works of art. This self-perfection is the goal of all of Wilde's artistic creations. Dorian Gray stands before his picture in a locked room in search of such integrity, a spectator of his own selfhood. Such figures might seem smug, yet they represent an eastern ideal found by Wilde in the writings of Chuang Tsu.[18] Shaw (Cat.148) might scoff at the quietism of eastern philosophy, but Wilde dedicated himself to uncovering an eastern undertow in western religious thought. He had always read St Augustine's *De Civitate Dei* as a description of an ideal state, free of governmental coercion, in which all were at liberty to enjoy the pleasures of holiness without stint. Likewise, his Christ is the very reverse of a Victorian do-gooder: when he advises a young man to give to the destitute, 'it is not of the state of the poor that he is thinking but of the soul of the young man'.[19] Under Wilde's Christian scheme, there will be no contradiction between helping the poor and becoming oneself: to do one will be to do the other.

Socialists and anarchists have always held that private charity can be no substitute for organised justice. As long as unequal relations based on private property persisted, charity would degrade both the giver and receiver. In such a system of savage inequality, the only immoral thing would be to remain acquiescent. If people revolted against industrial tyrannies, they would restore personal affection in

said that 'the form of government that is most suitable to the artist is no government at all'.[13] This put him at odds with the Fabians, for they believed in the state as the deliverer of social democracy and gradual reform. They also opposed the doctrine of the workers' revolt, but, in Wilde's eyes, civil disobedience was the first social virtue. He did not accept Marx's theory that social change would bring about a transformation in persons. Rather, he contended all change must begin with the individual, and the role of art in such a transformation was crucial.[14]

These ideas were outlined in a long essay, 'The Soul of Man under Socialism', published in the *Fortnightly Review* of 1891, just three years after a translation of the *Communist Manifesto*, had become widely available in England. Its flippant tone dismayed

Cat.186
George Frederic Watts
*Portrait of William
Morris*, 1870

'I have always thought that your work comes from the
sheer delight of making beautiful things; that no alien
motive ever interests you; that in its singleness of aim,
as well as in its perfection of result, it is pure art,
everything that you do.' Oscar Wilde to Morris, 1891

place of contractual relationships, and personal pleasure would again become a shared social experience. William Morris (p.108, Cat.186) had said that man 'must begin to build up the ornamental part of life – its pleasures, bodily and mental, scientific and artistic, social and individual'[20] to such a point that art would be merely the expression of a person's joy in labour.

Wilde agreed, arguing that men should be free to choose their work, which might then take on the creative character of play. Both he and Morris insisted that, far from deferring to public taste, artists should hold forth higher ideals, towards which people would inevitably subscribe once the cult of pleasure and the love of beauty had been restored as replacements for utilitarian values. If all were lovers of beauty, a poor, squalid being would be obnoxious, an unbearable rebuke to all who met him: and all would know what to do, if only out of self-interest. 'Living for others' in acts of programmatic charity was no way to create a society of Chuang Tsus and Augustines. It was ignoble because it assumed that egotism was man's natural condition (Matthew Arnold's 'doing as one likes'), and that it could be transcended only by woeful self-discipline. At its centre was a wholly Protestant gloom about one's natural instincts, but Wilde sought to counter this bleak,

mechanistic philosophy with a world in which all shared a good life, whose primary basis was the imagination rather than political activity. To make men socialists would be no achievement if one form of coercion was replaced by another, but to make socialism human would be a real breakthrough. Then a false egotism (each person marooned in the prison of seemingly selfish desires) would make way for a true individualism (by which personal pleasure became socially available). 'I hope', says Gwendolen to Jack in *The Importance of Being Earnest*, 'you will always look at me just like that, especially when there are other people present'.[21]

The figure in whom eastern serenity and western kindness were reconciled was the Jesus of the Middle East: but Wilde could find such blending also in an anarchist like Peter Kropotkin, 'a man with the soul of that beautiful white Christ that seems coming out of Russia'.[22] Jesus, however, was the ultimate rebel against tyranny over body, soul and mind. His insurrectionary programme had been without precedent. The Christ whom Wilde celebrates is the rather Catholic mystic of Ernest Renan: a true artist, rather than the breaker of false images beloved by Protestants. Less a didact than a guru, he was not a model for imitation so much as an example of self-becoming. His soul scarcely existed apart from his senses. Wilde's is the outcast Christ celebrated in the popular spirituality of the rural Irish tales and proverbs heard from peasants in Wilde's youth.[23]

James Joyce interpreted Wilde's apparent conversion to Catholicism as 'the repudiation of his wild doctrine',[24] but that is hardly true. Wilde had always been something of a cultural Catholic. If there is one element of his art that is even more subversive of late Victorian London culture than his anarchism, it may well be his ever-strengthening Catholicism. He had considered converting in his Oxford days, at a time when the 'bells and smells' wing of Anglicanism was becoming interested in the seemingly richer store of imagery and ritual of the Catholics. For his English contemporaries, that may have seemed like a way of embarrassing parents, but to an Irishman it was a serious act of solidarity with a peasant people who had endured poverty and death rather than worship a God in whom they could not believe.[25] Wilde was all but struck out of his half-brother's will and said to a friend: 'you see I suffer a good deal from my Romish leanings, in pocket and mind'[26] – for his punisher was deeply intolerant of such tendencies. His forebearance may have been connected with the recollection of being brought as a four-year-old boy by his mother for a second baptism at the Catholic church in Glencree, county Wicklow. (The desire for second baptism voiced by a character in *The Importance of Being Earnest* may have arisen from that experience.) Lady Wilde had taught her children to admire the Catholic church, which was the major patron of the arts in Victorian Ireland. Oscar never forgot their attendance at masses in Glencree, and the Catholic church's affinities with classic drama inspired him: 'it is always a source of

Cat.65
Emmeline Deane
Portrait of Cardinal
John Henry Newman,
1889

Cat.117
After Guido Reni
St.Sebastian,
17th century

pleasure and awe to me to remember that the ultimate survival of the Greek chorus, lost elsewhere to art, is to be found in the servitor answering the priest at mass'.[27] At Trinity, his classics teacher J.P. Mahaffy tried to distract Wilde from Romish involvements with the seductive alternative of pagan Greece, ignoring the obvious fact that the pupil's paganism 'merely reinforced his attraction to the sensual elements of Catholicism'.[28]

Although Catholics had been emancipated in England for most of the nineteenth century, they found it very hard to penetrate such core institutions as the law, the military and the police. As with the Jews, there was an unspoken implication that they were not fully integrable to the progress of the English middle class, their ultimate allegiance being imagined to be to a transnational force. This was especially true of Catholics with an Irish background: the invention of the 'Celt' as a category to account for Irish unreliability was consolidated after emancipation in 1829, when Catholicism could no longer be openly invoked to explain aberrant behaviour and when racial theories became ever more fashionable.

The young poetic rebels of the Rhymers' Club (a group of poets who met in the 1890s in the Cheshire Cheese pub of Fleet Street in London) expressed their distrust of the ruling Protestant ideology and their commitment to beauty. The culture of 'manliness' had created intolerable pressures for many sensitive men, who responded with spectacular conversions to Roman Catholicism. Its communal rituals seemed also to heal the awesome loneliness of Protestant self-election. Such conversions were even more subversive of the social consensus than was Catholicism itself: the word 'pervert', for example, had been used of converts to Catholicism long before it was applied to homosexuals (though, of course, as far back as Edmund Burke, the implied equation between Catholicism and homosexuality had been effected by those keen to break Irish careers in England). Wilde's cultural Catholicism was, therefore, an aspect of his subversion: and he shared Arnold's belief that sooner or later every decent English person must recognise the honorary Celt within himself.

For many intellectuals, Catholicism had the lure of forbidden fruit. Even the books of Cardinal Newman (Cat.65), the most famous convert of all, carried in their sinuous prose a *frisson* which Wilde openly acknowledged. The fear that secret agents in the Catholic interest might stealthily insert themselves into the social and political process was widespread: and the not-very-hidden Catholicism of Wilde's fairy tales might seem an inspired example of such programming, since it was aimed (at least in part) at a deeply susceptible audience – young children.[29] Wilde had once mocked his adult readers by saying to them 'you give the criminal calendar of Europe to your children under the name of history': but his stories, with their strange mapping of Irish onto Oriental settings, might function as an antidote by exposing some of the prevailing myths of European coloniasm.[30]

He was, after all, concerned with the human *soul*. The implied conflict between 'soul' and 'socialism' in the title of his essay 'The Soul of Man under Socialism' is dissolved in its actual argument. The Christlike figures of his children's stories embrace poverty, shame and social ostracism (as if their author foresaw his own final tragedy). There is a martyr-cult at work here, somewhat reminiscent of Saint Sebastian (Cat.117), whose story always haunted Wilde. For Wilde, the only way to get rid of a temptation was to yield to it.

The art of Bunburying, as practised in *The Importance of Being Earnest*, is based on the theory of *felix culpa*, the fault that is 'happy' because it becomes the basis of Augustinian self-correction and self-education. If experience is the name that a man gives to his mistakes, then Catholicism may well be the proper religion for a man, who is willing to go wrong in order to go right. On this aspect of Wilde's experience, Joyce got the balance right:

'He deceived himself into believing that he was the bearer of the good news of neo-paganism to an enslaved people. His own distinctive qualities, the qualities, perhaps, of his race – keeness, generosity and a sexless intellect – he placed at the service of a theory of beauty which, according to him was to bring back the Golden Age and the joy of the world's youth. But if some truth adheres to his subjective interpretation of Aristotle, to his restless thought that proceeds by sophisms rather than syllogisms, to his assimilations of natures as foreign to his as the delinquent is to the humble, at its very base is a truth inherent in the soul of Catholicism: that man cannot reach the divine except through that sense of separation and loss called sin'.[31]

That is, in fact, the link which Joyce could not otherwise find between the earlier and later works. If Bunburying is all about the educative effect of studying one's mistakes, then so also is *De Profundis*, the great letter to Lord Alfred Douglas (pp.101–2) written from gaol. The former is comic, the latter tragic. The Christ in 'The Soul of Man' is the same Christ extolled in *De Profundis*: an innocent man whose sin was the full artistic expression of himself. In the later text, he remains a guru rather than a preacher: 'he does not really teach one anything, but by being brought into his presence, one becomes something'.[32] The self-perfecting figure of the early essay is evoked again in *De Profundis*. 'To live for others as a definite self-conscious aim was not his creed', Wilde writes: 'when he says 'Forgive your enemies', it is not for the sake of the enemy but for one's own sake that he says so'.[33]

The redemptive potential of the child, uppermost in the fairy tales, is seen as providing a rare exception to the refusal of Jesus to enforce a direct moral: 'he held them up as examples to their elders, which I myself have always thought the chief use of children, if what is perfect can have a use'.[34] This is but another way of regretting that the old-fashioned respect for the young is fast dying out. At the core of *De Profundis* is a recognition of the tragic contradiction in Wilde's earlier thought: he had, after all, declared himself indifferent to society, but had then committed the unpardonable sin (for an anarchist) of appealing to society for vindication in his conflict with Douglas's father, the Marquess of Queensberry. He was the first to admit the poetic justice of condemnation by a law that he had flouted and then appealed to. Even after the failure of his action against Queensberry, he could have fled straight to France, but, as his mother expected, he stood his ground as a gentleman to take what was coming to him. Perhaps Wilde had a half-conscious desire to continue his reverse anthropology in new and more testing zones. Prison might be the ultimate university, where the weaknesses of a host society were most fully concentrated and exposed.

Wilde never portrayed himself as a gay martyr, least of all to Bosie. 'I am here,' he tells him in the letter from jail, 'for having tried to put your father in prison.'[35] (He had sued him for libel.) The artist's whole treatment of the Marquess of Queensberry

seems an almost formulaic inversion of Anglo-Saxon racism. Whereas the British upper class had considered the Irish reckless and criminal, he now reversed the charges, seeking to subvert the father/son relation on which the aristocracy based its claims of lineage. In court, he effectively tried to drive a legal wedge between the Marquess and his heir. Hundreds, possibly thousands, of homosexual men occupied powerful positions in the London of the time.[36] Wilde did not go to jail for homosexuality (except in the most technical sense). His real crime was, in the words of Mary McCarthy, 'making himself too much at home' in English society.[37] He was the ultimate social nightmare, a self-invited guest who had to be barred.

Gaol revealed to the writer the soul of man under capitalism, allowing him to 'see people and things as they really are'. It also confirmed his prior hunch about the educative effects of sin. To Bosie he writes: 'Suffering – curious as it may sound to you – is the means by which we exist, because it is the only means by which we

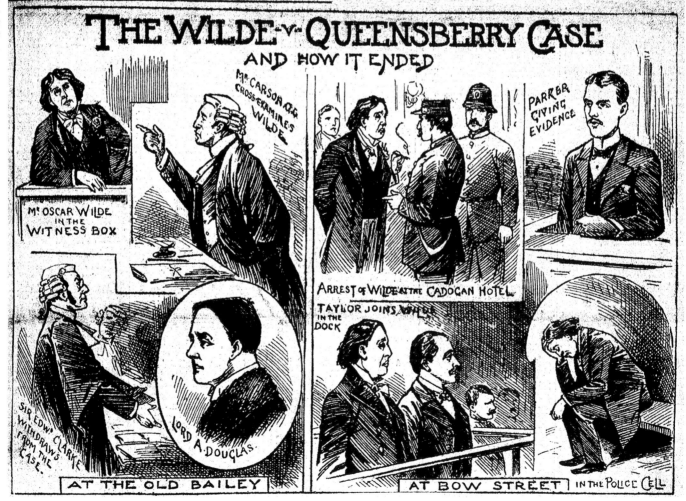

Fig.12
The Wilde–Queensberry Case and How It Ended
From *The Illustrated Police News*,
18 April, 1895

become conscious of existing'.[38] The experience also ratified the argument in 'The Soul of Man': that the punishments inflicted by the good were far more immoral than occasional outbreaks of crime, and that children were the major victims of such brutalisation. It also proved that work under such a regime, far from rehabilitating the person, would cause him to dread all labour forever. In gaol, Wide endured a hard pillow and plank bed. 'If this is how the queen treats her convicts', he told one warder, 'she doesn't deserve to have any'.[39] Solitary confinement was the worst of punishments. Designed to make offenders confront the nature of their sin, it was, in fact, a cynical device to destroy the sense of camaraderie with fellow inmates. In the prison sick-bay, Wilde so entertained inmates with quips and stories that a guard was placed by his bed, under strict instructions not to answer if the prisoner spoke. It was as if the whole process was designed to disconnect Wilde from all possible audiences.[40]

Yet the audience of fellow-lags was the one which, by now, he wanted most. Despite the official policy, he achieved deep friendships with the surrounding convicts, and told Bosie:

'The poor are wise, more charitable, more kind, more sensitive than we are. In their eyes prison is a tragedy in a man's life, a casualty, something that calls for sympathy in others. They speak of one who is in prison as of one who is 'in trouble' simply. It is the phrase they always use, and the expression has the wisdom of love in it'.[41]

The secret life of a London homosexual had inevitably led to clandestine contacts across the social divide with procurers and rent-boys, but these had always had a transgressive element (and some may have been frankly and horribly exploitative). In prison, on the other hand, the camaraderie was entirely sincere.

The extended letter to Bosie was Wilde's defiant response to the attempt by the authorities to prevent all but the most rudimentary communication. It was a viable and useful alternative to the madness which overcame many men in solitary confinement. The Christ who appears through its pages is an artist notable for his gift of giving voice to the lives of all who have been silenced: yet he transcends even that representative capacity, appearing once again as a wholly unconditioned being. At just that point when he appears to be about to project a knowable, believable personality, he eludes definition: 'To recognise that the soul of man is unknowable is the ultimate achievement of wisdom. The final mystery is oneself'.[42]

Notes

1   Oscar Wilde, 'The Critic as Artist', Richard Ellmann (ed), *The Artist as Critic*.

2   Regenia Gagnier, *Idylls of the Marketplace: Oscar Wilde and the Victorian Public* (Stanford, 1986), p.4.

3   Marina Warner, *From the Beast to the Blonde: On Fairy Tales and their Tellers* (London, 1994), p.20.

4   Even the Census of Ireland in 1901 found that 21% of persons could neither read nor write.

5   Owen Dudley Edwards, introduction to Prose section, *Collected Works of Oscar Wilde* (Glasgow, 1994), pp.14–5.

6   Rupert Hart-Davis (ed), *Selected Letters of Oscar Wilde* (London, 1962), p.208.

7   James Joyce, S. Deane (ed), *A Portrait of the Artist as a Young Man* (London, 1991), p.186.

8   Cyril Connolly, *The Unique Grave*: quoted by Edouard Roditi, *Oscar Wilde* (New York, 1947), p.157.

9   Gagnier, p.82

10   John Harrison, *The Reactionaries* (London, 1966), p.36.

11   Dominic Manganiello, *Joyce's Politics* (London, 1980).

12   David H. Greene and Edward M. Stephens, *J.M. Synge 1871-1909* (New York, 1961), p.66.

13   Wilde, *The Artist as Critic*, p.282.

14   E.H. Mikhail (ed), *Oscar Wilde: Interviews and Recollections*, Vol.1 (London, 1979), p.232.

15   Cited by Gagnier, p.31.

16   George Woodcock, 'The Social Rebel', Richard Ellmann (ed) *Oscar Wilde: A Collection of Critical Essays* (New Jersey, 1965), p.155.

17   Cited by Roditi, *Oscar Wilde*, p.158.

18   Wilde, *The Artist as Critic*, pp.221–8.

19   *Selected Letters*, p.208.

20   William Morris, *Collected Works*, p.111 and 173.

21   Oscar Wilde, *Field Day Anthology*, Vol.2, p.398.

22   Wilde, *Collected Letters* (London, 1962), p.488.

23   Yeats collected many of these later in the 1890s.

24   James Joyce, 'Oscar Wilde: The Poet of Salome', in *Oscar Wilde: A Collection of Critical Essays*, p.58.

25   H. Montgomery Hyde, *Oscar Wilde* (London, 1976), 38ff.

26   *Collected Letters*, p.43

27   Ibid., p.478.

28   Ronald Schuchard, 'Wlde's Dark Angel and the Spell of Dissident Catholicism',

29   This is the subject for a doctorial thesis being completed at University College Dublin By Jarlath Killeen.

30   Cited by Hesketh Pearson, *Oscar Wilde: His Life and Art* (New York, 1946), p.58.

31   James Joyce, 'Oscar Wilde' pp.59–60.

32   *Collected Letters*, p.878.

33   *Selected Letters*, p.205.

34   Ibid., p.213.

35   Ibid., p.184.

36   James Joyce, 'Oscar Wilde', p.59.

37   Mary McCarthy, 'The Unimportance of Being Oscar', *Oscar Wilde: A Collection of Critical Essays*, p.107.

38   *Selected Letters*, p.164.

39   Quoted by John Albert OSO, 'The Christ of Oscar Wilde', Regenia Gagnier (ed) *Critical Essays on Oscar Wilde* (New York, 1991), p.249.

40   Gagnier, *Idylls*, p.185.

41   *Selected Letters*, p.193.

42   Ibid., p.216.

DANDYISM,

decadence  & dissent:

STYLE & SENSIBILITY AMONG WILDE'S COTERIE

Oscar Wilde was a showman. He won an audience as a circus ringmaster draws in a crowd. He made people stop, look and listen – almost regardless of whether the audience understood his art. This showmanship that he exhibited was perfectly in keeping with the Irish oral tradition out of which he grew. A way with words – supplemented by bravura in the performance – could win admirers, as he learnt from the example of his mother, the nationalist poet Speranza, as well as from other practitioners of the art in Dublin.

JONATHAN FRYER

But his way with words also won him many enemies, especially in the more sceptical and staid environment of London. Nevertheless, as both admirers and enemies talked about him, Wilde had reason to be satisfied with the net result – until, by a mixture of accident and design, the two conspired to bring about his downfall.

A common assertion made about Oscar Wilde's fate is that he was destroyed by Lord Alfred Douglas (Fig.13 and pp.101–2). Yet a stronger case can, perhaps, be made for the proposition that Wilde destroyed himself, just as earlier he had made himself. His style injected a crucial contribution to both processes. A major reason why he is seen as an essentially modern figure is that he clearly appreciated that an individual can construct his or her own identity through style. That he did this in such a literally dramatic way in the highly conformist late Victorian era is undeniably remarkable. But that does not mean that he was entirely original. On the contrary, Oscar learned as well as taught when it came to projecting a persona – it was just that he did it better than anyone else. His triumphal success in this respect has resonated over the century since his death, even if for many years it was overshadowed by the perceived tragic failure of his life. That life – one could say, that performance – thus offered both a model and a warning to men and women of his own time, as it still does to people today. Yet when one analyses his life, it is riddled with unnerving contradictions. In fact, this should not surprise us, for as Wilde wrote: 'the wise contradict themselves'.[1]

Indeed, consistency is the last thing we should expect from Wilde. 'I have always been of the opinion that consistency is the last refuge of the unimaginative,' he declared.[2] How could one challenge the rigidity of the unimaginative, if one's counter-argument was rigid itself? Novelty and invention had to be ongoing. At the same time, there was an inherent peril in such a strategy: namely, that friends and admirers who were neither as quick nor as imaginative as Oscar could become confused, even

Fig.13
Oscar Wilde and Lord Alfred Douglas, 1893
Courtesy Mary Evans
Picture Library, London

Cat.19
Aubrey Beardsley
*Salomé: Enter Herodias,*1894
From *A Portfolio,*
published in 1906

Cat.149
William Rothenstein
*Portrait of Max
Beerbohm*, 1898

**Beerbohm once regretted that his satires in *The
Yellow Book* were often misunderstood: 'If only
I had signed myself D. Cadent or Parrar Dox.'**

alienated, by his inconsistency. Some of his strongest supporters fell by the wayside as his manner and mannerisms changed, especially when the message seemingly being conveyed became unpalatable.

From Horace Wilkins, Wilde's contemporary at Trinity College, Dublin, we know that Oscar was a 'queer, awkward lad… big, ungainly and clumsy to such a degree that it made him a laughing stock'.[3] If necessary, he could more than defend himself physically in violent encounters with belligerent detractors, as well-recorded incidents at Portora School and at Oxford confirm. But he also learned how to conquer adversaries with words. He discovered the power to surprise and to shock, as well as the effectiveness of wit. Later in life, he would become far more ambivalent about power, apprehending in prison the essential nature of pity towards the powerless. But as a young man, and as the butt of ridicule, the possibility of power (though not political power) held obvious attractions.

On his arrival at Oxford, Oscar initially adopted a pose of exaggerated conventionality in his dress. Careless of the bills he was running up at men's outfitters in the town (one of the few traits that did remain consistent throughout his adult life), he acquired a wardrobe of formal clothes, punctiliously following the codes set down by Society about what was appropriate for day or evening, town or country. It is no wonder that, in some quarters, he began to acquire a reputation as a parvenu and a snob. Yet soon the loudness of the checks of some of his leisure-wear, the cockiness of his hats and the flamboyance of his neckties indicated that he was aping the English gentleman, rather than trying to pass for one. As Joseph Pearce has rightly noted, Oscar's conformity was crystallising into *non*-conformity: he was becoming a dandy dilettante in disguise. 'Henceforth Wilde's disguise would be a statement, and his statements a disguise,' Pearce writes.[4] 'The truth and the mask would be one.'

In one of Wilde's less memorable aphorisms, he proclaimed that 'Dandyism is the assertion of the absolute modernity of Beauty'.[5] In saying this, and adopting the pose of a dandy, Oscar was actually harking back to another Oxford undergraduate, of eighty years earlier, George 'Beau' Brummell (1778–1840), an influence that some of Wilde's more percipient friends and acquaintances, such as Max Beerbohm (Cat.149 and pp.92–3), openly recognised. The influence of dandyism on Wilde's concept of the aim of life (defined by Lord Henry Wotton in *The Picture of Dorian Gray* as 'to realise one's nature perfectly') received a further boost from his study of the life and work of Thomas Griffiths Wainewright (1794–1847). This painter, belletrist and convicted criminal was the subject of Wilde's essay *Pen, Pencil and Poison* (see Cat.185). As Stephen Calloway has noted, Wilde discovered in Wainewright's character not only elements of his own nature but also 'the key to an essential quality of the Aesthetic and Decadent sensibility as it developed in England in the 1880s and '90s. That quality we might define as a Dandyism of the Senses – a self-consciously precious and highly fastidious discrimination brought to bear on both art and life.'[6]

There is often an element of aggressive self-parody in the style of the dandy, as well as a rebuke to the society in which he shines. This makes him a highly subversive creature, though not all of his contemporaries are astute enough to realise that. They may see only the surface of his presentation, not the motivation behind it. Therefore, their reaction to him is essentially superficial. There is a delicious paradox inherent in the situation, such as existed in late Victorian England, in which conventional style, behaviour and morality are considered 'deep', while dandyism and aestheticism are considered 'shallow'. Yet who was the 'deeper' character: a blustering, wholesome man like Rudyard Kipling, or the devious dandy Oscar Wilde?

Wilde derived enormous fun from playing with associated ideas, in particular the way that conventional London Society judged by form, rather than by substance. This was something he had been mulling over since before going up to Oxford. In an essay entered for the Oxford University Chancellor's Prize in 1879, he wrote: 'The new age is the age of style. The same spirit of exclusive attention to form which made Euripides often, like Swinburne (Cat.155), prefer music to meaning and melody to morality…'.[7] He returned to the theme again and again. 'It is only shallow people who do not judge by appearances,' Lord Henry Wotton tells Dorian Gray. 'In matters of grave importance, style, not sincerity, is the vital thing,' Gwendolen concurs in *The Importance of Being Earnest*.

While Wilde was amusing himself with his dandy aesthete's pose, Gilbert and Sullivan equally amused themselves by satirising him brilliantly in their operetta *Patience*. Similarly, he was an irresistible target for the publication *Punch*, though there the satire

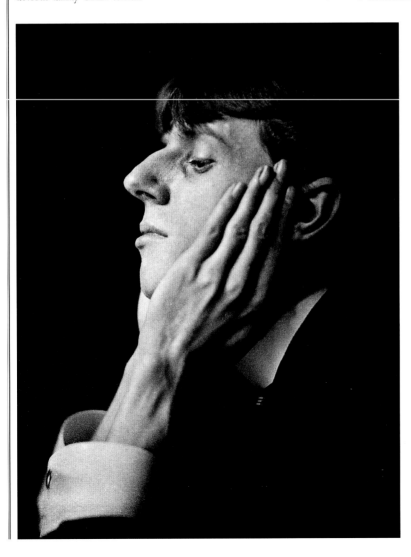

Fig.14
Aubrey Beardsley, 1895
Photograph by
Frederick H. Evans
Courtesy Stephen
Calloway, Brighton

55

For Wilde, Beardsley resembled 'a monstrous orchid' with 'a face like a silver hatchet and green grass hair'.

frequently betrayed a harder edge. Given that many of the readers of *Punch* would have considered themselves to be pillars of Victorian respectability, this is hardly surprising – especially as Wilde's aestheticism (partly seeded by Walter Pater) was so unmanly in their eyes. Manliness was seen as a great virtue at the time; a major mainstream objection to *fin-de-siècle* aestheticism was that it was 'effeminate'. As Alan Sinfield has pointed out,[8] being effeminate was *not* widely equated with being homosexual, at least not until Wilde's trials in 1895. After all, some of the most languid aesthetes and decadents, including Aubrey Beardsley, illustrator of Wilde's *Salomé* (Fig.14, Cats 39, 162 and pp.90–1), were not homosexual. Theirs was an act of defiance aimed at Victorian morality, but not necessarily at its heterosexuality.

In Wilde's case, however, the evolution of his style and sensibility involved forever crossing new frontiers and exploring new sensations, pushing himself and Society as far as they both could go. Wilde's sexual transgression[9] was, therefore, almost pre-destined, even before he was seduced by the seventeen-year-old Robbie Ross in 1886, or initiated into the world of working-class rent boys by the fatally alluring Lord Alfred Douglas. The

Fig.15
Anonymous
*André Gide at
21 years old*, 1891
Courtesy
Bibliothèque Nationale
de France, Paris

Fig.16
Pierre Louÿs, 1892
Courtesy Mary Evans
Picture Library,
London

"THE FIRST DUTY IN LIFE IS TO BE AS ARTIFICIAL AS POSSIBLE"

adventurous nature of Wilde's dissent from Society's norms explains much of the attraction he undoubtedly had in Douglas's eyes, even if in cementing his relationship with Oscar, 'Bosie' was following his own private agenda of hitting out at his father, the Marquess of Queensberry. It also explains why, for a while, Wilde was seen as a role model by other young friends and acolytes, by no means all of them homosexual.

The heterosexual French writer of erotic poetry Pierre Louÿs (Fig.16) is a case in point. He was initially enchanted by the nonchalant public behaviour of Wilde and his coterie. Louÿs cited to his friend André Gide (Figs 15, 25) the habit some of the group had of lighting a cigarette and then passing it from their own mouth to that of a friend. Some of the symbolism of this gesture was obviously lost on the young Frenchman, just as the wearing of green carnations by Wilde's circle of young admirers at the premières of his plays was seen by many as merely an aesthetic affectation. Wilde himself maintained that the green carnation had no significance, other than its startling artificiality. Nevertheless, for Robbie Ross and many other young men, the flowers were worn as a sign of inclusion within a secret fraternity. It was what W.H. Auden, in a later context, would christen the Homintern – an underground network of homosexuals across Europe, with their own signs and codes and lifestyles, which were invisible to the world at large.

It was when Wilde, through his lifestyle, made the sexually transgressive meaning of some of those signs and codes obvious – egged on by Bosie Douglas – that many former friends and admirers renounced him. Pierre Louÿs was shocked by the implications for Wilde's wife and children. Others were appalled by the idea of homosexuality itself. It was not just that male homosexuality had quite recently been criminalised; the act of sodomy itself was generally viewed in Britain with a degree of revulsion that is scarcely imaginable today. When the Marquess of Queensberry left his visiting card to Oscar Wilde, with the inscription 'posing as a somdomite (sic)', it was a very grave charge.

Even many homosexuals had cause for alarm at the way Wilde, through his style and bravado, rubbed Society's face in his private life, especially during the period 1894–5, thereby threatening their own safety as well as his. André Gide, who had been bowled over by Wilde when they first met in Paris in 1891, distanced himself as Wilde and Douglas's behaviour became ever more scandalous. The irony of this was that Gide, for whom Wilde was certainly a mentor, would go on to write far more explicitly about homosexuality than Wilde ever did. Yet in outward appearance, for much of his life, Gide cultivated a priest-like mask, more ascetic than aesthetic, utterly different from Wilde's.

Even Robbie Ross (Fig.17) maintained a façade that was at odds with any of Oscar's masks. Given Ross's key role as Wilde's first lover, devoted friend, literary executor and tomb-mate,[10] it is worthwhile contrasting their styles. A scion of a famous Canadian Liberal family, but born in France, Ross established himself as a highly-respected art critic and administrator in England, integrating himself into the London establishment to a degree that Wilde never managed (nor truly wanted to). Ross was 'clubable', in a way that Wilde most certainly was not. Moreover, Ross's dress and manner (after a certain juvenile exuberance) were generally conservative. He led what today would be called a double life, making him sympathetic to younger figures such as Harold Nicolson and Siegfried Sassoon, who also wanted to maintain a high degree of conventionality whilst enjoying forbidden fruits.

For Wilde, such a position would have been intolerably hypocritical, though he had every reason later to be grateful for Robbie Ross's ability to keep a foot in each camp: the 'straight' and the 'gay' worlds, to borrow terminology from modern discourse. Nonetheless, during his time in prison, Wilde had cause to reflect that he had perhaps gone too far in his pursuit of sensations. *De Profundis* contains several passages which convey regret, even remorse, for his self-identified excesses. During his confinement,

Fig.17
Robert Ross, reading 'De Profundis' by Oscar Wilde
Photograph by Elliot & Fry, c.1914
Courtesy The National Portrait Gallery, London

Robert Ross (1869–1918)
In 1895 Wilde wrote to Ross, praising his courage not only 'in going about with me in my days of gilded infamy, my Neronian hours, rich, profligate, cynical, materialistic' – but also 'in your coming to comfort me, a lonely, dishonoured man, in disgrace and obscurity and poverty'.

prison chaplains reminded him of the wages of sin, as widely perceived by the overwhelmingly church-going British public of the period. At times, *De Profundis* reads like a confessional, with Bosie Douglas cast as an agent of Satan. As with a confessional, writing the book also brought Wilde a degree of absolution. Certainly, soon after his release, and an aborted attempt to enter a religious retreat, he began to sin all over again, albeit with less style, in accordance with his reduced physical and financial circumstances.

It is significant that Wilde chose France as his place of exile. For France had displaced Ancient Greece as his spiritual home from the time of his first real contact with Gallic aestheticism, decadence and symbolism. The *coup de grâce* actually came during his honeymoon in Paris, in May 1884, when he read Joris-Karl Huysmans' newly-published novel *A Rebours* (see Cat.182). Wilde was not the only person dazzled by this portrait of the debauched aristocratic dandy-aesthete Des Esseintes (see Fig.18); Paul Valéry, for example, referred to the novel as his Bible.[11] But the direct influence of Huysmans' anti-hero on Wilde's world-view and work was colossal. One sees this reflected in the character of Dorian Gray, who reads a book clearly based on *A Rebours*, which seemed to 'contain the story of his own life, written before he had lived it'. Even more vividly, there are echoes in Wilde's play *Salomé*. Interestingly, both Dorian Gray and Salome come to sticky ends, which tends to undermine the accusation made both in court and in the press at the time of Oscar Wilde's disgrace that he was an immoral writer.

The enumeration of jewels and other costly objects, in salivatory detail, in both Huysmans and Wilde, reeks of decadence. It is worth pointing out, however, that Wilde, unlike Des Esseintes (or, indeed, Robbie Ross) was no connoisseur of art. It is the very words he uses in the descriptions, and the impression they convey, rather than the objects themselves, which resonate for Wilde. This is voluptuousness at play, rather than refined artistic sensibility.

In the setting of the Tite Street house, Constance, his wife, happy during the first years of the marriage to be a mannequin for Oscar's ideas about design and style (though this isn't to suggest that she was not an independent character). Professionally, his wife's complicity in this aesthetic display was useful to Wilde when he was editing *The Woman's World*. But he soon tired of such pre-occupations, not just because of his disinclination to be associated with an office. The idea of being an arbiter of style for Society quickly lost its attraction. Acutely aware of the potential *ennui* of life, he could only bear activities and ideas so long as they provided amusement. As he later recalled in *De Profundis*, 'I amused myself by being a *flaneur*, a dandy, a man of fashion.' Once the amusement had worn off, it was time to move on to the next thing. And, as he remarked with prescience to André Gide in Algiers shortly before his trials, having moved on so far, something dramatic had to happen.

Wilde ultimately made himself an outcast, not just because he flouted conventional morality, but also because even many of his

Cat.182
Félix Vallotton
Portrait of *Joris-Karl Huysmans*, 1896

friends could not keep up with him. The intensity of his own particular brand of dandyism, decadence and dissent, and the speed of their mutations, meant that he was increasingly seen as a threat, even by former allies. Yet it is that element of living dangerously, for the moment, in a perpetual search for his own true nature, that has helped turn him into an icon a hundred years after his death. Personally, he suffered by being premature. But, as he said himself: 'To be premature is to be perfect'.[12]

Notes

1   *Phrases and Philosophies for the Use of the Young*, first published in the *Chameleon*, December 1894, reprinted in *Complete works of Oscar Wilde*, Collins, London 1966, p.1205.

2   *The Relation of Dress to Art*, first published in *The Pall Mall Gazette* 28 February 1895, reprinted in *Aristotle at Afternoon Tea: The Rare Oscar Wilde*, (ed) John Wyse Jackson, Fourth Estate, London 1991, p.52.

3   Quoted in Joseph Pearce: *The Unmasking of Oscar Wilde* HarperCollins, London 2000, pp.21–2.

4   Pearce, L., op. cit., .31.

5   *A Few Maxims for the Instruction of the Over-Educated*, first published in the *Saturday Review*, reprinted in *Complete Works*, p.1204.

6   'Wilde and the Dandyism of the Senses', in *The Cambridge Companion to Oscar Wilde*, ed. by Peter Raby, Cambridge University Press, Cambridge, 1997, p.34.

7   *The Rise of Historical Criticism*, reprinted in *Collected Works*, p.1131.

8   *The Wilde Century*, Cassell, London, 1994

9   Brilliantly defined and discussed in Jonathan Dollimore: *Sexual Dissidence*, Clarendon Press, Oxford, 1991.

10 In 30 November 1950, on the 50th anniversary of Wilde's death, Ross's ashes were transferred to Wilde's tomb in the Père Lachaise cemetery in Paris, in accordance with Ross's will.

11 Quoted in Richard Ellmann's *Oscar Wilde*, Hamish Hamilton, London 1987, p.237.

12 *Phrases and Philosophies for the Use of the Young*, op.cit., *Collected Works* p.1205.

Fig.18
Giovanni Boldini
*Portrait of Comte de
Montesquiou-
Fezenac,* 1897
Courtesy Musée
d'Orsay, Paris

The inspiration of both Huysmans's Des Esseintes, the
hero of *A Rebours*, and M. Proust's Baron de Charlus, the
flamboyant Robert de Montesquiou-Fezenac was a patron
of both the jeweller René Lalique and Emille Gallé.

Salomé

THE LEGACY OF OSCAR WILDE

BY TOMOKO SATO

'Disobedience, in the eyes of anyone who has read history, is man's original virtue. It is through disobedience that progress has been made, through disobedience and through rebellion.'

(OSCAR WILDE, 'THE SOUL OF MAN UNDER SOCIALISM', 1891)

Among Oscar Wilde's dramatic work, the one-act play *Salomé* is unique. Firstly, it was written in French. And secondly, the subject is a Biblical story, in contrast to his four other plays from the same period, which were 'Society comedies' dealing with contemporary English life. *Salomé* has an unusual history as well: public performances were banned in England until 1931; and Wilde himself was never to see it performed. Nevertheless, as his literary executor Robert Ross appraised it later, '*Salomé* has made the author's name a household word wherever the English language is not spoken.'[1] Furthermore, the play had a strong impact on other forms of art and sub-culture at the turn of the century: Wilde's heroine Salome became an icon of the age, shaking up Victorian moral values and the traditional concept of womanhood. This article examines the history of Wilde's *Salomé* and its legacy in the twentieth century.

'I have one instrument that I know I can command, and that is the English language. There was another instrument I had listened to all my life, and I wanted once to touch this new instrument to see whether I could make any beautiful thing out of it.'[2] So

explained Wilde to a journalist when asked why he had written *Salomé* in French. Wilde was fluent in French and well read in its literature. He was familiar with Baudelaire, Edmond de Goncourt (Cat.41), Flaubert, Mallarmé (Cat.196) and, in particular, Huysmans (Cat.182). Since his first reading of Huysmans' novel *A Rebours* in a Paris hotel room on his honeymoon in 1884, it had become his bedside book. This book, widely acknowledged as 'the guidebook of decadence' at that time, had an enormous effect on Wilde. The impact was to be described later, in his novel of 1890, through his 'decadent' hero Dorian Gray: 'It was the strangest book that he [Dorian] had ever read. It seemed to him that in exquisite raiment, and to the delicate sound of flutes, the sins of the world were passing in dumb show before him.' The 'poisonous' world of *A Rebours* [*Against Nature*] had kept haunting Wilde's imagination for years, and it was to find another outlet in *Salomé*.

The subject of Salome meant something very personal to Wilde. Although we do not know when Wilde had become interested in this subject, obviously it had been close to his heart for years: Wilde had a vast knowledge of paintings depicting Salome, including those by Leonardo, Titian, Ghirlandaio, Dürer and Rubens. Mentioned in the Gospels of Mark (6, 14–29) and Matthew (14, 1–12), the legend of the dancing Jewish princess had been a popular theme in Christian art over the centuries. Wilde was also aware of the renewed interest in the subject in recent years, for instance in the works of Flaubert and Mallarmé. In the Bible, Salome is simply remembered as the immediate agent responsible for the death of John the Baptist – following the instructions of her mother, Herodias, Salome asked Herod for John's head as a reward for her dance. The story left plenty of room for new interpretations by the late nineteenth-century writers and artists.

Cat.9
Edward Armitage
Herod's Birthday Feast, 1868

61

'Yes, (she would be) utterly naked.
But with...interlacing strands of jewels...
On that burning flesh even the sapphire
must lose the unstained purity of its azure blue.'
Oscar Wilde, description of Salome in
conversation with Enrique Gomez Carrillo, 1891

Having also visited the city earlier that year, Wilde was rapidly extending his artistic network to the other side of the Channel. According to *L'Echo de Paris* (19 December 1891), Wilde was 'le "great event" des salons littéraires parisiennes' of the season. Paris was charmed by Wilde's wit and charisma, and in return Paris offered Wilde great opportunities to absorb the newest trends in French art and culture, and to formulate his ideas for *Salomé*.

Wilde was particularly attracted by the then current Symbolist ideas, which corresponded to his aesthetic philosophy that originated from the influences of Walter Pater (p.113 and Cat.170) and Whistler (pp.132–3 and Cats 114, 174). On his earlier trip to Paris that year, Wilde met Mallarmé, the leader of this new aesthetic, at his famous 'Tuesday' salon, *Mardis*. Wilde and Mallarmé shared the same views, especially about the supremacy of poetry, which could transform a painting into words, and the closeness of poetry to music. Bowing to his 'Master'[3], Wilde, wrote in Paris in his 'Preface' to *Dorian Gray*: 'All art is at once surface and symbol. Those who go beneath the surface do so at their peril. Those who read the symbol do so at their peril.' Further, Wilde was aware of one of Mallarmé's major works, still unfinished, 'Hérodiade', which also featured a subject that had been obsessing Wilde for years – the beheading of John the Baptist. Wilde was determined to write about it, but differently.

62

Wilde was also aware of 'Salome' paintings by Gustave Moreau (pp.110–11), whose sumptuous watercolour *The Apparition* (see Cat.106) had caused a sensation when exhibited at the 1876 Paris Salon. *The Apparition* was also exhibited in London in the following year at the Grosvenor Gallery's opening, and although Wilde, as a novice art critic, may have seen it, he did not make any comment on Moreau at that time. Nevertheless, fourteen years later, Moreau's Salome was to be interlocked with Wilde's image of Salome through Huysmans' descriptions in *A Rebours*. In Chapter Five, Huysmans had referred to two paintings: *Salome Dancing* (see Cats 104, 105) and *The Apparition*. In the novel, the decadent hero Des Esseintes would contemplate them every night. To Des Esseintes' eye, Moreau's Salome was not just a seductive dancing girl but 'the symbolic incarnation of undying lust, the goddess of immortal Hysteria', 'the curse of Beauty supreme above all other beauties' and 'a monstrous Beast of the Apocalypse, indifferent, irresponsible, poisoning'. Moreau's Salome was beautiful and sensual, yet cruel and monstrous. From this image, Wilde was to develop his own version of the Salome legend.

Wilde began writing his *Salomé* in the autumn of 1891 in Paris.

In the meantime, Wilde was expanding his contacts. At Mallarmé's *Mardis*, Wilde met the anarchist critic Félix Fénéon (see Fig.20), who had been the editor of *La Revue indépendante* as well as the recently launched *La Revue blanche* (see Cat.178). Fénéon was to become Wilde's loyal friend, who would continue to support Wilde after his downfall. Through his American friend and poet Stuart Merrill, Wilde met Jean Moréas, who had coined the term 'Symbolism' in his 'Symbolist' manifesto in 1886. Wilde also enjoyed the company of his young friends, such as André Gide (Figs 15, 25), Pierre Louÿs (see Fig.16), Marcel Schwob, William Rothenstein (Cat.33 and p.119) and Charles Conder (Cats 33, 144 and p.98). With them, Wilde could explore the Paris avant-garde sub-culture, visiting the Moulin Rouge and meeting the socialist singer Aristide Bruant (Cat.177) at Le Mirliton.

Inspired by a wide range of new encounters that would evoke images of Salome – from an obscure sculpture of a decapitated head to an exotic acrobatic dancer at the Moulin Rouge – Wilde wrote his play *Salomé* in French. Referring to his use of a foreign language to write the play, Wilde later talked about his interest in the 'curious effect' produced by the Belgian writer Maeterlinck, who wrote in 'an alien language'.[4] Wilde had a number of opportunities to discuss his ideas and text with Parisian friends such as Gide,

Pierre Louÿs and Marcel Schwob. With their help, he finished most of his play in December 1891 in Paris.

During early 1892, plans for the first London production of *Salomé* developed rapidly, with the leading French actress Sarah Bernhardt (p.94 and Cats 11, 38, 47, 110) in the title role. Wilde's friends Charles Ricketts (pp.114–6 and Cats 99, 147, 158) and Graham Robertson were the set designer and costume designer, respectively. Wilde was closely involved in both the stage direction and designs and he conceived the play as a 'total work of art', embracing poetry (word), music, dance and visual art (costumes and sets), where everything would be arranged symbolically, according to the progress of the play. For costumes, Wilde suggested yellow for the Jews, purple for the Romans, white for John and 'green like a curious and poisonous lizard' for Salome. He even thought about introducing scent: 'a violet sky and then, in place of an orchestra, braziers of perfumes.' Also, the moon would play a symbolic role, suggesting the mood of the scene with its changing colour: it would turn from virginal white (Salome: 'She [the moon] is cold and chaste. I am sure she is a virgin.') to blood-red (Herod: 'Ah! look at the moon! She has become red.') when Salome dances.

Cat.110
Alphonse Mucha
Sarah Bernhardt, 1896

Fig.19
'A Wilde Idea': Wilde as a 'poilu'
Caricature by Bernard Partridge
From *Punch*, 9 July, 1892

Wilde's treatment of Salome was also unique. Unlike his predecessors, including Mallarmé, Wilde regarded her as an independent woman, who would tell Herod: 'I do not heed my mother. It is for mine own pleasure that I ask the head of Jokanaan in a silver charger.' She had her own will. Having fallen in love with John, she simply desired him: 'Jokanaan, I am amorous of thy body!' She was articulate about her admiration for John's physical beauty: 'Thy body is white like the lilies of a field that the mower hath never mowed.' She was aware of her sexual desire, and she would act on it: 'It is thy mouth that I desire, Jokanaan … Let me kiss thy mouth.' Wilde's Salome was an assertive, modern woman. Unfortunately, her 'lover' was a saint, her opposite, and she would never be able to reach his spirit – so she would satisfy her wishes by kissing the lips of the lifeless head of John, who had rejected her.

Sarah Bernhardt was nearly fifty when she was set to play the role of Salome, yet to Wilde's eye she was 'that serpent of the Old Nile' with all her elegance and mystery, and the only one who could play his 'tragic daughter of passion.' Bernhardt even insisted in performing the 'Dance of the Seven Veils' herself, rather than having a stand-in. When asked about her plans for the dance by Graham Robertson, she replied with an enigmatic smile: 'Never

you mind.'[5] Also, she intended to play Salome with words that would fall 'like a pearl on a crystal disc, no rapid movements [and] with stylised gestures.'[6] According to Ada Leverson, *Salomé* was the only play about which Wilde really cared and in which he 'expressed *himself* in his innate love of the gorgeous and the unique.'[7]

Wilde's powerful vision, however, never materialised. The play was banned by the Lord Chamberlain towards the end of June, when rehearsals at the Palace Theatre were in full swing. The Censor refused to license the play because of an old English law that forbade the depiction of Biblical characters on stage. Wilde fiercely protested against this narrow view of artistic expression and the authorities' inconsistency in allowing painters and sculptors to depict such characters in their work. Wilde's view was supported by Bernard Shaw (Cat.148), Mallarmé, Maeterlinck and Pierre Loti, but few in England spoke out in his defence. Furthermore, his stance – 'I am not English. I am Irish which is quite another thing' – together with threats of emigrating to France (Fig.19), caused a storm of hostile comment.

Wilde was deeply hurt by the miscarriage of his play, but should he not have known this 'old English law' well? In Kerry Powell's view,[8] what was surprising to Wilde was the Censor's

Cat.179
Toulouse-Lautrec
*Oscar Wilde and
Romain Coolus*, 1896

rejection of his 'French' play. It was common knowledge in the theatre world of the 1890s that French plays had a better chance of being passed by the Censor, and maybe this is partly why Wilde wrote *Salomé* in that language. However, Wilde was a rebel: he publicly denounced the Examiner as an inept and 'commonplace' official. Wilde's provocative attitude certainly cannot have helped the examiner consider Wilde's case favourably, especially at a time when it was normal practice to negotiate with the Censor.

Nevertheless, Wilde was consoled by the publication of his *Salomé* as a book (Cat.95) in Paris and London in February1893. The book was beautifully bound in 'Tyrian purple' wrappers to go with the 'gilt hair' of Lord Alfred Douglas (Fig. 13 and pp.101–2), Wilde's lover and 'muse'. Wilde first met Alfred Douglas, the youngest son of the Marquess of Queensberry, in June 1891, just after the publication, in book form, of *The Picture of Dorian Gray*, in April the same year. Douglas was an ardent admirer of *Dorian Gray* and, just as Wilde/Dorian had become absorbed in the world of *A Rebours*, so Douglas was 'passionately absorbed' in *Dorian Gray*. In 1893, while he was still a student at Magdalen, Douglas was pursuing a literary career as poet and was the editor of an Oxford literary magazine, *The Spirit Lamp* (Cats 66, 67). The magazine was

also, covertly, an organ of a homosexual-rights movement, and Wilde contributed his poem 'The House of Judgement' to the February 1893 issue.

In April 1893, a strange drawing featured in the newly launched *Studio* magazine (Cat.14) caught Wilde's eye. It was a picture of Salome holding the severed head of St John the Baptist. The artist responsible for the drawing was twenty-year-old Aubrey Beardsley (see Fig.14, Cats 39, 162 and pp.90–91), whom Wilde had first met at Burne-Jones's house two years previously. Since then, Beardsley had been drawn to Wilde's circle, and on the publication of *Salomé*, Wilde had presented the book to the young artist, with the inscription: 'March '93. For Aubrey: for the only artist who, besides myself, knows what the dance of the seven veils is, and can see that invisible dance. Oscar.'[9] After reading it, Beardsley produced a drawing based on the climactic scene of the play, a shocking composition with lilies growing in a pool of blood dripping from John's head, confronting the monstrous face of Salome. Sinister but arresting, the drawing secured for Beardsley a commission to illustrate the English edition of Wilde's *Salomé*. Translated by Alfred Douglas (and corrected heavily by Wilde), the English edition of Wilde's play appeared in London in February 1894, accompanied

Fig.20
Toulouse-Lautrec
'The Moorish Dance' —
the right-hand panel for
*La Goulue's booth,*1895
Courtesy Musée
d'Orsay, Paris

In the panel, Lautrec monumentalised the
characters of *fin-de-siècle* Paris by bringing his
friends and associates together. Surrounding La
Goulue, performing a belly-dance, the onlookers in
the foreground include the conspicuous figure of
Wilde (centre left); the celebrated dancer Jane
Avril (centre); Félix Fénéon (far right) and
between Avril and Fénéon, Lautrec himself.

70

by Beardsley's illustrations (Cats 15, 19). Called 'unintelligible', 'repulsive', 'audacious' and 'extravagant', Beardsley's work caused a controversy in the London art world.[10] Wilde was hardly pleased by the extent of the public attention to his play's illustrator, but, in the public mind, the image of Salome and the names of Wilde and Beardsley were to become inseparable.

The year 1895 saw Wilde's most amazing drama of himself in real life: his great fall from fame to social disgrace. On 5 April, when Wilde was arrested at the Cadogan Hotel, London, for 'a charge of committing indecent acts', two of his plays, *An Ideal Husband* and *The Importance of Being Earnest* were being performed on West End stages, enjoying phenomenal box-office success. His arrest was quickly followed by a bailiff's sale of Wilde's possessions at his Tite Street house, and his name was removed from theatre bills. On 25 May, Wilde was convicted and sentenced to two-year imprisonment with hard labour, under Section 11 of the Criminal Law Amendment Act of 1885.

While homosexual activities had always existed in English history, this law for the first time defined all male homosexual activities, private or public, as acts of 'gross indecency' and made them illegal. The legislation was in response to a changing perception of sexuality at the time. As observed in the works of J.A. Symonds, Krafft-Ebing and Havelock Ellis, the concept of homosexuality began to take shape during this period.[11] Since this change to the law, male homosexual relationships had been conducted discretely or by living on a knife-edge, like Wilde and Douglas. As expressed in Wilde's defence speech during his first trial, the 'Love that dare not speak its name' was not just an issue of individual sexuality and lifestyle but that of art and aestheticism as well. Although the trials also brought up sordid details of male prostitutes and blackmailers, they uncovered the hitherto 'blind-eyed' reality of the Victorian underworld, which existed side by side with the 'decent' middle class. The Wilde affair as a whole highlighted an emerging conflict of aesthetic, social and ethical values in *fin-de-siècle* English society.

After his release from prison 1897, Wilde lived as an exile in Paris, Naples and elsewhere, under the pseudonym 'Sebastian Melmoth'. On 30 November 1900, Wilde died in poverty in Paris at the age of 46. He was buried at the Bagneux cemetery in Paris and so never returned either to England or to his native Ireland. Because of his premature death, Wilde had no time to recover from his disgrace or to regain his creative power; indeed, he was never able to see his greatest artistic vision, *Salomé*, on stage. However, after the publication of the English edition of the play, Wilde's Salome began to live her own life.

The first production of *Salomé* was staged in Paris in 1896, while Wilde was in Reading Gaol. Wilde's Parisian friends were sympathetic to his fate. The previous May, while the Wilde trials were going on , Fénéon's *La Revue blanche* featured Paul Adam's

article 'L'Assaut malicieux' in defence of Wilde. The article was accompanied by a portrait of Wilde by Toulouse-Lautrec (Cat.145 and pp.128–9).[12] It was also a gesture of solidarity with Wilde that Lugné-Poë produced *Salomé* at his avant-garde Théâtre de l'Oeuvre, against all odds: the author's permission was unobtainable due to his imprisonment, and there was a risk of the English court's intervention. Despite discrete publicity, tickets for the premiere on 11 February 1896 were sold out.

According to Beardsley and the poet Ernest Dowson, who attended the premiere, it was a 'triumphant performance', with Lina Munte as Salome and Lugné-Poë himself as Herod.[13] The programme (Cat.179) was designed by Lautrec, with another Wilde portrait, which had been painted in London during the Wilde trials. On hearing news of the success of his play whilst in prison, Wilde was grateful to Lugné-Poë, but he also expressed the numbness of his feeling to his friend Robert Ross (Fig.17): 'I wish I could feel more pleasure: but I seem dead to all emotions except those of anguish and despair.'[14]

Regardless of Wilde's feeling and his absence from the world, this Paris production triggered a Salome boom, and inspired many derivative art forms (eg. 109, 111). Less than two years after Wilde's death, *Salomé* was translated into German. Max Reinhardt

Fig.22
Maud Allan as Salome, c.1907
Courtesy Mary Evans
Picture Library, London

Fig.23
Maud Allan as Salome, c.1907
Courtesy Mary Evans
Picture Library, London

'It is as if a wildly jerking sensuality were driven
into the slender body, as if it began to blossom
and swell forth and glow through her skin...'.
From a review of Maud Allan's performance
in Prague, c.1907

produced the first German production in Berlin in 1902 and, inspired by this, Richard Strauss produced his operatic version of *Salomé* in Dresden in 1905. The resulting book and play royalties allowed the Wilde estate to be declared solvent in 1906 and his bankruptcy was annulled.[15] *Salomé* was translated and performed in many other European countries, as well as in the United States. It even reached Japan (e.g. Cat.129), where Wilde's name became synonymous with Salome, which had a great impact on the country's young avant-garde writers.

By contrast, in England, Wilde's artistic rehabilitation was slow. His books were not easily obtainable, except illegally pirated editions, until the discharge of his estate from bankruptcy in 1906. The public performance of his plays was banned for a long time: occasionally they were staged in the provinces, but without publicising Wilde's name. The first presentation of *Salomé* in England was in 1905. It was a private performance by the New Stage Club and it took place at the Bijou Theatre in Bayswater, London. According to Robert Ross, Wilde's executor, press response ignored its then popularity in Germany, referring to how the production was 'dragging [the play] from its obscurity'.[16] In the audience was Wilde's old friend Charles Ricketts, who was the set designer for the ill-fated first London production. The following year, Ricketts directed and designed another private *Salomé* production by the Literary Theatre Society (Cat.128). In 1907, an attempt at a London production of Strauss's opera added only notoriety to Wilde and his play, and the performance was only allowed in 1910 after some modification.

Jacob Epstein's tomb for Oscar Wilde (Fig.21 and pp.103–5) was another reminder of the controversial nature of Wilde's position at the time. When Epstein's sculpture was transported from London to the Père Lachaise cemetary, Paris, in 1912, following the reburial of Wilde's remains, the French authorities objected to it. The tomb, a winged male nude, was banned as 'indecent', and eventually Epstein had to modify his work significantly and a bronze plaque was fixed over the statue's genitals like a fig leaf. Wilde's tomb remained covered until the outbreak of the First World War. Ross sarcastically called this 'surprising' act of the French authority 'a graceful outcome of the Entente Cordiale and a symptom on the part of our allies to prove themselves worthy of political union with our great nation, which ... they think has always put Propriety before everything'.[17]

In 1918, another attempt to put on a public production of *Salomé* was nearly thwarted by the Independent right-wing MP Noel Pemberton Billing. Billing's attacks on the celebrated 'Salome dancer' Maud Allan resulted in her and her collaborator Jack Grains suing Billing. Billing was an MP who rose to power on the back of wartime hysteria. His Vigilante group campaigned against 'corruption' and 'decadence', which would detract from the nation's war efforts. In effect, Wilde was tried again in his absence, and the episode ended with Billing's acquittal, won partly through the testimony of Alfred Douglas – by then in his late forties, married, drawn to Roman Catholicism, with a loathing of his past. The verdict was greeted with loud cheers and the *Morning Post*, agreeing with the Judge that the play should not be produced, wrote:

'the play is not merely immoral; it is morbid and leads to the black and hopeless portals of criminal insanity...These perversions of sexual passion have no home in the healthy mind of England'.[18]

Nevertheless, the Billing trial was soon forgotten after the war and its memory was pushed into a narrow margin of history. What was not forgotten, however, was Wilde's legacy, which re-emerged through the open discussions of his work and art in the trial. His art, outrageous personality and non-conformist and rebellious attitude lived on beyond this repression and they continued to inspire artists as well as social and sexual revolutionaries in the twentieth century. As Wilde said in his 'Preface' to *The Picture of Dorian Gray*, 'Diversity of opinion about a work of art shows that the work is new, complex and vital.' The mysterious image of Salomé had kept Wilde's spirit alive and new through the years of imprisonment and disgrace. After his death, his most controversial character continued to provoke 'diversity of opinion', as it does to this day.

Notes

1 Robert Ross 'A Note on "Salome"' in Oscar Wilde, *Salomé* (Faber Drama series, London, 1989), p.xv.

2 Richard Ellmann, *Oscar Wilde*, Hamish Hamilton, London, 1987, p.352.

3 Ellmann, pp.316–7.

4 Ellmann, p.352.

5 Ellmann, p.351.

6 Ellmann, pp.350–51.

7 Quoted from E.H. Mikhail (ed), *Oscar Wilde, Interview and Recollections* (Macmillan Press: London, 1979).

8 Kerry Powell, *Oscar Wilde and the Theatre of the 1890s* (Cambridge University Press, 1990), pp.34-35.

9 Rupert Hart-Davis (ed), *Collected Letters of Oscar Wilde* (OUP, 1962), p.115, ft 4.

10 Miriam J. Benkovitz, *Aubrey Beardsley: An Account of His Life* (Hamish Hamilton, London, 1981), pp.87–8.

11 Elaine Showalter, *Sexual Anarchy: Gender and Culture at the Fin de siècle* (Viking, New York), p.14.

12 Sos Eltis, *Revising Wilde: Society and Subversion in the Plays of Oscar Wilde* (Clarendon Press, Oxford), p.18.

13 Ellman, p.466.

14 Letter to Robert Ross, 10 March 1896, Hart-Davis, p.139.

15 H. Montgomery Hyde, *Oscar Wilde* (Methuen Paperbacks, London, 1977), p.484.

16 Robert Ross, 'A Note on "Salome"' in Oscar Wilde, *Salome* (Faber Drama series, London 1989), p.xvii.

17 Robert Ross, *The Pall Mall Gazette*, 28 September, 1912, quoted by Montgomery Hyde, p.488.

18 *Morning Post*, 6 June 1918, quoted by Philip Hoare, *Oscar Wilde's Last Stand* (Arcade Publishing, New York), p.182.

OSCAR WILDE

· DIEPPE · ✠ · BernEVAL

MICHAEL BARKER

In the early hours of Thursday 20 May 1897, *La Tamise*, a French operated Cross-Channel boat steamed slowly into the Normandy port of Dieppe, berthing at 4.30 am in front of the eighteenth-century arcades in the heart of the town. From the jetty, next to the tall crucifix erected for the local fishermen who risked their lives in the treacherous Channel, two Englishmen, Robbie Ross and Reggie Turner, awaited the arrival of their friend Oscar Wilde, released from prison in England the previous day. His distinctive silhouette, head and shoulders above his fellow passengers on the deck, was easily discerned. Recognising them, Wilde smiled and waved as they ran towards the landing stage. When he came down the gangway, Wilde handed Ross a large sealed envelope containing the manuscript of his long epistle, ostensibly to his lover Lord Alfred Douglas, eventually to be published with the title *De Profundis*. The meeting might have been awkward since, only a week earlier, Wilde had accused Ross and More Adey (with whom he had just crossed the Channel) of mismanaging his financial affairs, but the welcome was warm nevertheless. They thought he looked well, for the forty-three-year-old had lost some of his fleshiness while incarcerated. Wilde waited with his fellow passengers in the buffet of the Gare Maritime on the Quai Henri Quatre while Reggie Turner cleared his luggage through Customs, including the 'blessed bag' embossed with the initials S.M. (Sebastian Melmoth). This was the name Wilde adopted in exile, taken from Sebastian the Martyr (Guido Reni's *San Sebastiano* in Genoa was one of his favourite paintings: Cat.117) and from *Melmoth the Wanderer*, a novel written by his great-uncle Charles Maturin.

The friends proceeded the few hundred yards to the Hôtel Sandwich in the Rue de l'Hôtel de Ville behind the seafront and close to the church of St. Rémy, run by Titine Lefèvre, who provided good home cooking and a motherly figure for English bachelors. Wilde's room was filled with flowers, and books that he

had asked for were arranged on the mantelpiece. Only the previous day Wilde had been released from Pentonville at 6.10 am — secretly transferred from Reading Gaol to avoid demonstrations and the attentions of the press. He had served a sentence of two years with hard labour without remission, despite petitions, and had now arrived in France in self-imposed exile, never to set foot again in England. On reaching the hotel, after a great deal of talk with his friends, Wilde stayed up and wrote letters: to Ada Leverson to thank his 'Sphinx' for being the first to greet him; to Frank Harris to thank him for 'lovely clothes and for the generous cheque'; and to his wife Constance, a letter she described as 'full of penitence'.

Dieppe, so close to England but so firmly abroad, was an obvious choice for Wilde — a habitué in earlier, happier days — to escape from the bitterness of England. In 1884, he had much enjoyed a week of his honeymoon there on the way back from Paris to London. The town was the first fashionable seaside resort in France, thanks in part to the new craze for the medicinal benefits of sea-bathing, and was well placed to become a favourite rendezvous of English and French artists, writers and composers. Ruşkin merely passed through the town, but Courbet came to paint and Flaubert took a villa, which Turgenev visited. On the recommendation of Georges Sand, Alexandre Dumas *fils* came and built a villa at Puys — where his father died and where he entertained Carpeaux.

Dieppe was not a typical Normandy town, with picturesque half-timbered houses and towering gables so beloved of nineteenth-century artists. The old houses had been destroyed by the Anglo-Dutch bombardment of 1694, and the town had been rebuilt between 1696 and 1720 all of a piece in brick. The buildings on the quai, which appear in Turner's huge painting exhibited at the Royal Academy in 1825, *The Harbour of Dieppe* (Frick Collection, New York), also look much the same now as in the 1890s.

Cat.48
Charles Conder
The Beach and Cliffs, Dieppe, 1893

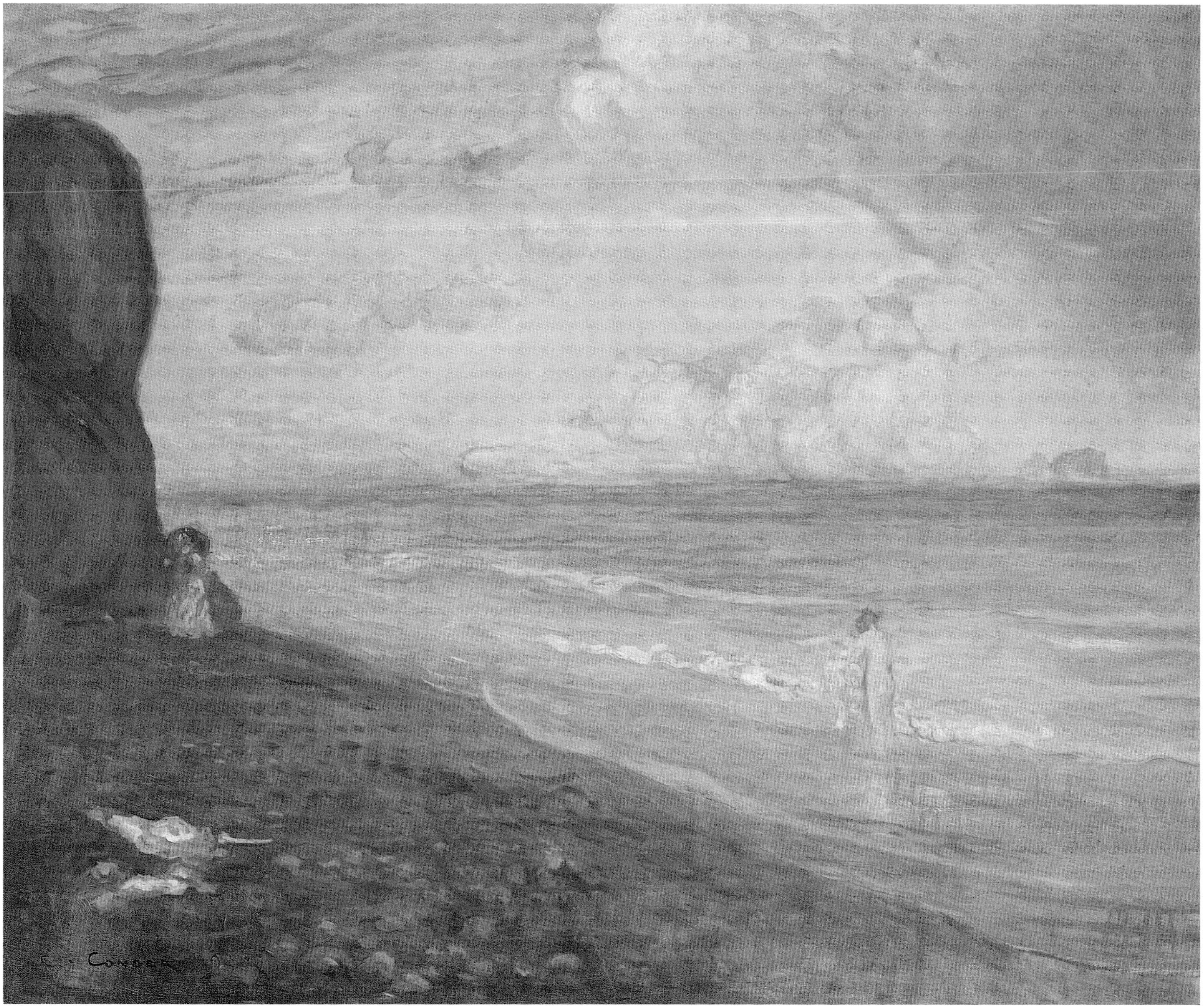

76

Once the humiliation of German occupation during the Franco-Prussian war had passed, Dieppe entered a new era of astonishing popularity with both the English and the French which lasted from the late 1870s until the Great War. Strindberg, Henry James, George Moore, Proust (Fig.24), Max Beerbohm (Cat.149 and pp.92–3), Saint-Saëns, Dubussy, Fauré, Grieg, Percy Grainger and Diaghilev (see Cat.18) all came for the bracing sea air and lively social life. They met at the Café Suisse (Cat.163) and the Café des Tribunaux which both survive although not their opulent Belle Epoque interiors. Aristocratic visitors from Paris: de Polignac, Greffulhe, Caraman-Chimay and de Montesquiou who, transposed, later became characters in Proust's *A la recherche du temps perdu*, welcomed artists and writers to their summer retreats, while Dieppe became part of Proust's composite seaside town, Balbec.

While in Dieppe, Whistler (Cats 114, 174 and pp.132–3) painted Olga Alberta, daughter of the Duchessa de Caracciolo (and almost certainly the natural daughter of the Prince of Wales) – probably in 1883 (he sold the painting to Jacques-Emille Blanche in 1885). Olga would have been thirteen at the time of the portrait, but she looks older and is clearly aware of her attractions. It certainly launched her among fashionable painters, including Helleu and Giovanni Boldini.

Blanche (pp.94–5) was the pivotal figure of Dieppe. The son of a very successful alienist based in Paris who treated de Nerval and de Maupassant. Blanche seems to have known and painted everyone of note and was at ease on both sides of the Channel, as his memoirs amply testify. From the 1880s, at his family's new holiday villa in Dieppe at the Bas Fort Blanc, below the cliffs and the castle, Blanche gathered writers and artists, among them Degas, Renoir, Helleu, Pissarro, Manet, Whistler, Sickert (p.124), Conder (Cats 33, 144 and p.98) and Beardsley (Fig.14, Cats 39, 162 and pp.90–91). The last two described Dieppe as 'Balzac-ian' while Henry James said to Blanche: 'Your Dieppe is a reduced Florence, Every type of character for a novelist seems to gather there'. Sickert (1860–1942) and Blanche (1861–1942), thus almost exact contemporaries, met each other in 1882 and became life-long friends. For significant periods of their lives, both were residents of Dieppe or its hinterland.

When still a schoolboy, Blanche first met Wilde in Paris in 1879 and again in 1883 during Wilde's sojourn from January until May at the Hôtel Voltaire on the Left Bank. Wilde had first stayed at the hotel with his mother in 1874 to celebrate his scholarship from Magdalen College, Oxford, and he returned to it on his honeymoon with Constance in 1884. Blanche exhibited a portrait in 1883 of a young girl reading Wilde's poems, which brought an effusive letter of thanks dated 5 April. Wilde accepted an invitation to tea at Blanche's studio in Auteuil – then outside Paris – his letter praised (its) ' … peacock blue door, the little green and gold bedroom … a fresh oasis of beauty in the desert of

Fig.24
Marcel Proust, c.1900
Courtesy Mary Evans
Picture Library, London

77

Louis Seize which I find at Paris'. The fashion in Paris at the time was actually for a flamboyant neo-Louis Quinze style – a curious slip for an aesthete to make.

During the same stay in 1883, the young Walter Sickert, en route to deliver to the Salon his master Whistler's famous portrait of his mother, lodged at the hotel as Wilde's guest. He had first met Wilde in 1879 at a Sickert family holiday at Dieppe, where Wilde and the actor-impresario Johnston Forbes-Robertson had been house-guests of Sickert's parents. Their fifteen-year old daughter Helena, known as Nelly, was utterly captivated by Wilde. But both Sickert and Blanche (who first met each other in London in 1882) had mixed feelings about him. Blanche had many homosexual friends, notably Proust and Gide (Figs 15, 25), yet was a friend of the hell-raising, womanising Charles Conder among other more or less louche artists, and his close friend Sickert was equally adventurous with women. His own sexuality was rather neutral, though he eventually married his slightly older childhood friend Rose Lemoinne, just five days before the death of his beloved but dominating mother, whose three other children all died young. Rose was unable to bear children, yet they waited until 1938, a year before her death, to adopt her nephew – already married with his own children. Blanche's world was principally *beau monde*; while broad-minded, kindly and sociable, he kept away from scandal. He admired Wilde's talent but his extravagant aura and

Cat.45
Eugène Carrière
Paul Verlaine, 1896

Cat.13
Aubrey Beardsley
Emile Zola, 1893

78

whiff of danger is not likely to have been to Blanche's fastidious taste for too prolonged a contact.

Flushed with the success of his recent tour in America, Wilde returned to London on 27 December 1882, and very quickly decided to go to Paris, ostensibly to write a play (*The Duchess of Padua*), but more importantly to take literary Paris by storm. On arrival in Paris at the end of January 1883, he took a suite of rooms at the Hôtel Voltaire, overlooking the Seine. Fluent in French – though William Rothenstein described it as having a strong English accent – he sent fulsome letters with copies of his *Poems* to many of the best-known French writers, receiving in return invitations to their salons. He met with only partial success. Although the talk of the town, his extravagant manner, his odd style of clothes and Neronian haircut, did not always go down well. The aged Hugo dropped off to sleep, he did not get on with Zola (Cat.13) and found the hard-drinking Verlaine (Cats 5, 45) altogether too much. He was, however, on good terms with Henri de Regnier and was welcomed at the famous *Mardis* – the Tuesday afternoon literary gatherings at the home of the Symbolist poet Stéphane Mallarmé (Cat.196). As for Edmond de Goncourt (Cat.41), a gossip with a malicious tongue, he described Wilde in his *Journal* as ' an individual of doubtful sex who talks like a third-rate actor'. Alphonse Daudet's son Léon was equally unenthusiastic: 'his voice was at once pallid and fat, the words came tumbling out of his frightful slack mouth and when he finished he would roar with laughter like a fat, satisfied, gossipy woman.' Degas' tart comment was 'that he has the look of an amateur playing Lord Byron in a suburban theatre'. Nevertheless the four months spent in Paris until funds ran low were not without success socially. Sarah Bernhardt (p.94 and Cats 11, 38, 47, 110) entertained him at her house and he managed to complete his play. Although no collector of pictures, Wilde's views on art were listened to attentively by Degas, Cazin and Pissarro at the house of the painter Giuseppe de Nittis, a generous host. In the company of Whistler, he was allowed a visit to Degas' studio.

The arrival in Dieppe of Wilde from prison was greeted with little enthusiasm by Sickert and Conder. In a discussion with Blanche as to what their attitude should be, Conder wanted to shun Wilde as an outlaw and exhibitionist, whereas Blanche thought they ought to be more understanding. In the event, when Blanche and Sickert passed the Café Suisse where Wilde was sitting as was his custom, Blanche pretended not to notice him beckoning, to his later remorse. Sickert seems not to have liked Wilde greatly, nor did he consider him particularly witty. He did, however, concede that Wilde provided a warm and generous audience for others. In 1908, declining to speak at a dinner at the Ritz in honour of Ross to celebrate his successful winding up of the Wilde Estate, Sickert wrote to Ross explaining that, in spite of an old friendship with Wilde, his writings seemed to him 'a sort of glorification of nonsense'.

Cat. 41
Félix Bracquemond
Edmond de Goncourt, 1882

Wilde enjoyed his first few days of freedom in Dieppe. With £800 raised by Ross to draw upon, he entertained a group of young poets and students from Paris at the Café des Tribunaux, as ever the social hub of the town. Their party was so boisterous that the Sub-Prefect warned Wilde against repeating such orgies, with an official letter threatening expulsion from France. The staid English colony that largely inhabited the Faubourg de la Barre soon showed their displeasure by ostentatiously walking out when he entered a café or restaurant, or by complaining to the proprietor. On one such occasion, a local resident, Mrs Arthur Stannard, the author with the nom-de-plume 'John Strange Winter', invited him to dinner. On another occasion, observing a further snubbing, she said loudly, 'Oscar, take me to tea'. They then repaired to the Pâtisserie Grisch (now Divernet's) in the Grande Rue to eat ice-cream on the balcony.

Another sympathiser was the Norwegian artist Frits Thaulow, who also lived in the Faubourg, but had nothing in common with the tut-tutting English residents. He approached Wilde and said in a clear voice for all to hear: 'Mr Wilde, my wife and I would feel honoured to have you dine with us en famille this evening'. This gentle bearded giant of a man, married to Alexandra, a statuesque Russian Countess with Marxist sympathies, were often to be seen bicycling around with their two striking blond children. Thaulow was the brother-in-law (by his first wife) of Gauguin, and a friend of Monet and Rodin. He spent most of his life in France and was one of the few Scandinavians to be regarded as an Impressionist. A prolific artist, he was highly successful in his lifetime, with his studies of the effect of moonlight or sunlight on snow and water regularly dispatched to dealers in several capitals. While Grieg, Strindberg, the violinist Joachim and such stars of the Paris theatre as Sarah Bernhardt and Coquelin were entertained at the Thaulows' Villa des Orchidées, the open-hearted, free-thinking, pacifist family also welcomed with champagne and copious dinners local dignitaries, such as doctors, lawyers and town councillors. This was the setting in which Wilde found himself at dinner. Also present was Conder, a regular guest, who soon recovered from his confusion having avoided Wilde in recent days and then renewed their friendship.

While the French writers Hugues Rebell and Tristan Klingsor sent him their latest works, Wilde's first French visitor at the hotel on 25 May was Lugné-Poë (see p.71), the producer of *Salomé* in Paris the previous year (Cat.179). He was keen to put on Wilde's next play but, unfortunately for Wilde, he was unable to advance any money. Within just a week of his arrival in France, unpleasantly aware of being shadowed by a private detective in the pay of his persecutor the Marquess of Queensberry, Wilde thought about moving out of Dieppe. First, however, he wrote a long, impassioned letter to *The Daily Chronicle* on the cruelties of prison life for children. Published on 28 May, it made a strong impression and

80

Cat.144
William Rothenstein
L'homme qui sort:
Charles Conder, 1892

undoubtedly had some influence on the Prisons Act of 1898, which brought reform to the prison system.

Driving in a horse-drawn carriage north-eastwards along the coast, the more windswept, less wooded and less fashionable side of Dieppe, Wilde happened upon the village of Berneval, six miles from Dieppe. Or, as he related whimsically, the white horse drawing the carriage followed his nose home and determined his fate. This small agricultural village, consisting largely of thatched cottages around a pond, which served as a precious reservoir in case of fire and provided the farm horses with water, was attempting also to become a summer resort. Using the name of Sebastian Melmoth, Wilde moved into Hôtel de la Plage on 26 May, taking the two best rooms at 7 francs a day *en pension*, while a valet was engaged at 35 francs a month. He hung on the wall a portrait of his revered Queen Victoria and arranged his books, including the novels of Flaubert, Dumas, Dostoyevsky, the Gospels and Renan's *La Vie de Jésus*. Two days later, alone once more, his pen was soon active and he wrote to Max Beerbohm to thank him for a copy of his *Happy Hypocrite*.

Monsieur Bonnet, proprietor of Hôtel de la Plage, was something of a dabbler in property, and he suggested finding a plot of land for Wilde to build a villa. Wilde enthused in a letter to Ross with the idea of a place of his own, which he envisaged in the style of an old English farmhouse. But it was an unrealistic dream, as Ross pointed out, for Wilde had not the funds and was more likely to spend his time in Paris.

For the time being, Wilde enjoyed the calm of a simple life in a remote village of some five hundred souls, rising at 7.30 am, in bed by 10 pm; the apple trees were in blossom and the sun shone for his daily walk down through the ravine in the cliffs to the beach for a swim before attending Mass. He convinced himself that he might end his days at Berneval, at least as so expressed in a letter to Robert Ross, to whom he wrote almost daily – usually beseeching money but also revealing that Bosie telegraphed frequently. Meanwhile, he had cards engraved: 'Mr Sebastian Melmoth, Berneval-sur-Mer, près Dieppe'. The former atheist charmed the Abbé Trop-Hardy, the elderly *curé* of the parish, who offered Wilde a permanent pew in the church. Wilde proposed, unsuccessfully, that the priest should celebrate Mass on Sundays at the tiny, little-used stone chapel near the hotel dedicated to Notre-Dame de Liesse; the chapel contained a statue of the Black Virgin and was a place of pilgrimage on 15 August, the Feast of the Assumption. The bankrupt but ever beneficent Wilde even contemplated donating stained glass windows. He befriended the local fishermen with whom he played cards or dominoes and the Customs officers, posted here to guard the beaches against smugglers, to whom he lent novels to relieve the tedium of their vigils in their lonely cabins. While continuing to take his main meals at the hotel produced by its excellent chef, he rented for the summer season,

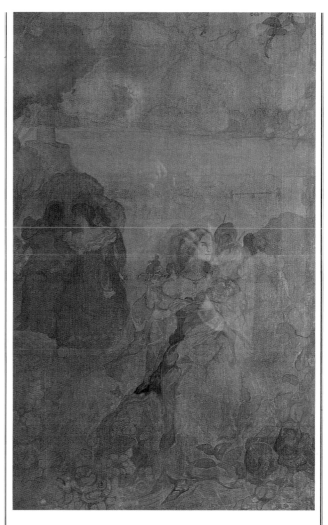

Cat.49
Charles Conder
Screen painting:
'Homage à Villon'

for the sum of £32, a nearby villa with three bedrooms and sea-views, the Chalet Bourgeat (later to be rented by Renoir).

Visitors soon made their welcome appearance. On 3 June, the young poet Ernest Dowson arrived with Conder and Dalhousie Young. They talked well into the night, and Young even proposed giving Wilde the money to build a house, but Wilde felt uneasy about accepting such a large gift from a comparative stranger. However, he did accept a handsome cheque from the actor Charles Wyndham, who came to Berneval ostensibly to commission an adaptation of a French play for the English stage. But he was aware that the play was never likely to materialise. Wilde had little enthusiasm for serious work, turning down a proposal by the editor of *Le Journal* for a weekly column on literary topics – his excuse was that it would be read only out of morbid curiosity. Later, on 20 June, André Gide, a long-standing acquaintance, arrived unannounced at Berneval. As Wilde was absent, Gide spent an evening alone in the hotel until Wilde arrived late from Dieppe,

"ONE NEEDS MISFORTUNES TO LIVE HAPPILY"

chilled to the bone having somehow mislaid his coat. Once revived with hot grog, they talked until late into the night, and in the morning he took Gide to see the Chalet Bourgeat, which he was beginning to furnish. Gide was later to reproach Wilde for leaving Berneval without writing a play.

At the Chalet Bourgeat on 22 June, perhaps pining for his sons, Wilde organised a tea-party in the garden for some fifteen boys (no girls!) of the village with their teacher to celebrate Queen Victoria's Diamond Jubilee. Marcel Bary, a young local carpenter, was engaged to install decorations, including lanterns and flags of both countries; he also removed from the guest list those boys of whom he did not approve. Wilde's valet served strawberries and cream and chocolates but the *pièce de résistance* was an enormous confection by the local *pâtissier* Monsieur Lauvergeat, adorned with red and green roses and the inscription in icing-sugar: 'Jubilé de la Reine Victoria'. Distributing presents of musical instruments to the boys, Wilde demanded that they sing the *Marseillaise* and then *God Save the Queen*, which inevitably presented a problem. The feast ended with cries of 'Vive la Reine d'Angleterre', 'Vive la France, mère de tous les artistes' and, to Wilde's amusement as a recent jail-bird to

have his name so coupled, 'Vivent le Président de la République et Monsieur Melmoth'.

All the while, the villagers had been unaware of the real identity of this exotic English gentlemen in their midst. When exposed, Wilde was shunned once more, forcing him to seek company in Dieppe, or occasionally at Martin-Eglise, just south of the town, at the still picturesque Auberge du Clos Normand, its orchard gardens watered by a pretty stream. His expenditure was reckless as ever, and whatever little money came to him soon flowed through his hands. He even made loans to the likes of Ernest Dowson, to whom he was physically attracted, then with Conder living at Arques. It was Dowson who persuaded Wilde to visit a prostitute in Dieppe 'to acquire a more wholesome taste in the sex line' as he put it. It was not a success. 'The first these ten years, and it will be the last. It was like cold mutton' said Wilde but exhorted Dowson to 'tell it in England, for it will entirely restore my character'.

During July, he at last made an effort to divert his creative powers from writing amusing or importuning letters. Despite refusing to discuss his life in gaol with Sherard and Ross, who came to stay at the Chalet Bourgeat in August (a visit spoilt for Sherard

82

Cat.51
Charles Conder
Fan Painting:
Two women in
landscape,
late 1890s

Fig.25
Jacques-Emile Blanche
André Gide, 1912
Courtesy Musée des
Beaux-Arts, Rouen

when he espied, or so he told Smithers, Wilde and Ross in sexual embrace), he had largely completed what he called his swan song – his great polemic poem *The Ballad of Reading Gaol* – dedicated to a soldier condemned to hanging for killing his mistress. Later revised and extended, it was indeed to be his last important literary work, achieving great success when published the following year, albeit in limited print-runs, by the raffish Leonard Smithers (Fig.26 and p.125), publisher of erotica as well as *The Savoy* (Cat.17), the quarterly hatched at the Café des Tribunaux.

Another figure of Wilde's past was spending the summer in Dieppe while trying to avoid him: the sickly Aubrey Beardsley, who was to die from tuberculosis in Menton the following March at the age of twenty five. Once close, their relationship had soured;

moreover, Beardsley was being supported financially by Wilde's enemy André Raffalovich. Beardsley was staying at the Hôtel Sandwich, which was rather odd given that it was Wilde's known Dieppe base and forwarding address, but he then moved to the Hôtel des Etrangers in the Rue Aguado, at the quieter end of the seafront. Since Dieppe is so small and its meeting places so few, it was inevitable that their paths would cross. It happened at a dinner on 19 July at the Thaulows' villa, where they greeted each other as old friends, although only recently Beardsley, in the company of Conder and Blanche, had snubbed Wilde in the street. On 3 August, they went on a spree in Dieppe when Wilde persuaded Beardsley to buy a hat 'more silver than silver'. But when Beardsley failed to turn up for dinner at Berneval on a later occasion, Wilde

84

Wilde wrote to Smithers in May 1898:
'You are accustomed to bringing out books limited to
an edition of three copies, one for the author, one for
yourself, and one for the Police that I really feel you
are sinking beneath your standards in producing a
sixpenny edition of anything ...Perhaps, as I want the
poem to reach the poorer classes we might give away
a cake of "Maypole" soap with each copy; I hear it dyes
people the most lovely colours, and is also cleansing.'

bitterly commented, 'it was too *lâche* of Aubrey.' Beardsley, however, received his own snub: the prickly Whistler, a Dieppe regular, who had quarrelled with Wilde (and, indeed, with many members of their milieu) was in Dieppe in July with the Pennells but, significantly, did not accompany them when they called on Beardsley.

The weather became vile during August. After ten solid days of rain and wind, with no friends for company and conversation and oppressed at the thought of a winter alone in Berneval, Wilde was at low ebb, to the point of feeling suicidal. Despite his penury – his finances effectively were controlled by his wife and Ross on the condition that Wilde kept away from Lord Alfred Douglas – his initial fear of rekindling his relationship with Bosie gradually dissolved. His assurances to Ross at the end of May that to be with Bosie again would be a return to the hell from which he had been released gave way, in just a few days, to affectionate letters to Bosie. Within a fortnight, his 'My dear boy' became 'dear honey-sweet boy' and an invitation to Bosie to come to Berneval, bringing lots of cigarettes and books. This reached the ears of Ross, and Wilde was warned off by his solicitor. In panic, he put off the visit but continued to write to 'my own darling boy'. Their joyful reunion at last took place on 28 August, at the Hôtel de la Poste, Rouen.

The charms of Berneval exhausted, Wilde departed on 14 September 1897 to flee to Italy with Bosie. It is unlikely that he ever returned to the village, although it seems he did make one final excursion to Dieppe in June 1900. After a peripatetic five months in Naples, Capri, Sicily and Rome, Wilde lived out the last three years of his life in Paris, sliding more or less downhill to his death at the age of forty-six in the modest Hôtel d'Alsace on 30 November 1900. Wilde expired holding Ross's hand and cared for by the hotel's kindly proprietor, Monsieur Dupoirier.

Bibliography

Principal works consulted:

Bialek, Mireille *Jacques-Emile Blanche*, Offranville, 1997.

Blanche, Jacques-Emile *Dieppe*, Emile-Paul Frères, Paris, 1927.

Blanche, Jacques-Emile *Portraits of a Lifetime 1870-1914*, Dent, London 1937.

Jacques-Emile Blanche, Peintre (1861-1942) – Exhibition catalogue Rouen 1997.

Caillas, Alin *Oscar Wilde, Tel que Je l'ai connu*, La Pensée Universelle, 1971.

Croft-Cooke, Rupert *The Unrecorded Life of Oscar Wilde*, WH Allen, London 1972.

The Dieppe Connection – A Town and its Artists from Turner to Braque – Exhibition catalogue, Brighton 1992.

Ellman, Richard *Oscar Wilde*, Hamish Hamilton, London 1987.

Pearson, Hesketh *The Life of Oscar Wilde*, Penguin, London 1960.

Pakenham, Simona *Quand Dieppe était Anglais 1814-1914* – Les Informations Dieppoises 1971.

Sturgis, Matthew *Aubrey Beardsley*, Flamingo 1999.

Sutton, Denys *Walter Sickert*, Michael Joseph, London 1976.

Sweetman, David *Toulouse-Lautrec and the Fin-de-Siècle*, Hodder and Stoughton, London 1999.

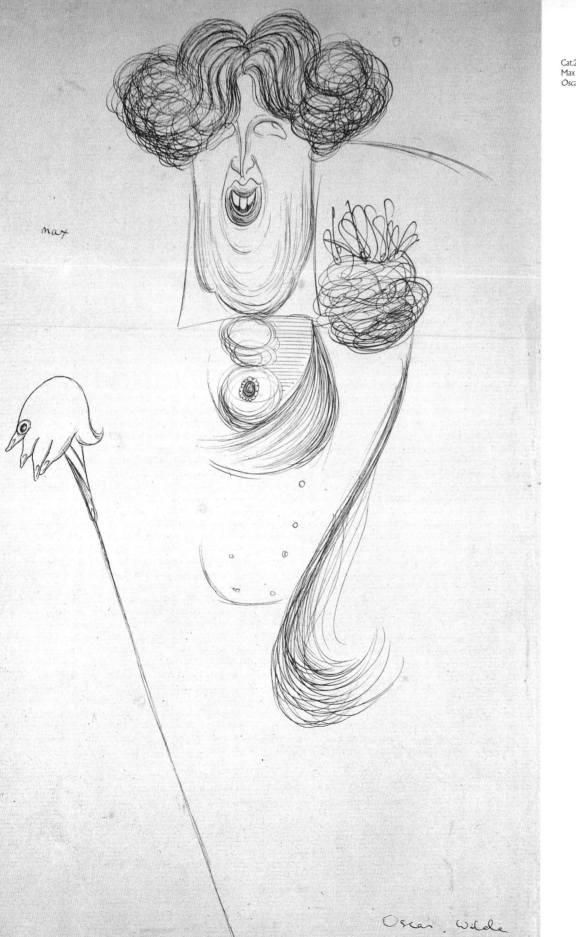

max

Oscar. Wilde

Cat.25
Max Beerbohm
Oscar Wilde,1894

Catalogue

COMPILED BY: LIONEL LAMBOURNE (LL)

TOMOKO SATO (TS)

VICTOR ARWAS (VA)

LOUISE VAUGHAN (LV)

THE ARTISTS

THE PERSONALITIES

ASSOCIATED WITH OSCAR WILDE

◆ ◆ ◆ ◆ ◆ ◆ ◆ ◆ ◆ ◆ ◆ ◆ ◆ ◆ ◆ ◆ ◆ ◆ ◆

Notes to users:

The authors of the catalogue entries are noted by the initials in brackets, at the end of biographies, which appear in the ALPHABETICAL order of names. Due to the mixture of British and foreign artists, writers and publishers, in the interests of consistency, formal titles and memberships of societies have not been used.

Following each biography, works are listed chronologically, grouped under the same artist, writer or publisher.

Measurements are in centimetres. For two-dimensional works, image sizes are given height before width. For three-dimensional works, height (H) before width (W) or diameter (D), followed by depth (D). Widest dimensions are given for the measurements of the objects of irregular shapes.

The placing of signatures and inscriptions on the work is indicated by the following abbreviations: t.r. – top right; b.r. – bottom right; r.c. – right centre; t.c. – top centre; b.c.-bottom centre; l.c. – left centre; t.l. – top left; u.l. – upper left; b.l. – bottom left; l.l. – lower left.

Cat. 3

Alastair
[pseudonym of Hans Henning Voigt or von Voigt]
1887–1969

Born in Karlsruhe, he took the title of Baron and often claimed to be the illegitimate son of various members of European royalty, including King Edward VII. Alastair was a highly talented pianist and accompanied Yvette Guilbert in several recitals, as well as playing with Pablo Casals and Alfred Cortot.

He was a creative and original draughtsman, and was considered as Aubrey Beardsley's (pp.90–91) successor by John Lane (p.109), founder of The Bodley Head Press and publisher of *The Yellow Book* (Cats 16 a-b, 96). He illustrated many books and exhibited in many places, including New York, Paris, Brussels and Geneva. Alastair's drawings were all inspired by literary works and he produced several variations for books that interested him. His first published book was Oscar Wilde's *The Sphinx* (Cat.1) in 1920, though the drawings had been executed before the war. He also illustrated Wilde's *Salomé* in the original French (Cat.2), which was published in 1922; *The Birthday of the Infanta* in both English and French editions in 1928; and *The Picture of Dorian Gray* (Cat. 3), which was never published. (VA)

1 Oscar Wilde
Illustrated by Alastair
Sphinx
Published in London and New York, John Lane and The Bodley Head, 1920 (one of 1,000 copies)
Book, white cloth, blocked in gold and blue, 30.5 x 23.5 cm
Simon Wilson, London

2 Oscar Wilde
Illustrated by Alastair
Salomé
Published in Paris, Les Editions G. Grès et Cie, 1922
Book, paper wrappers, 19.1 x 14.3 cm
Private Collection

3 ***Dorian Gray in Catherine de Medici's mourning bed***, early 1920s
Pen and ink and watercolour on paper, 16.8 x 11.5 cm
Victor and Gretha Arwas, London

=+=+=+=+=+=+=+=+=+=+=+=+=+=+=+=+=+=+=+

Lawrence Alma-Tadema
1836–1912

Alma-Tadema was born in Holland and in 1869 came to England, where he became very much part of the English establishment. He was essentially a Classicist painter, and his paintings depict the life of ancient Greece and Rome, concentrating on the domestic rather than the dramatic. He was highly praised for his accurate rendering of archaeological detail and technical accuracy, but there was little passion in the figures he painted. He emphasised the outward rather that the inward character.

Alma-Tadema was a regular exhibitor at the Grosvenor Gallery, which was opened in 1877. His depiction of a priestess of Bacchus dancing before a Genii-nostra altar (Cat. 4), was exhibited in 1880. In Oscar Wilde's review of the first Grosvenor Gallery exhibition in 1877, where Alma-Tadema showed eight pictures, he described the artist's works as 'good examples of that accurate drawing of inanimate objects which makes his pictures so real from an antiquarian point to view'. In a letter to the article's publishers, he commented that he and other artists of his acquaintance felt that Alma-Tadema's drawing ability was disgraceful. However, a recently discovered letter

to the artist, probably dating from 1880, reveals Wilde in friendlier vein: 'I hope that whenever you want any kind of information about Greek things, in which I might help you that you will let me know. It is always a pleasure for me to work at any Greek subject, and a double pleasure to do so for anyone whose work mirrors so exquisitely and rightly, as yours does, that beautiful old Greek world.' (LV/LL)

4 ***A Garden Altar***, 1879
Oil on panel, 44.5 x 22 cm
Signed t.c. by frieze: L.Alma-Tadema OP.CCV
Inscribed r.c. (on altar): GENIO I NOSTRI FELIX L [To the Genius of our Emperor Felix his Freedman]
Aberdeen Art Gallery and Museums

=+=+=+=+=+=+=+=+=+=+=+=+=+=+=+=+=+=+=+

Edmond-François Aman-Jean
1858–1935/6

This most eclectic of artists studied at the Ecole des Beaux Arts and shared a studio with Georges Seurat for several years. He also studied and worked with Puvis de Chavannes before obtaining the Prix de Rome in 1886. On his return, he became involved with the Symbolist poets Mallarmé (Cat.196), Villiers de l'Isle Adam, and Paul Verlaine (Cats 5, 45). Wilde admired Aman-Jean's work, and compared it favourably with the paintings of Burne-Jones (p.96). (LL)

5 ***Paul Verlaine***, c.1892
Lithograph on chine collé, 19.5 x 12.8 cm
Signed (in stone)
Richard Hollis, London

Paul Verlaine's stormy relationship with the poet Arthur Rimbaud (1854–91) culminated in imprisonment in 1873 for wounding Rimbaud with a revolver. While in prison, Verlaine became a devout Catholic. In 1886, believing Rimbaud to be dead (he was living in Abyssinia), Verlaine published his poems under the title of *Les Illuminations*, a work which played a major role in launching the Symbolist and Decadent Movements.

6 ***The Girl with a Peacock***, 1895
Oil on canvas, 150 x 104 cm
Signed b.l.
Musée des Arts Décoratifs, Paris

Aman-Jean specialised in depicting languid young women in gardens with peacocks. He also produced pastels wrought in a style which led to him being described as a latter day Pre-Raphaelite, a judgement shared by Wilde.

=+=+=+=+=+=+=+=+=+=+=+=+=+=+=+=+=+

Louis Anquetin
1861–1932

Born in 1861, Anquetin moved to Paris in 1882 where he met and worked with leading avant-garde painters of the day, including Toulouse-Lautrec (pp.128–9), Gauguin, Van Gogh and Bernard.

In exploring alternatives to Impressionism and naturalism, Anquetin and Bernard studied Japanese prints (in vogue at that time), the early work of Van Gogh and stained glass windows. By the summer of 1887 they had created a new style, which were to be coined 'Cloisonnism' by the critic Edouard Dujardin in 1888.

Cat.7

Anquetin established a reputation as an innovatory artist and expressed his search for the new, not only through this style but also through the modernity of his subject matter. The latter included Parisian townscapes, café-cabaret scenes, racecourses and fashionable women (e.g. Cat.7) who frequented places such as the Moulin Rouge and the Moulin de la Galette.

Wilde made two visits to Paris in 1891 and was warmly received by the literary salons. He was introduced to many leading artistic figures of the period, including Stéphane Mallarmé (Cat.196), the central figure related to Symbolism, which was current during the 1890s. (LV/LL)

7   *Girl reading a Newspaper*, 1890
     Pastel on paper mounted on mill board,
     54 x 43.5 cm
     Signed and dated b.l.
     Board of Trustees of The Tate Gallery, London

This remarkable study in green, the colour of the 1890s, was one of a series of 'women in hats full of flowers' and chosen, like his friend Lautrec's models, from environments such as the Moulin Rouge. Wilde was also fascinated by the colour green, a colour associated with perversity. As Wilde put it in his essay 'Pen, Pencil and Poison', subtitled 'A Study in Green', Thomas Griffiths Wainewright (Cat.185) 'had that curious love of green, which in individuals is always the sign of a subtle artistic temperament, and in nations is said to denote a laxity, if not a decadence of morals', a quotation which puts Wilde's adoption of the green carnation as a symbol in a new perspective.

=+=+=+=+=+=+=+=+=+=+=+=+=+=+=+=+=+

'Ape' [pseudonym of Carlo Pellegrini]
1838–89

Pellegrini was a diminutive Neapolitan caricaturist, who as a youth fought for Garibaldi. He came to London in 1865, and his coloured lithograph of Disraeli established the 'house style' of the long-running journal *Vanity Fair* (1869–1913). Pellegrini was also a close friend of Whistler (pp.132–3) and the Prince of Wales. (LL)

8   *'English Music' Sir Arthur Sullivan*
     Published in *Vanity Fair*, 14 March 1874
     Colour lithograph, 35.5 x 23.2 cm
     Signed b.r.
     Catherine Haill, London

The son of a bandmaster at the Royal Military School of Music, Arthur Sullivan (1842–1909) attended the Chapel Royal and Royal Academy of Music before studying at Leipzig. While working as an organist he began to compose operettas, linking up with the librettist W.S. Gilbert (Cat.172) in 1871. For twenty years their collaboration went from triumph to triumph, notably with *Patience* in 1881 and *The Mikado* in 1885.

=+=+=+=+=+=+=+=+=+=+=+=+=+=+=+=+=+

Edward Armitage
1817–96

Born into a wealthy Leeds family, Armitage studied in Paris under Paul Delaroche. His first painting, exhibited in Paris in 1842, was described as 'well drawn but brutally energetic', a statement in a sense true of all his later works. He painted two frescoes in the House of Lords of scenes from the works of Alexander Pope and Sir Walter Scott. In later years, he turned to Crimean war themes and also depicted the suppression of the Indian Mutiny of 1857 in *Retribution*. (LL)

9   *Herod's Birthday Feast*, 1868
     Oil on canvas, 154.9 x 276.9 cm
     Guildhall Art Gallery
     (The Corporation of London)

Armitage selects a theme from the middle of the story told in St Mark, Chapter 6, and creates a careful reconstruction of Herod's palace. He also ventures upon the erotic element of the tale, when Salome dances for Herod, although she seems to be far from discarding any of her seven veils. Armitage also avoids any reference to Salome's request for the head of John the Baptist, the aspect of the story that particularly appealed to French artists of the period (see pp.60–65).

=+=+=+=+=+=+=+=+=+=+=+=+=+=+=+=+=+=+

Jules Barbey d'Aurevilly
1808–89

Born into a Royalist Roman Catholic family, he was equally extreme in his dandyism and his ultramontane Catholicism. His prolific works provide an exotic blend of flamboyant sensationalism, fervent spirituality, and a romantic affirmation of the values of tradition, especially of the monarchy and the literary classics. But like Oscar Wilde he was himself his own most fascinating creation – generous, proud, idolised, highly influential and extremely quarrelsome with great powers of invective. He denounced Zola (Cat.13) as 'this mud-stained Hercules who wallows in the Augean dung and adds his little bit to it...' Essays, novels and short stories poured from his pen, notably the famous story *Les Diaboloques* in 1874. (LL)

10   Translated by Sebastian Melmoth [Oscar Wilde]
     What Never Dies
     Published in Paris, privately printed by Charles Carrington, 1902
     Book, purple cloth with gilt cross device and initials 'OW', 18.9 x 13.1 cm
     Stephen Calloway, Brighton

=+=+=+=+=+=+=+=+=+=+=+=+=+=+=+=+=+=+

Jules Bastien-Lepage
1848–84

Bastien-Lepage's work was once described by Emile Zola (Cat.13) as 'Impressionism corrected, sweetened and adapted to the taste of the crowd'. He is chiefly remembered today for his rural subjects, and small full-length studies of children going to school or having been wrapped in sacks to protect them from the elements while guarding their flocks. Bastien-Lepage was also a distinguished portrait painter. (LL)

11   *Portrait of Sarah Bernhardt holding a statue of Orpheus*, 1879
     Line engraving after a painting in oil on canvas
     Signed and dated t.l.
     Inscribed t.l.: 'A SARAH BERNHARDT'
     Victor and Gretha Arwas, London

=+=+=+=+=+=+=+=+=+=+=+=+=+=+=+=+=+=+

Aubrey Vincent Beardsley
1872–98

His highly controversial black and white drawings and his tragically early death from consumption at the age of twenty five made Beardsley a legend of the 1890s. The celebrated reviewer of the period Holbrook Jackson said that Beardsley had been 'as necessary a corner-stone of the Temple of the Perverse as Oscar Wilde'.

Born in Brighton, Beardsley moved to London in 1888, where he developed his career as an artist while working as a clerk in the City. Largely self-taught, the only formal training he had received was in 1891–2 when he attended Frederick Brown's night classes at the Westminster School of Art. Beardsley's style evolved from his personal response to a variety of influences ranging from Burne-Jones (p.96) and Puvis de Chavannes to Whistler (pp.132–3) and Japanese prints. In 1892, he was commissioned by the publisher J.M. Dent to illustrate and design Sir Thomas Malory's *Le Morte D'Arthur*, which established his reputation.

Beardsley first met Wilde in July 1891 in Burne-Jones's home, and he soon became friendly with Wilde and his circle. Perhaps with Wilde's influence, Beardsley's style became more satirical and sinister, as evident in his illustrations to Wilde's play *Salomé* (see p.68 and Cats 14, 15, 19). Wilde used to say that Beardsley was his creation, and also in the public's mind Beardsley's name became inseparable from that of Wilde. Such a strong association, however, had an adverse effect on Beardsley at the time of Wilde's disgrace in 1895, and led to his resignation from *The Yellow Book* (Cats 16 a-b, 96), the art magazine he had founded the previous year with Henry Harland.

In 1896, Beardsley was involved in another new magazine, *The Savoy* (Cat.17), with Arthur Symons, but his health was declining with the onset of consumptive attacks. Beardsley spent much of this period abroad, in Brussels, Paris, Dieppe and

Menton, where he died in 1898. Beardsley's attitude towards Wilde was not always cordial: Wilde was displeased by Beardsley's impudent caricatures of him, cleverly incorporated in the *Salome* illustrations. Also Wilde was deeply hurt when Beardsley avoided him in Dieppe (see pp.83–5), where they happened to stay in the same hotel following Wilde's release from prison in 1897. Nevertheless, Wilde held Beardsley's art in high esteem. He reckoned that Beardsley had brought 'a strangely new personality to English art'(Hart-Davis, *Letters*, p.410), and he was shocked by the news that Beardsley had died, in Wilde's words, 'at the age of a flower' (Ellmann, p.535). (TS)

12   *Miss Terry: Caricature of Ellen Terry as Rosamund in Tennyson's 'Becket', produced by Henry Irving at the Lyceum Theatre, London, 6 February 1893*
     Published in *The Pall Mall Budget*, 9 February 1893
     Pen and ink on paper, 20.5 x 11 cm
     Signed b.r.
     Inscribed b.l.: 'Miss Terry'
     Merlin Holland, London

Cat.12

13 *The Disappointment of Zola*: *Caricature of Emile Zola on being refused entry to the Académie Française*
Published in *The Pall Mall Budget*, 9 February 1893
Pen and ink on paper, 24 x 13 cm
Signed b.r.
Inscribed t.c.: 'L'ACADÉMIE FR'
Merlin Holland, London

In Paris in March, 1891, Wilde visited Zola, the great realist novelist who was working on his novel *War* and preparing himself by reading heaps of documents about the Battle of Sedan before visiting the battlefield. Zola declared: 'There is no good novel which is not based on documents'. Surprisingly, Wilde agreed, saying 'in writing my Dorian Gray I studied long lists of jewellery … you cannot draw a novel from your brain as a spider draws its web out of its belly'.

14 *The Studio*, Volume I, Number I
London, April 1893
Magazine, 30.2 x 21.1 cm
Green paper wrappers with design by Beardsley
Containing Joseph Pennell's article 'Aubrey Beardsley; A New Illustrator' reproducing Beardsley's original *Salomé* design, 'J'ai baissé ta bouche, Jokanaan.'
Stephen Calloway, Brighton

15 Oscar Wilde, translated from the French of Oscar Wilde, illustrated by Aubrey Beardsley
Salomé, A Tragedy in One Act
Published in London, Elkin Mathews and John Lane, 1894
Book, rough blue cloth, stamped with front and rear cover device by Beardsley, 21.6 x 15.2 cm
The first English edition (one of 500 copies)
Stephen Calloway, Brighton

16 Aubrey Beardsley (as Art Editor)
Two volumes of
The Yellow Book, An Illustrated Quarterly

a. Volume I
Published in London, Elkin Mathews and John Lane, April 1894
Book, yellow cloth, blocked with design by Beardsley, 20.8 x 15.9 cm
Stephen Calloway, Brighton

b. Volume 4 (the last volume to appear under Beardsley's art editorship)
Published in London, Elkin Mathews and John Lane, January 1895
Book, yellow cloth, blocked with design by Beardsley, 20.8 x 15.9 cm
Stephen Calloway, Brighton

17 Aubrey Beardsley (as Art Editor)
The Savoy, Number I
Published in London, Leonard Smithers, January 1896
Magazine, pink paper-covered boards with design by Beardsley, 26.6 x 19.4 cm
Includes Arthur Symons's article 'Dieppe' illustrated by Beardsley
Stephen Calloway, Brighton

18 *Six Drawings Illustrating Theophile Gautier's Romance Mademoiselle de Maupin*
Published in London, Leonard Smithers, 1898
Portfolio of six designs, printed in photogravure on separate sheets (one of 50 sets)

Cat.18

Sheet size 38.2 x 28 cm each
Stephen Calloway, Brighton

These illustrations were greatly admired by the Russian impresario Sergei Diaghilev (1872–1929), who met Beardsley in Dieppe and later Wilde in Paris. To oblige Diaghilev, Wilde on 4 May 1898 wrote to his friend and publisher Leonard Smithers (p.125): 'Have you a copy of Aubrey's *Mademoiselle de Maupin*? There is a young Russian here who is a great amateur of Aubrey's art, who would love to have one. He is a great amateur, and rich. So you might send him a copy and name your price, and also deal with him for drawings by Aubrey…'

19 *A Portfolio of Aubrey Beardsley's Drawings illustrating Salomé by Oscar Wilde*
Published in London, John Lane, 1906
16 plates printed on separate sheets of Japan vellum paper
Sheet size 34.6 x 27.4 cm each
Stephen Calloway, Brighton

Cecil Beaton
1904–80

Photographer, stage and film designer, draughtsman, painter and writer, Beaton established a reputation as an arbiter of beauty from the mid-1920s, publishing the *Book of Beauty* and working on *Vogue* magazine. Beaton was fascinated by the gorgeous raiment worn by late Victorian high society ladies, an interest which made him ideally suited for designing productions of Wilde's plays for stage and screen. Of all the many revivals of plays such as *Lady Windermere's Fan*, *An Ideal Husband*, *A Woman of No Importance* and *The Importance of Being Earnest*, productions with costumes designed by Beaton were by far the most glamorous. Wilde's plays were also made into extremely successful films, *The Importance of Being Earnest* (1952) preserving for posterity the performance of the famous actress Dame Edith Evans and her definitive reading of the role of Lady Bracknell. The photographs seen here show how successful he was at creating costumes that recall the silky elegance of a Sargent painting, even though Beaton was then working at the height of the post-war austerity, conditions associated with the then Chancellor of the Exchequer, Sir Stafford Cripps. Clothing was still rationed and Beaton needed special government permission to buy materials for these gowns. Although his creations were exaggerated and idealised versions of the clothes that women really wore in the early 1890s, Beaton's hope was that film audiences 'will be so struck by their beauty that they will begin thinking fondly and enviously of the epoch'. (LL)

20 *Isobel Jeans as Mrs Erlynne in 'Lady Windermere's Fan'*
New York, 1946
Modern copy print
Courtesy Sotheby's, London

21 *Isobel Jeans as Mrs Erlynne, playing with 'Lady Windermere's' fan*
New York, 1946
Modern copy print
Courtesy Sotheby's, London

22 *Cecil Beaton as Cecil Graham in 'Lady Windermere's Fan'*
New York, 1946
Modern copy print
Courtesy Sotheby's, London

With great panache, Beaton himself acted in the New York production the minor role of Cecil Graham. He is seen here with Penelope Ward as Lady Windermere.

23 *Lord Darlington's Room in Act 3 of 'Lady Windermere's Fan' with Cecil Beaton as Cecil Graham*
New York, 1946
Modern copy print
Courtesy Sotheby's, London

=+=+=+=+=+=+=+=+=+=+=+=+=+=+=+=+=+

Max Beerbohm
1872–1956

The most aphoristic of the aesthetes, Beerbohm, whilst still an undergraduate at Merton College, Oxford, contributed to *The Yellow Book* (Cats 16 a-b, 96). In 1896, in a mock farewell to literature, he published *The Works of Max Beerbohm*, declaring himself a trifle outdated and a member of the 'Beardsley Period'. In 1898 he succeeded Bernard Shaw as drama critic for the prestigious *Saturday Review*, a post he held for twenty years, before retiring to Rapallo, Italy, where he remained, apart from sojourns in England during both world wars. He was knighted in 1939, and during the Second World War perfected the broadcast talk into an art form.

As a draughtsman, Beerbohm's creative methods were fascinating. Using as a mental point of departure the profile figures made familiar by 'Ape' (p.89) and 'Spy' (p.126) in *Vanity Fair* he evolved a *faux-naif* likeness of remarkable analytical power. In a private character notebook, he would first write down a penetrating analytical verbal portrait, before making the finished drawing alone at night in the privacy of his room. (LL)

24 *Beerbohm's Undergraduate drawings of Oscar Wilde*
Published in *Pick-Me-Up*, 22 September 1894
Pen and ink on paper, 30.9 x 19.2 cm (HD 1779)
Visitors of the Ashmolean Museum, Oxford

25 *Oscar Wilde*, 1894
Published in *Pick-Me-Up*, 22 September 1894
Pen and ink on paper, 30.8 x 19 cm (HD 1778)
Signed u.l.
Visitors of the Ashmolean Museum, Oxford

26 *Oscar Wilde*, c.1894
Pen and ink on paper, 30 x 18 cm
Collection Barry Humphries, London

27 *Self-portrait*, c.1895
Pen and ink and watercolour on paper, 19.7 x 9.5 cm (HD 1402)
Signed
The Warden and Fellows of Merton College, University of Oxford

28 *Robert Hichens – the Author of 'The Green Carnation'*, 1898
Published in *The Sketch*, 18 May 1898
Pen and ink on paper, 19 x 12.6 cm (HD751)
Board of Trustees of the Victoria and Albert Museum London (E.3774-1914)

The Green Carnation (Cat. 89), a parody of Wilde's lifestyle, gets its title from Oscar's circle of friends who wore this botanically impossible flower as buttonholes at his first nights. *The Green Carnation* was published anonymously in 1894, when literary London became agog to learn who was the author. Even Wilde himself was accused of penning the work, but, while admitting inventing 'that magnificent flower', stated: 'The flower is a work of art. The book is not.' It was withdrawn from circulation in 1895 during the trials.

29 *Mr W.B. Yeats, presenting Mr George Moore to the Queen of the Fairies*, 1904
Pen and wash on paper, 31.8 x 19.1 cm (HD 1827)
Signed l.c.
Hugh Lane Municipal Gallery of Modern Art, Dublin

The poet and dramatist William Butler Yeats (Cats. 29, 32, 93) was preoccupied with the occult and Celtic symbolism, rather to the alarm of the realist novelist George Moore (1852–1933).

I was often called upon for sympathy when Conder was in difficulties. Sober men are, alas, poor comforters and sorry companions for men crowned with vine leaves. 'Will, don't look so sensible,' said Oscar Wilde one evening as I sat with him and Conder and Max at the Café Royal.

Is this what you would imply, Will?

Max 1929

Cat. 33

30   *Caricature of Edward Carson*, 1912.
     Pencil and wash on paper, 31.1 x 19.4 cm
     (HD247)
     Board of Trustees of the National Portrait Gallery,
     London (Reg.no. 3852)

Of commanding presence, magnetic in appearance and speaking with a musical brogue, Carson – then a Q.C. acting for Queensberry – demolished Wilde in the brilliant cross-examination of the libel case. But, after the jury disagreed in the first criminal trial, Carson pleaded with the Solicitor General, 'cannot you let up on the fellow now? He has suffered a great deal.' By 1912, the date of this cartoon, Carson had become leader of the Ulster Unionist Party.

31   *The Name of Dante Gabriel Rossetti is heard for
     the first time in the Western States of America*,
     1916
     Pen and ink and watercolour on paper,
     40 x 36.8 cm
     Board of Trustees of the Tate Gallery, London
     (A 01060)

Beerbohm had first planned a novel upon the theme of the Pre-Raphaelite Movement entitled *A Peep into the Past*. Although the project remained unrealised, it served as inspiration for the famous series of caricatures entitled *Rossetti and his Circle*, of which this is one of the most famous. Beerbohm completed the series in the Cotswolds during the First World War.

32   *Some Persons of 'the Nineties'*, 1925
     Pen and ink and watercolour, on paper,
     35 x 33 cm (HD 1650)
     Visitors of the Ashmolean Museum, Oxford

From left to right, back row: Richard Le Gallienne (1866–1947) poet; Walter Sickert (1860–1942); George Moore (1852–1933); John Davidson (1857–1909) poet; Oscar Wilde (1854–1900); William Butler Yeats (1865–1939), front row Arthur Symons (1865–1945) poet and critic; Henry Harland (1861–1905) novelist; Charles Conder (1868–1909); William Rothenstein (1872–1945); Max Beerbohm (1872–1956); Aubrey Beardsley (1872–98).

The full caption reads: *Some persons of 'the Nineties' little imagining, despite their Proper Pride and Ornamental Aspect, how much they will interest Mr Holbrook Jackson and Mr Osbert Burdett, 1925*. The books referred to are Holbrook Jackson's *The Eighteen Nineties* (1913) and Osbert Burdett's *The Beardsley Period* (1925). Just at the top on the right, Yeats seems to be talking to the shadowy figure of Enoch Soames, the main character in Beerbohm's brilliant satire of the aesthetes and decadents of the nineties.

33   *'Is this what you would imply, Will?': Oscar Wilde
     and His Circle of Friends, Max Beerbohm, Charles
     Conder and William Rothenstein*, 1929
     Signed and dated l.l.
     Pen and ink on paper, 20 x 28 cm (HD1322)
     Collection Barry Humphries, London

Pasted on to the drawing is a cutting of some words by W. Rothenstein (pp.119–20): 'I was often called upon for sympathy when Conder was in difficulties. Sober men are, alas, poor comforters, and sorry companions for men crowned with vine leaves. "Will, don't look so sensible" said Oscar Wilde one evening, as I sat with him and Conder at the Café Royal.' In the drawing, all are tipsy except for William Rothenstein, who sits primly upright, his bowler hat under his chair. The drawing was once owned by the great wine expert and cricket commentator John Arlott.

=+=+=+=+=+=+=+=+=+=+=+=+=+=+=+=+=+

Jean Béraud
1849–1935

Though born in St Petersburg, from the age of four Béraud lived in Paris. After the Franco-Prussian War, he enrolled in the studio of Louis Bonnat, and, like his master, began his career as a portrait painter. In the 1870s, he began to depict the daily life of the Parisian boulevard, which he saw with a clarity that recalls the objective cynicism of the stories of Guy de Maupassant. Urbane and sophisticated, this most Parisian of artists achieved great success in the Salon, where he exhibited from 1873 to 1889. But in the 1890s, he turned to religious themes transferred to contemporary settings, and these paintings were considered scandalous. (LL)

34 *The Ground-floor box at the Théâtre des Variétés* (*La Baignoire au Théâtre des Variétés*), c.1883
Oil on canvas, 49 x 40.5 cm
Signed and dated b.r.
Musée Carnavalet, Paris (Inv.P.1743)

35 *The Boulevard Montmartre, facing the Théâtre des Variétés in the afternoon* (*Le Boulevard Montmartre, devant le Théâtre des Variétés, l'après-midi*), c.1886
Oil on canvas, 45.5 x 55 cm
Musée Carnavalet, Paris (Inv.P.1657)

In this study the theatre is seen from the Café de Madrid, opposite, on the Boulevard Montmartre. In his last years, Wilde would haunt the locality of the 'grands boulevards' looking for friendly faces from his past whom he could touch for a 'loan'.

=+=+=+=+=+=+=+=+=+=+=+=+=+=+=+=+=+=+

Sarah Bernhardt
1844–1923

This great French actress made her début at the Comédie Français in 1862. She first visited London in 1879, when Oscar Wilde is reported to have welcomed her with an armful of lilies. The next year, she visited New York, which may have prompted her to suggest Wilde's lecture tour. Herself an impressive sculptor and artist (eg. Cat.36), she inspired many fine portraits (Cats 11, 38, 47, 110), notably the series of posters for her plays, commissioned from Alfonse Mucha (p.112).

Cat.36

Even in old age her stage presence was remarkable. During the First World War, in aid of the Red Cross, her famous 'Voix d'Or' rang out in huge theatres when she appeared in symbolic roles as the Rivers and Cathedrals of France. She remained active, experimenting with the new medium of film, right up to her death in Paris on 26 March 1923.

36 *Self-portrait*, c. late 1870s
Terracotta mask, 24.1 x 16.5 cm
Victor and Gretha Arwas, London

37 Selection of archives photographs

a. W&D Downey
Sarah Bernhardt in 'Théodora', 1884
14 x 9.5 cm
Victor and Gretha Arwas, London

b. W&D Downey
Two photographs of *Sarah Bernhardt in 'La Dame aux Camélias', 1896*
14.5 x 10 cm each
Victor and Gretha Arwas, London

c. Paul Boyer
Two photographs of *Sarah Bernhardt in 'L'Aiglon'*, 1900
14.5 x 10 cm each
Victor and Gretha Arwas, London

Cat.37a

=+=+=+=+=+=+=+=+=+=+=+=+=+=+=+=+=+=+

Paul François Berthoud
1870–1939

Born in Paris, Berthoud studied at the École des Beaux-Arts. He exhibited at the annual Salons of the Société des Artistes Français, where he was awarded an Honourable Mention in 1898. He was a founder member of the Salon d'Automne, exhibiting there between 1907 and 1931. He was elected Full Member of the Société Nationale des Beaux-Arts, and exhibited in its annual Salons between 1926 and 1939.

He exhibited sculpture in marble, bronze, plaster and multimedia, particularly bronze and marble. Several of his bronzes were given two or more contrasting patinations, particularly in his powerfully Art Nouveau portrait heads and busts, such as Cat. 38. (VA)

38 *Sarah Bernhardt as Jeanne d'Arc*, c.1890
Bronze and gold leaf, 57 x 56 x 31 cm
Victor and Gretha Arwas, London

=+=+=+=+=+=+=+=+=+=+=+=+=+=+=+=+=+=+

Jacques-Emile Blanche
1861–1942

Born in Paris, Blanche was the son of an eminent pathologist. He trained under Henri Gervex and was closely associated with Manet and Degas. From the early 1880s Blanche had been a frequent visitor to London, where he spent a formative period working closely with Whistler (pp. 132–3) and Sickert (p.124), and exhibiting with the New English Art Club from 1887. During the 1890s he became a successful portrait painter of fashionable society, exhibiting with the Société Nationale and winning a gold medal at the Exposition Universelle of 1900.

Blanche first met Wilde in Paris in 1883, while Wilde was trying to gain a footing in the French capital, after his tour of America. He became one of the first admirers of Wilde in the Parisian artistic circle and produced a painting of a young woman reading Wilde's *Poems* (location unknown). Blanche was an important Parisian contact for Wilde, through whom he met Marcel Proust in 1891. Wilde and Blanche shared many friends, including Beardsley (pp.90–91 and Cat.39), Conder (p.98), Sickert and Rothenstein (pp.119–20).

A regular visitor to Dieppe where his family had a villa, Blanche entertained and painted many of his friends. In Cat. 39, Beardsley sat as a dandy on the occasion of his stay in Dieppe with Conder, Arthur Symons, Ernest Dowson and Leonard Smithers (p.125) during the summer of 1895. Two years later in Dieppe, Blanche had chance meetings with Wilde, who had recently been released from prison, but, like Beardsley, Conder and Sickert, he rather ignored Wilde out of embarrassment. (TS)

Cat.40

39 *Portrait of Aubrey Beardsley*, 1895
Oil on canvas, 90 x 72 cm
Signed and dated b.r.
Board of Trustees of the National Portrait Gallery, London (Reg. no.1991)

40 *Sir Coleridge Kennard sitting on the sofa, or 'The Portrait of Dorian Gray'*, 1904
Oil on canvas, 117 x 95 cm
Private Collection

The sitter, better known as Roy Kennard, was the son of Mrs Carew, a great friend of Wilde's, who instigated the commission of the Wilde memorial by Jacob Epstein (pp.103–5) with her donation to Robert Ross in 1909. Roy Kennard, renowned for his good looks in the fashionable societies of Paris and London, is captured here as a young dandy, who would exemplify the image of the English aristocracy. His elegance, luxurious taste and good breed are eloquently depicted in Blanche's 'English-style' free, fluid brushwork, influenced by Gainsborough. However, his mother strongly disapproved of this portrait, and it was not exhibited between 1908 and 1924. When it was shown in an exhibition at Jean Charpentier's gallery in Paris in 1924, it was conditioned that the sitter's name should not appear in the catalogue. Charpentier, therefore, simply invented the title 'The Portrait of Dorian Gray' for the exhibition, without thinking how curiously the image of Wilde's hero would correspond to that evoked by this portrait (J. Roberts in Pétry et al – Exh. Cat: pp.115–6).

95

=+=+=+=+=+=+=+=+=+=+=+=+=+=+=+=+=+

Félix Bracquemond
1833–1914

Bracquemond is best known as a print-maker and designer. Along with his friend Charles Meryon, he was one of the principal inspirations for the etching revival in France. In the early 1860s, Bracquemond became the centre of an artistic circle that included Gautier, Baudelaire and Gavarni. Later, he participated in the Impressionists exhibitions and was a close friend of Edouard Manet. His main claim to posthumous fame is his possession of the first copy of Hokusai's *Manga*, from which he borrowed extensively for motifs in his etchings and ceramics, notably in the 'Rousseaux' service. For the

1900 Exposition Universelle, he also designed furniture, gold and silver jewellery, bookbindings and tapestries, collaborating with Rodin (pp.116–7) and Chéret (p.97). (LL)

41 *Edmond de Goncourt*, 1882
Contemporary print from etching, 51.3 x 33.8 cm
Board of Trustees of the British Museum, London (Acc.no. 1900-4-11-351)

The print depicts the great French art historian, whose *Journals* are a major source for the history of his time – just before he first met Wilde in 1883. The two men were later, in 1891, to differ vehemently on the poetic importance of Swinburne (Cat. 155), and to discuss Goncourt's forecast of the hydrogen bomb. In prison at Reading, Wilde succeeded in obtaining the latest volume of the *Goncourt Journal*.

=+=+=+=+=+=+=+=+=+=+=+=+=+=+=+=+=+

Edward Coley Burne-Jones
1833–98

When Burne-Jones went up to Oxford in January 1853, it was with the intention of entering the Church. But there, he met his lifelong friend William Morris (p.111), and together they joined with Rossetti, whom they both admired, in painting the Oxford Union frescoes. In 1860, he married Georgiana Macdonald and two years later accompanied John Ruskin (p.121) to Milan and Venice. For Morris & Co he designed stained glass windows whose tall upright compositions may have influenced such paintings as *The Golden Stairs* (1872–80), *King Cophetua and the Beggar Maid* (1884) and *The Annunciation* (1876–9). (LL)

42 *Sidonia von Bork*, 1860
Watercolour and gouache on paper, 33 x 17.1 cm
Board of Trustees of the Tate Gallery, London (N 05878)

Sidonia the Sorceress, a historical romance by Wilhelm Johann Meinhold (1797–1851), is a perverse and erotic novel set in the early seventeenth century and based on the witch hysteria of northern Europe. It was first published in Germany in 1847, and in an English translation by Lady Wilde, Oscar's mother, in 1849 (Cat.197). The novel became extremely popular in Pre-Raphaelite circles, and Burne-Jones painted two scenes from it in 1860. In Cat. 42, Sidonia, an evil witch, is seen planning a crime at the court of the Dowager Duchess of Wolgast, who approaches in the distance. The striking dress is said to have been inspired by Giulio Romano's portrait of Isabella d'Este at Hampton Court, and the hairstyle by a Lucas Cranach portrait.

43 *The Sleeping Princess*, 1872–4
Oil on canvas, 126 x 232 cm
Hugh Lane Municipal Gallery of Modern Art, Dublin

Burne-Jones once remarked, 'I mean by a picture a beautiful romantic dream of something that never was, never will be – in a light better than any light

Cat.42

that ever shone – in a land no one can define, or remember, only desire.' These words help to explain the mysterious beauty of this work, a version of the last painting in *The Briar Rose* series, one of the finest of all aesthetic works of art. To accompany the paintings, Morris wrote some verses describing how:

'The fateful slumber floats and flows
About the tangle of the rose.'

This final image of the sleeping Princess is described by Morris thus:

'There lies the hoarded love, the key
To all the treasures that shall be;
Come fated hand the gift to take
And smite this sleeping world awake.'

Like Burne-Jones, Wilde used the imagery of the briar rose in his fairy story *The Nightingale and the Rose*. But in Wilde's story, the symbolism turns sour. The beautiful white rose, stained red with the blood of the nightingale, is scorned by the lovers who throw it 'into the gutter, and a cartwheel went over it...'

44 Félix Jasinki after Burne-Jones
The Annunciation, 1897
Engraving (trial proof), 50.2 x 20.3 cm
The Maas Gallery Ltd, London.

Cat. 44 is a print made after Burne-Jones's painting *The Annunciation*, 1876–9 (Lady Lever Collection, Port Sunlight), which was first shown at the Grosvenor Gallery in 1879. The model for the Virgin was Mrs Leslie Stephen, the mother of Virginia Woolf and Vanessa Bell. Of the painting, Wilde wrote: '... the Virgin Mary, a passionless, pale woman, with that mysterious sorrow whose meaning she was soon to learn mirrored in her wan face, is standing, in grey drapery, by a marble fountain, in what seems the open courtyard of an empty and silent house, while through the branches of a tall olive tree, unseen by the Virgin's tear-dimmed eyes, is descending the Angel Gabriel with his joyful and terrible message not painted as Angelico loved to do, in the varied splendour peacock-like wings and garments of gold and crimson, but somewhat sombre in colour, set with all the infinite grace of nobly-fashioned drapery and exquisitely ordered design.'

=+=+=+=+=+=+=+=+=+=+=+=+=+=+=+=+=+=+=+

Eugène Carrière
1849–1906

Born in Gournay Saint-Denis, Carrière grew up in Strasbourg, where he was apprenticed to a lithographer. However, in 1869 he decided to become a painter, and moved to Paris to study under Cabanel at the École des Beaux-Arts. In order to support himself financially, he continued to work as a commercial lithographer in Jules Chéret's studio (p.97) in 1872–3, among others. In 1876–7, he stayed for six months in London, where he saw and admired Turner's work.

Carrière's early paintings were naturalistic in style but subdued in colour, and he began exhibiting at the Paris Salon in 1879, with his first *Maternité* (Musée des Beaux-Arts, Avignon). Throughout his career, he was to restrict himself in subject matter, preferring the themes of family life, mother and child or children. Towards the end of the 1880s, he developed a distinctive style with a monochrome mist enveloping vaguely transcribed forms. The effect created a sense of mystery that particularly appealed to the Symbolist artists and writers, such as Rodin (pp.116–7), Gauguin and Charles Maurice.

Cat. 45 was made after his oil portrait of Verlaine painted in 1890 (Musée d'Orsay, Paris), which is 'the only worthwhile and faithful portrait of the old Verlaine' (cf. Cat.5), according to Maurice, the first biographer of the poet in 1888. At the time of his sitting for Carrière, Verlaine was already ill in hospital but travelled across Paris to the painter's studio, where he was restless and kept 'talking at the top of his voice'. Only a few months later on 25 May 1891, Verlaine, in a state of considerable poverty, wrote to Carrière, apologising for having to sell 'such a beautiful portrait' out of financial necessity. (TS)

45 *Paul Verlaine*, 1896
     Lithograph in chine collé from two stones,
     52 x 40.5 cm
     Signed b.l.
     Richard Hollis, London

=+=+=+=+=+=+=+=+=+=+=+=+=+=+=+=+=+=+=+

Jules Chéret
1836–1932

This great poster designer was dubbed by Manet 'the Watteau of the streets' and by Degas as 'the Tiepolo of the Boulevards'. Wilde, too, greatly admired his art, and particularly the effect produced by his advertisements on the illuminated kiosks that decorate Paris. They are, declared Wilde, 'as lovely as a fantastic Chinese lantern, especially when the transparent advertisements are from the clever pencil of M. Chéret.' (LL)

46 *Loïe Fuller: The Dance of Fire (Danse du Feu,*
     La Loïe Fuller Folies-Bergère), 1893
     Poster, colour lithograph, 120 x 82.2 cm
     Board of Trustees of the Victoria and Albert
     Museum, London (E.112 -1921)

Chéret designed this poster for the Folies-Bergère in four different colourways, trying to capture a spectacle vividly described by W.B. Yeats (Cats 29, 32, 93) as 'an agony of flame that cannot singe a sleeve'.

=+=+=+=+=+=+=+=+=+=+=+=+=+=+=+=+=+=+=+

Georges Clairin
1843–1919

Little is known about the life of Clairin, but his name is remembered through the numerous portraits he produced for the 'divine' Sarah Bernhardt. He was a devoted follower of the celebrated actress and met her sometime around 1876. He was initially one of her many lovers, but with his warm, cultivated, rational yet amusing character, he ended as the 'brother of her heart' and a lifelong friend. Clairin was a gifted artist and became Bernhardt's 'court painter', observing her eventful career. Through his paintings and drawings, we gain a view of how Bernhardt looked on stage in her various roles, as well as at home in her private life.

Clairin's best-known portrait of Bernhardt (Musée de Petit Palais, Paris) was exhibited at the Paris Salon in 1876, where it attracted a large crowd. It was a large oil, showing the actress dressed in white satin, seated on a luxuriously cushioned, brightly red divan, with a plumed fan in her hand. Before her on a bearskin lies a borzoi, one of the

Cat.47

most aristocratic and elegant of dogs. Cat. 47 depicts Bernhardt, probably in the title role of Victorien Sardou's highly successful play *Théodora* (also Cat.47a). Set in sixth-century Istanbul, Bernhardt played a whorish dancing girl who would rise from a life of debauchery to the Empress of Byzantium. Premièred in Paris in December 1884, it was performed 300 times in Paris and more than 100 times in London. As the critic Jules Lemaître commented, Bernhardt's exotic princess evoked the image of Salome and Salammbo, 'a distant chimerical creature, sacred and serpentine with a fascination both mystic and sensual' (Gold and Fizdale: p.215), and Wilde might have had the same image in his mind when writing his *Salomé*. (TS)

47 *Sarah Berhnardt*, c.1884
     Oil on canvas, 99 x 47 cm
     Signed b.l.
     Victor and Gretha Arwas, London

Cat.52

=+

Charles Conder
1868–1909

Born in London, but brought up in India until the age of nine, Conder was sent to Australia at the age of sixteen, after being educated at Eastbourne. There, in the 1880s, his robust but sensitive Impressionist oil paintings were acclaimed. Conder then went to Paris, where he painted subtle designs for fans in watercolour on silk (Cats 51, 52, 53). For a brief period he shared a studio with Phil May and became a friend of Toulouse-Lautrec (pp.128–9), who used him several times as a model. Rothenstein (pp.119–20) records Oscar Wilde saying 'Dear Conder! With what exquisite subtlety he goes about persuading someone to give him a hundred francs for a fan, for which he was fully prepared to pay three hundred!' Married and settled in Chelsea in 1901, he died on 9 February 1909. (LL/TS)

48 **The Beach and Cliffs, Dieppe**, 1893
  Oil on canvas, 59 x 72 cm
  Signed and dated b.l.
  Collection Barry Humphries, London

49 **Screen painting: 'Hamage à Villon**, 1894
  Watercolour on silk, stretched onto canvas,
  61.5 x 38.5 cm
  Signed and dated
  Collection Barry Humphries, London

One of Conder's earliest panel paintings, Cat. 49 originally was produced for Siegfried Bing's shop, L'Art Nouveau, which opened in Paris in 1895. Poem on panel to read: 'Homage to Villon'.

50 **Beach Scene, Dieppe**, c.1895–9
  Oil on wood, 33 x 44.5 cm
  Sheffield Galleries and Museums Trust

51 **Fan painting: two women in landscape**, late 1890s
  Watercolour on silk, 21.5 x 45.5 cm
  Signed b.l.
  Collection Barry Humphries, London

52 **La Vie Champetre**, late 1890s
  Watercolour on silk, 22 x 47 cm
  Collection Barry Humphries, London

53 **The Grey Fan**, late 1890s
  Watercolour on silk, 11.4 x 41.9 cm
  The Hugh Lane Municipal Gallery of
  Modern Art, Dublin (Inv. No. 565)

54 **A Tocatta of Galuppi's**, 1900
  Watercolour on silk, 29 x 20.5 cm
  Signed b.r.
  Collection Barry Humphries, London

One of Conder's finest works, inspired by a poem by Robert Browning with the same title, which describes the mood of melancholia conjured by the music of the eighteenth-century Venetian composer Baldassare Galuppi (1706–85). Conder seizes the essence of the poem:

Cat.54

'Dear dead women, with such hair too –
what's become of all the gold
Used to hand and brush their bosoms?
I feel chilly and grown old.'

Like his fans, Cat. 54 has qualities described by Ricketts (pp.114–6), as 'delightful in colour, design and the sense of wit and romance which they evoke, the sense of luxury which they express, and the love for beautiful things that pass away, like laughter and music, the mirage of noon, the magic of night, the perfume of flowers, and youth and life'.

=+

Walter Crane
1845–1915

Crane exhibited his first painting at the Royal Academy in 1862 and, between the years 1863 and 1912, illustrated many children's books, notably *Baby's Bouquet, The Baby's Opera* and *Pan-Pipes*. He also wrote and illustrated several books on design. In 1888, he became the first President of the Arts and Crafts Exhibition Society. He was a prolific designer of wallpapers, carpets, ceramics, furniture and tapestries, which are all now better remembered than his oil paintings of allegorical and figurative subjects. Closely connected with William Morris (p.111 and Cat.186), whose socialist views he shared, Crane toured America with an exhibition of his work in 1891 and managed to scandalise Chicago with the radical views he expressed in his lectures. He was also Principal of the Royal College of Art in 1898–9. (LL)

55 **Love's Sanctuary (also known as 'Love's Altar')**, 1870
  Oil on canvas, 77.3 x 54.8 cm
  Signed (monogram) and dated
  William Morris Gallery
  (London Borough of Waltham Forest)

When first exhibited, cat. 55 was adversely criticised as irreverent for its explicit ritualism. It depicts a handsome male pilgrim kneeling in prayer before an altar. On the altar stands the icon-like portrait of Walter Crane's betrothed, Mary Frances Andrews. The altar is an elaborate mixture of a celebration of the mass and pagan sacrifices to Venus, variously symbolised by the illuminated missal, singers and musicians, the smoking censer and the flight of doves.

56 *Costume Design for 'Patience'*, early 1880s
    Watercolour on paper, 34 x 24.1 cm
    Signed (monogram) c.r.
    Tullie House Museum and Art Gallery, Carlisle
    (Acc.no.1949.125.455A).

This painting may be a study for the costumes
of the 'love sick maidens' in Gilbert and Sullivan's
Patience who, in the finale of Act 1, escort
'Bunthorne, crowned with roses and hung about
with garlands, and looking very miserable'. The
maidens are 'dancing classically, and playing on
cymbals, double pipes, and other archaic
instruments while singing'.

57 Oscar Wilde
    Illustrated by Walter Crane
    and Jacomb Hood
    The Happy Prince and Other Tales
    Published in London, David Nutt, 1889
    (second edition)
    Book, cream parchment-covered boards
    ('japon vellum') with design in red and black,
    22.7 x 16.9 cm
    Stephen Calloway, Brighton

58 *A selection of three facsimile plates from Cartoons
    for the Cause 1886–96*
    Produced 1976 (originally produced in London,
    Twentieth Century Press, 1896)
    Process engraving, 31.5 x 18.8 cm each sheet
    Tish Collins, London

a. *Cover for the Portfolio* (Plate IX)
b. *The Worker's Maypole – An offering for
May Day 1894* (Plate IX)
c. *A Garland for May Day – Dedicated to the Workers
by Walter Crane* (Plate XI)

Containing twelve designs, the portfolio was
published as a souvenir of the International and
Trade Union Congress of 1896. Crane made similar
drawings for a variety of periodicals, pamphlets
and societies, from broadsheet newspapers to Trade
Union banners. Socialist, communist, anarchist and
even nihilist views were frequent concomitants of
a taste for aesthetic designs and ideals. In 1891,
Wilde contributed his long political essay on the
theme of *The Soul of Man under Socialism*.

Crane's commitment to the socialist cause can be
seen practically in Cat. 58b showing the 'Worker's
Maypole', a graceful evocation of a worker's Utopia,
akin to those envisaged in William Morris's prose
romances. In the spring of 1894, Wilde remarked:
'We are all of us more or less socialists now-a-days
… I think I am rather more than a Socialist. I am
something of an Anarchist.' Wilde admired the
Labour politician John Burns (Fig.10: 1858–1943),
whom he described as 'a splendid personality' and in
1898 suggested that Burns might write a preface to
The Ballad of Reading Gaol.

99

Cat. 58c was originally published in a special May Day number of *The Clarion* on 27 April 1895. Amongst the slogans on the banner are several with a distinctive Wildean ring, 'Art and Enjoyment for All' in particular being a sentiment he shared.

=+=+=+=+=+=+=+=+=+=+=+=+=+=+=+=+=+

Frederick Holland Day
1864–1933

Day was a wealthy American publisher and photographer who acted as co-publisher with John Lane of *The Yellow Book* (Cats 16a–b, 96). He made frequent visits to Europe, meeting his idols Wilde and Beardsley (pp.90–91). In 1898, on a hill twenty miles from Boston, he made a series of photographs of *The Crucifixion* in which he posed as Christ. In the early 1900s, he specialised in the male nude, creating soft-focus images that derived compositionally from drawings by Simeon Solomon (pp.125–6). (LL)

59   *Hypnos* (*also known as 'Boy with a Flower'*), c.1896–7
     Modern copy print
     The Royal Photographic Society, Bath
     (RPS 3578)

60   *In the Glade*, 1905
     Modern copy prints from the triptych
     The Royal Photographic Society, Bath
     (RPS 3509)

A youthful male figure embraces the Herm of Pan, a symbol of the penis and fertility. The photograph was probably inspired by a Beardsley drawing.

=+=+=+=+=+=+=+=+=+=+=+=+=+=+=+=+=+

Georges de Feure [pseudonym of Georges Joseph Van Sluijters]
1868–1943

Of Dutch and Belgian parentage, de Feure was the pupil of Jules Chéret (p.97). He was a prolific magazine illustrator and poster designer, and, as a key figure in the move from Symbolism to Art Nouveau, played an important part in the creation of the Art Nouveau Pavilion at the Paris Exhibition of 1900. He also exhibited at the Salon and in the Secessionist show in Munich. The portrayal of women plays a major role in his work, as evinced in his posters for Loïe Fuller's *Salomé* (Cat. 61) and Sarah Bernhardt's performance as *Joan of Arc* (cf. Cat. 38). (LL)

61   *Poster for Salomé – spectacle de Loïe Fuller*, 1895
     Colour lithograph, 127 x 88.9 cm
     Board of the Trustees of the Victoria and Albert Museum (E.161-1921)

Loïe Fuller's own dance drama *La Tragédie de Salomé* at the Comédie Parisienne in 1895 did not meet with universal approval. One critic described the lead as 'sweating and with make-up ... a laundress misusing her paddles ... with the grace of an English boxer and the physique of Oscar Wilde ... a Salomé for Yankee drunkards'. Robert Ross, writing on 6 April 1905 regarding a projected performance of Wilde's play, declared: 'The artist who sustains the role of Salome should also, if I may be allowed to say so, abstain from introducing in the dancing scene anything in the nature of Loïe Fuller's performances.'

=+=+=+=+=+=+=+=+=+=+=+=+=+=+=+=+=+

Evelyn De Morgan
1855–1919

Evelyn De Morgan (née Pickering) was one of the earliest female students to attend the Slade School of Fine Art, London, in 1873. She then lived and worked in Italy with her uncle the painter Spencer Stanhope between 1875 and 1877.

Her work was clearly influenced by Burne-Jones (p.96) and the Pre-Raphaelites as well as by her time in Italy, where she looked to the Florentine School and greatly admired the work of Botticelli (cf. Cat. 151), an influence that can be seen in her soft fresco-like colours and composition.

She did not exhibit widely during her lifetime, mainly contributing to the newly opened Grosvenor Gallery. Despite the gallery's commitment to promoting women artists, she was one of very few women to show work there. Wilde included a description of Cat. 62 in his review of the 1879 Grosvenor Gallery exhibition.

De Morgan established herself as a painter of symbolic pictures based on classical mythology, and her work reflects fashionable ideas of the time, such as the incorporation of the sunflower in Cat. 64, an iconic symbol in the aesthetic movement. She also responded to the growing representation of 'male youth beauty' in her depiction of *Phosphorus and Hesperus* in Cat. 63. (LV/LL)

62   *Night and Sleep*, 1878
     Oil on canvas, 106.7 x 157.5 cm
     The De Morgan Foundation, London

When shown at the Grosvenor Gallery, Wilde admired 'a large picture of *Night and Sleep*, twin brothers floating over the world in indissoluble embrace, the one spreading the cloak of darkness, while from the other's listless hands the Lethean poppies fall in a scarlet shower'.

63   *Phosphorus and Hesperus*, 1881
     Oil on canvas, 59.1 x 43.8 cm
     Signed and dated b.r.
     The De Morgan Foundation, London

64   *Clytie*, 1885
     Pastel on paper, 104.1 x 44.5 cm
     Wightwick Manor, Staffordshire (The National Trust)

Cat. 63

=+=+=+=+=+=+=+=+=+=+=+=+=+=+=+=+=+=+=+

Emmeline Deane
fl. 1890

65   *Portrait of Cardinal John Henry Newman*, 1889
    Oil on canvas, 111.8 x 89.5 cm
    Board of Trustees of the National Portrait Gallery,
    London (Reg.no. 1022)

This touching portrait of the most spiritual of
religious figures, John Henry Newman, (1801–90)
the leader of the Oxford Movement a year before
his death, is by a talented but little known woman
artist. Newman made his conversion to Roman
Catholicism in 1845 and founded the Oratories
at Birmingham (1847) and London (1850).
He was not created cardinal until 1879. His
charismatic personality endeared him to the young
Oscar Wilde, who wrote in 1877, 'I have dreams
of a visit to Newman, of the Holy sacrament in
a new church, and of a quiet peace afterwards in
my soul …. I am awfully keen for an interview,
not of course to argue, but merely to be in the
presence of that divine man.' Years later in Reading
Gaol, Wilde requested and read Newman's works,
and it is possible that Newman's *Apologia pro vita sua*
may have played a part in Wilde's formulation
of *De Profundis* as well as his deathbed conversion
to Roman Catholicism. (LL)

=+=+=+=+=+=+=+=+=+=+=+=+=+=+=+=+=+=+=+

Lord Alfred Douglas
1870–1945

The son of the Marquis of Queensberry, who
elaborated the rules that govern professional boxing,
Douglas was introduced to Wilde at Oxford by
Lionel Johnson. While still an undergraduate, he
edited *The Spirit Lamp* (Cats 66, 67). The passionate
friendship of Wilde and Douglas led to bitter family
quarrels with Douglas's father, who provoked a libel

suit by describing Wilde as acting as a sodomite, an action which led to the Wilde trials, imprisonment for the writer, and the subsequent estrangement of Wilde and Douglas. In 1902, Douglas eloped with his childhood friend Olive Custance, with whom he remained on close terms after their separation. He became a Roman Catholic in 1911 but was constantly embroiled in libel litigation concerning his relationship with Wilde, as well as other matters. In 1923, for instance, he was imprisoned for six months for libelling Winston Churchill. (LL)

66   Edited by Alfred Douglas
     The Spirit Lamp, Volume 3, Number 11
     Published in Oxford, 17 February 1893
     Magazine, paper wrappers, 22.7 x 14.5 cm
     Contains poems by J.A. Symonds, Douglas and
     'The House of Judgement' by Oscar Wilde
     Sheila Colman, Lancing
     (The Lord Alfred Douglas Literary Estate)

67   Edited by Alfred Douglas
     The Spirit Lamp: An Aesthetic, Literary and Critical Magazine, Volume 4, Number 1
     Published in Oxford, May 1893
     Magazine, blue paper wrappers, 22 x 17.5 cm
     Contains contributions from J.A. Symonds, Lionel Johnson, Lord Henry Somerset, 'Sonnet' by Pierre Louÿs and 'Salomé – A Critical Review' by Alfred Douglas.
     Sheila Colman, Lancing
     (The Lord Alfred Douglas Literary Estate)

68   *Poems*
     Privately printed in Paris, 1896 (one of 20 copies)
     Book, hand-made paper, bound in cream and gold boards, 19.2 x 14.7 cm
     Sheila Colman, Lancing
     (The Lord Alfred Douglas Literary Estate)

The book bears an inscription by Douglas to Walter Spindler, who produced his portrait (Cat.171) in November 1895: 'The portrait of my soul in return for the portrait of my face. Naples 23 Sept. 1897'.

69   Selection of two photographs associated with
     Lord Alfred Douglas

a. *Francis Archibald Douglas*, *Viscount Drumlanrig*, early 1890s
14 x 10 cm
Sheila Colman, Lancing
(The Lord Alfred Douglas Literary Estate)

b. *Lord Alfred Douglas in Egypt*, 1895
24.3 x 12.2 cm
Sheila Colman, Lancing
(The Lord Alfred Douglas Literary Estate)

=+=+=+=+=+=+=+=+=+=+=+=+=+=+=+=+=+

Edmund Dulac
1882–1953
Born in Toulouse, where he studied law and later attended the Ecole des Beaux Arts, Dulac made his way to London in 1906 and remained there until his death. His brilliant illustrations for *The Tempest*, *The Rubaiyat of Omar Khayam* and fairy stories such as *The Arabian Nights* led publishers to regard him as a successor to Arthur Rackham. He also designed stamps, and was commissioned by Charles De Gaulle to create posters, bank notes and stamps for the Free French forces. Dulac's caricatures, first exhibited in 1914, were brilliantly stylised portraits – the detailed miniaturist technique used in Cat. 70 being particularly effective. Dulac also caricatured Ricketts and Shannon as Indian gods. (LL)

Cat.70

70   *Ricketts and Shannon as Mediaeval Saints*, 1920
     Tempera on linen – covered panel,
     38.7 x 30.5 cm
     Syndics of the Fitzwilliam Museum, Cambridge

=+=+=+=+=+=+=+=+=+=+=+=+=+=+=+=+=+

George Du Maurier
1834–96
Du Maurier studied painting in Paris before moving to London, where he turned to book illustration and social caricature in the 1860s. For two decades he charted the fashions and foibles of the Aesthetic Movement. His characters – the 'Cimabue Browns' and their friends, the critic Maudle and the poet Postlethwaite are major creations, and their taste embraced everything fashionable from Liberty silks to peacock feathers. Du Maurier's caricatures provide the background to Wilde's early career. (LL)

71   *Acute Chinamania*
     Published in *Punch*, 1875
     Pen and ink on paper, 14 x 22.9 cm
     Birmingham Museums and Art Gallery
     (Inv. no. 242'34)

The caption reads:
May: 'Mamma!, mamma! don't go on like this, pray!!'
Mamma: (who has smashed a favourite pot)
    'What have I got left to live for?'
May: 'Haven't you got me, mamma?'
Mamma: 'You, child! you're not unique!! there are
    six of you – a complete set!!'

72   *Pet and Hoby*
     Published in *Punch*, 26 August 1876
     Pen and ink on paper, 11.2 x 13.9 cm
     Board of Trustees of the Victoria and Albert
     Museum, London (E.399-1948)

73   *Public Opinion*
     Published in *Punch*, 21 June 1879
     Pen and ink on paper, 36.2 x 25.4 cm
     Bristol Museums and Art Gallery

The caption reads:
Public Opinion Pictor Notus: 'Ha! Ha! Ha! You and
    a critic! Why, how old are you my lad?'
Our Pet Critic: (sternly) 'If you dare talk in that

way to me sir I'll be hanged if I don't publish it
as my conviction that your picture is the one
supreme, and crowning Masterpiece of
Contemporary Art!'
(Appalled by the threat, Pictor subsides).

74   *Artistic Amenities*
Published in *Punch*, 26 July, 1879
Pencil, pen and ink on paper, 15.2 x 10.5 cm
Birmingham Museums and Art Gallery
(Inv. no. 236'31)

Bellamy Brown (pictor ignotus) on a picture
by Rigby Robinson:'Quite a Poem! Distinctly
precious, blessed, subtle, significant and
supreme!'
Jordan Jones (to whom a picture by R. Robinson
is as a red rage to a bull, as B.B. knows): 'Why,
hang it, Man, the Drawing's vile, the colour
beastly, the composition idiotic, and the subject
absurd!'
Brown: 'Ah, *all* works of the *highest* genius have faults
of that description!'
Jordan Jones: 'Have they? I'm glad to hear it, then,
for there's a chance for *you* old Man!'

75   *The Height of Aesthetic Exclusiveness*
Published in *Punch*, 1 November 1879
Pen and ink on paper, 15.9 x 24.4 cm
Board of Trustees of the Victoria and Albert
Museum, London (E.396-1948)

The caption reads:
'Mamma: 'Who are these
extraordinary looking children?'
Effie: 'The Cimabue Browns Mamma – they're
aesthetic you know!'
Mamma: 'So I should imagine. Do you know them
to speak to?'
Effie: 'Oh *Dear* no, Mamma – they're most
exclusive – why, they put out their tongues at us
if we only *look* at them!'

Du Maurier's aesthetic and 'chinamania' cartoons
boosted Wilde's initial career. They relate to Wilde's
early notoriety as an undergraduate caused by his
remark, 'I find it harder and harder every day to live
up to my blue china,' the first of all his aphorisms
to gain international notice. Cat. 75 recalls an incident
in the life of Wilde's children when, tired of waiting
in aesthetic garb, they took off all their clothes.

Jacob Epstein
1880–1959

Born in New York to a Jewish family of Polish
origin, Epstein went to Paris in 1902. Initially
he spent six months at the Ecole des Beaux-Arts
and then went on to study at the Académie Julian.
During this period, he was strongly influenced
by Rodin (pp.116–7), especially his modelling
in *St John the Baptist* (1878–80). Later he also
learnt the ideas of abstraction and simplification
from non-European sources, as well as from
Modigliani, Brancusi, and Picasso's Cubism.

While maintaining his contacts in Paris,
Epstein moved to London in 1905, carrying
a letter of introduction from Rodin. Virtually
unknown in the London art world, his early years
were not easy, but he quickly expanded his network.
His earliest supporters included Bernard Shaw
(Cats 148), Augustus John (pp.108–9 and Cats 92,
150) and William Rothenstein (pp.119–20). A
close associate of the Carfax Gallery (under Robert
Ross's directorship), Rothenstein was keen to
promote young avant-garde artists, and he provided
financial help to Epstein. Shaw introduced Epstein
to his friends and British contacts, and John offered
Epstein a modelling job at his newly founded
Chelsea Art School.

In 1908, Epstein became a controversial figure
with a frieze of eighteen figures, all naked or semi-
naked, carved for the British Medical Association
building (which is still visible today on the walls
of Zimbabwe House) in the Strand. Called 'vulgar'
and 'offensive', his work provoked a storm of
attacks from the public and the press as well as
from religious organisations. However, this *succès
de scandale* might have been a contributing factor to
his next major commission at the end of that year,
Tomb of Oscar Wilde. Mrs Helen Carew (see Cat.40),
Wilde's old friend, donated £2,000 anonymously to
Ross, asking him to place 'a suitable monument to
Wilde at Père Lachaise', on condition that the work
should be carried out by 'the brilliant young
sculptor Mr Jacob Epstein' (Gardiner: p.70). A great
admirer of Wilde and an outstanding collector and
connoisseur of art, Mrs Carew may have been
inspired to support the revolutionary young sculptor
by the criticism of the Strand sculptures.

103

Cats 76–8 illustrate the development of Epstein's concept of the *Tomb of Oscar Wilde* from a group of Greek youths to a single, winged male figure, inspired by ancient Assyrian tomb-sculptures, which Epstein studied in the British Museum. Completed in 1912, the monument bears an inscription from Wilde's *Ballad of Reading Gaol*:

'And alien tears will fill for him
Pity's long-broken urn,
For his mourners will be outcast men,
And outcasts always mourn.'

In 1950, on the occasion of the fiftieth anniversary of Wilde's death, the ashes of Wilde's devoted friend Robert Ross were, according to his own wishes, placed in the monument together with those of Wilde (Montgomery Hyde, pp.490–91). (TS)

76 *Sketch for the Tomb of Oscar Wilde, with a group of Greek youths*, 1910–11
Pencil on paper, 27.9 x 29.2 cm
Simon Wilson, London

104 77 *Sketch for the Tomb of Oscar Wilde, with the inscription on pedestal by Eric Gill*, 1910–11
Pencil on paper, 27.9 x 29.2 cm
Simon Wilson, London

78 *Sketch for the Tomb of Oscar Wilde*, 1910–11
Pencil on paper, 50.8 x 38.1 cm
Inscribed: (b.l.)
'covetousness/envy/jealousy/anger/sloth/
wandering thoughts/fornication/slander
sodomy/evil;
(b.r.) 'circlet of/sins for double/crown'
Mr and Mrs Michael W. Wilsey, San Francisco

79 *Letter to Auguste Rodin, concerning his Tomb of Oscar Wilde*, 19 September 1912
Manuscript, ink on paper, 25.2 x 20.2 cm
Musée Rodin, Paris (Inv. 1231)

80 Anonymous
Tomb of Oscar Wilde, c.1912
Two photographs, 16 x 11 cm each
Musée Rodin, Paris (Inv. Ph 13577 and Ph13578)

Epstein sent these photographs to Rodin with Cat. 79.

Cat. 78

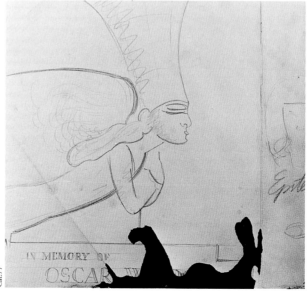

Cat. 77

'And alien tears will fill for him
Pity's long-broken urn,
For his mourners will be outcast men,
And outcasts always mourn.'
Oscar Wilde, *Ballad of Reading Gaol*, 1897

Fig. 27
Jacob Epstein
Tomb of Oscar Wilde,
Père Lachaise, Paris
Courtesy Simon Wilson, London

Cat. 76 (far right) and verso (right)

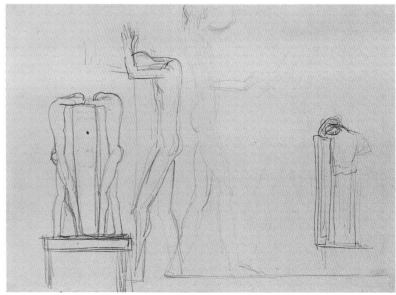

Edward Onslow Ford
1852–1901

Ford initially studied painting on the Continent but on his return to London in 1874 decided to become a portrait sculptor and, under the influence of Alfred Gilbert, became a central figure of the New Sculpture Movement.

Cat. 81 is a study for his Manchester Statue as well as being an independent work, for which the Queen gave official sittings. So pleased was she with the work that she gave several replicas in marble and bronze to members of the Royal Family.

Oscar Wilde greatly admired Queen Victoria and declared that she was one of three great personalities of the nineteenth century, along with Napoleon and Victor Hugo. During his editorship of *The Women's World* he asked the Queen to contribute one of her poems, 'but the indignant regal response was that she had never written one' (Ellman: p.275). However, the first edition of the magazine in January 1888 opened with a long poem, 'Historic Women' by Lady Wilde (p.133), which included a eulogy of the Queen; it was sent to Queen Victoria and it was reported that Her Majesty had liked it very much.

Wilde, who 'would have married her with pleasure', celebrated the Queen's Diamond Jubilee at Berneval in 1897, shortly after his release from prison, with a party for 'fifteen gamins' with 'a huge iced cake with *Jubilé de la Reine Victoria* in pink sugar just rosetted with green, and a great wreath of red roses round it all'. (LV/LL)

81　*Queen Victoria*, 1896
　　Bronze, (H) 35.3 cm
　　Inscribed on base: 'VRI'
　　Private Collection

=+=+=+=+=+=+=+=+=+=+=+=+=+=+=+=+=+

Louis Edouard Fournier
1857–post-1900

Fournier, who studied with Cabanel, was a painter of historical subjects, a designer and an illustrator. He won the Prix de Rome in 1881, and medals at the exhibitions of 1889 and 1900. A mural painter, he created the long *History of Art*, which ran along the cornice of the Palais des Beaux Arts on the Champs-Elysées in Paris. He also illustrated Petronius. In the Walker Art Gallery is his *Incineration of the body of Shelley*. (LL)

82　*Monnet Sully making up as Oedipus*, 1893
　　Oil on canvas, 46 x 65 cm
　　Signed b.r.
　　Musée Carnavalet, Paris (Inv.1159)

Wilde saw the great French actor Monnet Sully, star of the Comédie Français, when he appeared as Hippolyte in *Phédre* with Sarah Bernhardt (p.94) on her visit to London with the company on 2 June 1879. She wrote later of her stage fright on that occasion: 'when I began to speak I pitched my voice too high and could not bring it down. My tears flowed, scorching and bitter. I implored Hippolyte for the love that was killing me, and the arms that stretched out to Monnet Sully were the arms of Phédre, writhing in cruel longing for his embrace … When the curtain fell, Monnet carried my inert body to my dressing room.'

Wilde was at the first night and commented, 'it was not until I heard Sarah Bernhardt in *Phédre* that I absolutely realised the sweetness of the music of Racine'. He wrote a sonnet to her, and the incident began his long fascination with the French language, culminating in *Salomé* (see pp.60, 65). (LL)

=+=+=+=+=+=+=+=+=+=+=+=+=+=+=+=+=+

William Powell Frith
1819–1909

As a boy, Frith wanted to become an auctioneer not an artist, and there is something of the viewpoint of the auctioneer, high above the crowd on his rostrum, in all three of his major pictorial records of his time. It was not until his summer holiday at Ramsgate in 1851 that he embarked on what became his most successful themes – crowded scenes of contemporary life. These works, *Life at the Seaside* (1851), *Derby Day* (1858), *The Railway Station, Paddington* (1863) and *The Private View at the Royal Academy, 1881* (1881–2: see right) provide an invaluable record of Victorian life. (LL)

83　*Retribution*, 1878
　　Oil on canvas, 30.8 x 34.9 cm
　　Birmingham Museums and Art Gallery

Frith was fascinated by the evil social effects of gambling, which he explored in two series, each consisting of five paintings, *The Road to Ruin* (1878) and *The Race for Wealth* (1880). In the latter series Frith wished 'to illustrate … the common passion for speculation, and the destruction that so often attends the indulgence of it, to the lives and fortunes of the financier's dupes'. The storyline was based on the career of the Kensington entrepreneur Baron Albert Grant, which also inspired Anthony Trollope's novel *The Way We Live Now*, serialised from 1874 to 1875. In the fifth painting, *Retribution*, the fraudulent financier is portrayed at exercise in the yard of Millbank Prison. The scene inevitably resonates with Oscar Wilde's experiences while at Reading Gaol.

84　*The Private View of the Royal Academy, 1881*, 1881–2
　　Oil on canvas, 102.9 x 195.6 cm
　　A Pope Family Trust, St Helier, Jersey

In *My Autobiography and Reminiscences* (1888), Frith recalled that his main motivation for painting this work was 'the desire of recording for posterity the aesthetic craze as regards dress'. But he also 'wished to hit the folly of listening to self-elected critics in matters of taste, whether in dress or art. I therefore planned a group, consisting of a well-known apostle of the beautiful, with a herd of eager worshippers surrounding him. The main figure is supposed to be expounding his theories to willing ears, taking some picture on the Academy walls for his text. A group of well-known artists are watching the scene … The rest of the company is made up of celebrities of all kinds, statesmen, poets, judges, philosophers, musicians, painters, actors, and others.' Years later, in 1890, Wilde wrote in *The Critic as Artist*, a dialogue between two critics, 'Ernest' and 'Gilbert'. Ernest describes a lady who once gravely asked the remorseful Academican 'if his celebrated picture of "A Spring-Day at Whiteley's" or "Waiting for the Last Omnibus", or some subject of that kind, was all painted by hand'. To which Gilbert replies: 'And was it?'

Giotto
1267–1337

The Arena Chapel at Padua was begun in 1303. Giotto's frescoes of the life of Christ and the Virgin Mary in the Arena Chapel are usually dated c.1305–06/9. Before then Giotto had probably painted the life of St. Francis located in the upper Church of S. Francesco at Assisi, although his authorship is denied by some critics on stylistic grounds. In any event they are clearly the work of a great master, works regarded as the founding artefacts of the Western tradition. They introduce a new sense of naturalism, imbued with the humanity which St Francis himself brought into the religious life of the thirteenth century. (LL)

85 Edward Kaiser, after Giotto
   St. Francis preaching to the Birds, 1877
   Watercolour, made for reproduction as an Arundel Print, 57.1 x 41.6 cm
   Board of Trustees of the Victoria and Albert Museum, London (E.121-1995)

In 1848 when foreign travel was still the privilege of the few, the Arundel Society was founded by John Ruskin (p.121) and others with the aim of giving some idea of paintings available to those unable to visit Italy themselves. George Baxter's experiments in printing in oil colours and the emergence of chromolithography enabled the Arundel Society to publish from 1856 to 1897 a series of some two hundred coloured prints, the first coloured reproductions of Italian old masters. Great pains were taken over the process, by making careful copies directly from the original works.

In June 1875 Wilde travelled to Italy and visited Padua to see Giotto's works, admiring their 'clear transparent colour, bright as the day it was painted', and the harmony of the whole building. He wrote home to his mother, Lady Wilde, saying that he considered Giotto 'the first of all painters'. Wilde formed an extensive collection of these Arundel prints which were all sold off in the Bailiff's sale of his possessions which took place between the trials. In one of the most moving passages in *De Profundis* he discusses Giotto's role in 'Christ's own renaissance'.

Edward William Godwin
1833–84

Architect, stage designer, interior decorator, furniture and tile designer, Godwin remains one of the most enigmatic figures in Oscar Wilde's life. His influence on the contents of Wilde's lectures and the design of Whistler's exhibitions was highly significant. Yet, although Godwin's diaries record many evenings spent with Wilde and Whistler, we can only guess at their conversations. Godwin and Wilde were probably introduced by Frank Miles (1852–91), a fashionable portrait painter who had commissioned a house from Godwin. Miles's close friendship with Wilde, with whom he briefly shared a flat in the summer of 1880, ended when Miles's father, a clergyman, criticised Wilde's lifestyle. Wilde left for America shortly afterwards, and Miles had a nervous breakdown and was eventually sent to a lunatic asylum near Bristol, where he died in 1891. Godwin's friendship with Wilde was to continue and be deeply influential. He designed the interior decoration for Wilde's home in Chelsea – 'the house beautiful'. In writing to thank him, Wilde wrote: 'Each chair is a sonnet in ivory, and the table is a masterpiece in pearl.' (LL)

86 ***Designs and plans for the front elevation
   of a house and studio for Frank Miles at
   44 Tite Street, Chelsea, London***, 1878
   Pencil and watercolour, 38.7 x 28.9 cm
   Board of Trustees of the Victoria and Albert Museum, London (E.556-1963)

Godwin considered his initial designs for the Frank Miles house to be 'the best thing I ever did', but the Metropolitan Board of Works, the planning authority, sadly turned it down.

Walter Greaves
1846–1930

The son of a Chelsea boatman who had instructions to awaken the painters J.M.W. Turner or John Martin when there was particularly spectacular lightning or a moonlight effect, Greaves fulfilled the same function for Whistler (pp.132–3). Greaves was a real English primitive, as evident in his *Hammersmith*

Bridge on Boat Race Day (Tate Gallery, London). But under the spell of the charismatic Whistler, he produced strange, ghostly pictorial echoes of Whistlerian nocturnal subjects. (LL)

87 ***The Lawn and Fireworks Gallery, Cremorne
   (or James McNeill Whistler in Cremorne
   Gardens, Chelsea)***, 1869
   Pencil, black chalk and ink on paper, 61.5 x 49 cm
   Private Collection, courtesy The Fine Art Society, London

A view of the site from which was launched the rocket that provoked the famous libel case between Ruskin (p.121) and Whistler (pp.132–3). The famous Victorian pleasure grounds at Cremorne, a notorious nightspot, opened in 1845 as a rival to the Vauxhall Gardens. The land was formerly a Chelsea farm, the property of Viscount Cremorne. It became a popular venue for entertainment such as outdoor dancing and was celebrated for its firework displays on Saturday nights. These pyrotechnic displays inspired several Nocturnes by Whistler as well as drawings by Greaves. The Gardens were closed in 1877 after many local complaints.

Walter Hamilton
1844–99

Hamilton was an English writer and book collector. His most important book, the first chronicle of the Aesthetic Movement, *The Aesthetic Movement in England* (1882: see p.108) discussed Wilde's early life and theories. In his book Hamilton complains bitterly of the unfairness of all the satires of the Aesthetic Movement, singling out Du Maurier's cartoons (pp.102–3) for special opprobrium. But Hamilton himself also wrote several parodies of Wilde's works which he published in *Parodies of English and American Authors* (6 vols. 1884–9). On this subject Wilde wrote to Hamilton on 29 January, 1889 saying 'I have never collected the parodies of my poetry, collecting contemporaneous things is like trying to catch froth in a sieve … Parody, which is the muse with her tongue in her cheek, has always amused me; but it requires a light touch … and oddly enough, a love of the poet whom it caricatures. One's disciples can parody one – nobody else.' (LL)

88 *The Aesthetic Movement in England*
Published in London, Reeves and Turner, 1882
(first edition)
Book, green cloth stamped with title and gilt
device, 21.9 x 14 cm
Stephen Calloway, Brighton

Cat. 88 contains Hamilton's 5pp. MS of the
'Preface' to the second edition, thanking Lady
Wilde (p.133) for the 'very complete account' of
'her son, Mr Oscar Wilde about whom at present
considerable curiosity exists, both at home and
in the United States'.

=+=+=+=+=+=+=+=+=+=+=+=+=+=+=+=+=+

Robert Smythe Hichens
1864–1950
When visiting Egypt, Hichens (Cat.28) met Lord
Alfred Douglas (pp.101–2), who in turn introduced
him to Oscar Wilde when they were back in
London. Hichens, later a prolific novelist, enjoyed
great success with his first book, the witty skit *The
Green Carnation*, in which Wilde was portrayed as
Esmé Amarinth and Douglas as Reggie Hastings.
(LL)

89 *The Green Carnation*
Published in New York, D. Appleton and
Company, 1894
The first American printing, precedes English
edition
Book, green cloth 17.8 x 11.6 cm
Stephen Calloway, Brighton

=+=+=+=+=+=+=+=+=+=+=+=+=+=+=+=+=+

Frederick Hollyer
1837–1933
Hollyer was primarily a portrait and landscape
photographer, who from the 1870s became
particularly identified with the second phase of the
Pre-Raphaelitism. He produced many extremely
successful reproductions of works by Burne-Jones
(p.96) and Simeon Solomon (pp.125–6) (LL)

90 *John Ruskin aged 75*, 1894
Photograph, 19 x 23 cm
Ruskin Foundation
(Ruskin Library, University of Lancaster)

=+=+=+=+=+=+=+=+=+=+=+=+=+=+=+=+=+

William Holman Hunt
1827–1910
Holman Hunt was born in London and entered
the Royal Academy schools in 1844, where he met
and became good friends with John Everett Millais
and later Dante Gabriel Rossetti. In 1848 – in a
combination of youthful enthusiasm and as a
reaction to what they saw as the formulaic painting
of the Royal Academy – Hunt, Millais and Rossetti
established the Pre-Raphaelite Brotherhood. Their
primary aim was to paint nature with complete
fidelity combined with noble ideas.

Hunt's paintings are nearly all religious or
moralistic and are characterised by extreme detail
as well as a brightness of light and colours. Loyal
to his commitment to painting directly from nature,
he travelled to the Middle East, in 1854, to find
exact historical and archeological backgrounds for
his religious paintings. It was during this period
that he began to paint Cat. 91. Shown at the 1877
Grosvenor Gallery exhibition, Wilde responded to it
as a superb study of colour and described Holman
Hunt as 'probably the greatest master of colour that
we have ever had in England, with the single
exception of Turner'. (LV)

91 *The Afterglow in Egypt*, 1854–63
Oil on canvas, 185.4 x 86.3 cm
Southampton City Art Gallery

=+=+=+=+=+=+=+=+=+=+=+=+=+=+=+=+=+

Cat.92

Augustus Edwin John
1878–1961
Born at Haverfordwest
in Wales and the younger
brother of Gwen (see
p.117 and Cat.134), John
studied at the Slade School
in 1894–8. There he and
William Orpen (p.113) were the most promising
students of their generation. Between 1901 and
1904 he was Professor of Painting at Liverpool
University; at the same time, with Orpen, he ran
the Chelsea Art School, a private teaching studio.
The greatest hope of modern British art, he was
featured in the New York Armory Show of

Cat.93

1913 with over forty oils and drawings.
John met Wilde in September 1899, while
he was staying in Paris with his friends, including
Rothenstein (pp.119–20). Both men formed strong
impressions of each other: Wilde called John 'the
charming Celtic poet in colour' (Montgomery
Hyde, p.466); and later John was to include his
recollections of Wilde in his autobiography
Chiaroscuro (1952). Also, as a friend, he would attend
the commemoration ceremony of the centenary
of Wilde's birth in 1954, when a blue and white
plaque was placed on the outside wall of Wilde's
former residence at No.16 (now 34) Tite Street.
Cat. 93, of Yeats, is the earliest of a series of
portraits of famous contemporaries, which primarily
established his fame. Writer and a leading figure
of Irish nationalism, Yeats (1865–1939) first met
Wilde in December 1888. Remarking on their
Irish background, Wilde said to Yeats: 'we Irish are
too poetical to be poets; we are a nation of brilliant
failures but we are the best talkers after the Greeks'
(Montgomery Hyde, p.145). Yeats was a great
admirer of Wilde and he wrote many articles on
Wilde and his work. (TS)

92 *Self-portrait*, c.1901
Chalk on paper, 26 x 17.8 cm
Board of Trustees of the National Portrait Gallery,
London (Reg.no.4577)

93 *William Butler Yeats*, 1907
Oil on canvas, 75 x 49.5 cm
Manchester City Art Galleries (Inv. no.1928.79)

=+=+=+=+=+=+=+=+=+=+=+=+=+=+=+=+=+

Cat.94

Fernand Khnopff
1858–1921

Born in Grembergen
near Dendermonde,
Khnopff briefly
studied law in 1875
at the University
of Brussels but soon
gave up to pursue
his artistic career.
A great reader of
Flaubert, Baudelaire and Leconte de Lisle, he also
had a passion for literature. Trained under Xavier
Mellery, he studied painting at the Academy of Fine
Arts in Brussels in 1876–9, where he met James
Ensor. He was a frequent visitor to Paris, where he
discovered Burne-Jones (p.96), John Everett Millais,
and Gustave Moreau (pp.110–11) at the Exposition
Universelle of 1878. He also attended Jules
Lefebvre's open studio and the Académie Julian.

Following a début at the exhibition of L'Essor
in Brussels in 1881, Khnopff became a founding
member of the avant-garde group Les XX in 1883,
which was to be reconstituted as La Libre Esthétique.
Led by Octave Maus, the group aspired to unite
art, music and literature. Admired by the French
Symbolist circle, especially the Sâr Péladan, Khnopff
regularly exhibited with Salon de la Rose + Croix
during the 1890s. He was also an anglophile,
friendly with Burne-Jones, Holman Hunt (p.108)
and Watts (pp.130–31), and contributed regularly
to *The Studio* magazine (Cat. 14). Wilde regarded his
work highly, and hoped to commission Khnopff
for the illustration of his *Ballad of Reading Gaol*
(Hart-Davis: p.637).

Cat. 94 was probably inspired by Flaubert's short
story 'Hérodias' (1877). The story was also a source
of inspiration for Wilde's *Salomé* (see p.60). (TS)

94 *Herodias*, 1880s?
Charcoal on paper, 19 x 12.5 cm
Victor and Gretha Arwas, London

=+=+=+=+=+=+=+=+=+=+=+=+=+=+=+=+=+

John Lane
1854–1925

Born in Devon, Lane came to London in 1868
and worked as a railway clerk at Euston station
before turning to publishing. In 1887 he went
into partnership with Charles Elkin Matthews
(1851–1921) who had begun his career as a
bookseller in Exeter. They started a bookselling
business under the sign of the Bodley Head in Vigo
Street in London, although Lane's name did not
appear in its publications until 1892. He and Wilde
never liked each other, and Wilde called the
manservant in *The Importance of Being Earnest* 'Lane' to
show his contempt. In 1895, during the trials, Lane
swiftly withdrew all Wilde's books from circulation
(also Cats 1, 14, 15, 16, 19, 125). (LL)

95 Oscar Wilde
Salomé
The original French edition, published in Paris,
Librarie de L'Art Indépendant, and London,
Elkin Matthews and John Lane, 1893
Book, cloth-bound (one of 600 copies)
Julia Rosenthal, Oxford

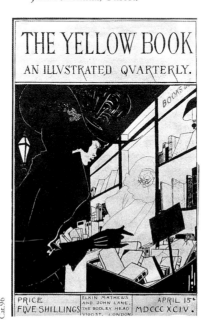
Cat.96

96 *Prospectus for The Yellow Book:
An Illustrated Quarterly*, Volume 5
Issued in London, John Lane, April 1895
Booklet, yellow paper wrappers, with design
by Beardsley, 19.4 x 15.6 cm
Stephen Calloway, Brighton

97 *Catalogue of Publications in Belles Lettres*
Issued in London, John Lane, The Bodley Head,
1897
Booklet, paper wrappers, with the illustration of
the Vigo Street offices by E.H. New,
17.6 x 11.1 cm
Stephen Calloway, Brighton

=+=+=+=+=+=+=+=+=+=+=+=+=+=+=+=+=+

Cat.98

Louis Legrand
1863–1951

Legrand initially
studied at the Ecole
des Beaux-Arts in
his home town of
Dijon, before moving
to Paris, where
he studied with
Félicien Rops
(pp.117–8). Like
Toulouse-Lautrec
pp.128–9), Steilen
and Forain, he supplied several journals with regular
drawings, many of them commenting satirically on
current politics, art and literature. He illustrated a
number of books with original etchings, designed
several book-bindings, executed cut, etched,
drawn and burned leather panels, produced some
embroideries, and painted a few oil paintings as well
as many more pastels, watercolours and drawings.
Many of his subjects were drawn from the ballet,
music hall and theatre, as well as from life in cafés,
boudoirs and bedrooms. (VA)

98 *Death and a Maiden*, mid-1890s
Pencil and pastel on paper, 49 x 39 cm
Signed b.l.
Victor and Gretha Arwas, London

109

Alphonse Legros
1837–1911

Legros is perhaps one of the most underrated of nineteenth-century draughtsmen and etchers. His work was praised by Baudelaire, and Degas thought highly enough of his work to hang one of his drawings between a Raphael and an Ingres. In the late 1850s, on Whistler's advice, he moved from France to London, where he taught for many years at the Slade School of Art. (LL)

99 *Portrait of Charles Ricketts*, 1896
Silverpoint on pink prepared paper,
27.6 x 21.9 cm
Signed and dated t.l.
Syndics of the Fitzwilliam Museum, Cambridge
(Inv. no.2095)

=+=+=+=+=+=+=+=+=+=+=+=+=+=+=+=+=+=+=+

Frederic Leighton
1830–96

110

Elected to the Presidency of the Royal Academy in 1878, Leighton was a highly influential figure among the establishment circle. However, privately he was less conventional, admiring the work of younger artists such as Charles Ricketts (pp.114–6), Charles Shannon (p.123) and Aubrey Beardsley (pp.90–91), artists who shared many of his own interests.

In his career, Leighton made only three sculptures. One of these, *The Sluggard*, was inspired by having seen a model, Guiseppe Valon, stretching. The bronze was originally called *An Athlete awakening from Sleep* but was renamed *The Sluggard* because the implied laziness of the languid figure expresses moral weakness, the boy's lack of ambition being suggested by the laurel wreath which he is treading underfoot. The figure became famous through the extensive reproductions of this small-scale version (Cat. 100). It has been seen as an homage to Donatello but is surely more Hellenic in inspiration. For Wilde, Greek sculptures were 'always modern, always of our time'.

Towards the end of the nineteenth century, Classical Greek sculpture's depiction of the idealised male nude as an object of beauty provided inspiration to many artists. (LV/LL)

Cat.100

100 *The Sluggard*, 1885
Bronze, (H) 51.8 cm
Signed on base
Inscribed on front of base: 'THE SLUGGARD'
Private Collection

=+=+=+=+=+=+=+=+=+=+=+=+=+=+=+=+=+=+=+

Mortimer Menpes
1855–1938

Born in Australia, Menpes was educated in England and France, studying under Poynter (p.113) at South Kensington, and at the Pont Aven artists' colony in the winter of 1881–2, where he met Whistler (pp.132–3) and became his assistant and biographer. He was also a friend of Wilde, becoming godfather to Oscar's second child, Vyvyan. But Menpes's friendship with Whistler ended when, without consulting the temperamental artist, Menpes visited Japan in 1887 for eight months to learn 'all the methods of Japanese art'. On his return, he exhibited 137 oils but refused to sign his works 'Pupil of Whistler'. Menpes's exhibition was reviewed by Wilde in *The Decay of Lying*, published in January 1889:

'… do you really imagine that the Japanese people, as they are presented to us in art, have any existence? … One of our most charming painters went recently to the Land of the Chrysanthemum in the foolish hope of seeing the Japanese. All he saw, all he had the chance of painting, were a few lanterns and some fans … if you desire to see a Japanese effect, you will not behave like a tourist and go to Tokyo. On the contrary, you will stay at home and steep yourself in the work of certain Japanese artists and then, when you have absorbed the spirit of their style, and caught their imaginative manner of vision, you will go some afternoon and sit in the Park or stroll down Piccadilly, and if you cannot see an absolutely Japanese effect there, you will not see it anywhere.' (LL)

101 *Flags*, c.1888
Oil on panel, 15.1 x 10.8 cm
Collection of Andrew McIntosh Patrick Esq.,
London

102 *A Japanese Boy*, c.1888
Oil on panel, 15.9 x 17.8 cm
Private Collection, courtesy
The Fine Art Society, London

=+=+=+=+=+=+=+=+=+=+=+=+=+=+=+=+=+=+=+

Gustave Moreau
1826–98

Born in Paris, Moreau studied under François Picot at the Ecole des Beaux-Arts. His early paintings show strong influences from his friend and mentor Theodore Chassériau as well as from Delacroix. He visited Italy twice, in 1841 and in 1857–9, where he painted landscapes and copied Carpaccio, Leonardo and Mantegna; there he became friendly with his fellow French students in Rome, Degas, Puvis de Chavannes and Elie Delaunay.

With his great success at the Paris Salon of 1864–6, Moreau became known, in particular, for his mythological paintings, with sumptuous colours and rich, arresting imagery, such as *Jason* (Musée d'Orsay, Paris) and *Orpheus* (Musée d'Orsay, Paris). However, after 1869, Moreau temporarily stopped showing his work in public exhibitions.

Moreau returned to the Salon in 1876, with his most celebrated paintings, *Salome Dancing* (Armand Hammer Museum of Art and Cultural Centre, Los Angeles, California) and *The Apparition* (Musée du Louvre, Paris). Cat. 105 is one of the variations of the former and Cat. 106 is a contemporary print from *L'Art* magazine. Causing a great sensation in the Parisian art world, they were also shown at the Exposition Universelle of 1878. His treatment of Salome was probably inspired by the Carthaginian priestess in Flaubert's novel *Salammbo* (1862) and Baudelaire's *Les Fleurs du Mal* (1857). In return, Moreau's *Salome* paintings had a strong impact on the Symbolist literary circle. This is especially evident in Huysmans's long descriptions of Moreau's paintings at the 1876 Salon in *A Rebours*,

a book that provided inspiration for Wilde's *Salomé* (see pp.60–62).

Following his last showing at the Salon in 1880, Moreau retreated into a private world. On the death of his friend Elie Delaunay in 1891, however, he took over his atelier at the Ecole des Beaux-Arts, where he taught until his death. In the early twentieth century, his influences continued to be felt by the painters Georges Rouault and Matisse, as well as by André Breton and the Surrealists. (TS)

103 *The Beheading of St. John the Baptist*, c.1872–5
　　Oil on canvas, 85 x 60 cm
　　Musée Gustave Moreau, Paris (Cat. 581)

Cat.107

104 *Salome*, c.1874–5
　　Charcoal and black
　　crayon on paper,
　　60 x 36 cm
　　Signed b.r.
　　Musée Gustave Moreau,
　　Paris (Des.4831)

105 *Salome (or 'Tattooed
　　Salome')*, c.1874–5
　　Oil on canvas, 92 x 60 cm
　　Musée Gustave Moreau,
　　Paris (Cat. 211)

106 After Gustave Moreau
　　The Apparition, c.1876
　　Contemporary print
　　reproduced in *L'Art*
　　Board of Trustees of the
　　British Museum, London
　　(Acc.No.1879-5-10-
　　120)

107 *Sappho*, late 1880s
　　Watercolour over pencil
　　on paper, 20 x 13 cm
　　Signed b.l.
　　Board of Trustees of the
　　Victoria and Albert
　　Museum, London
　　(P.11-1934)

=+=+=+=+=+=+=+=+=+=+=+=+=+=+=+=+=+

William Morris
1834–96

Designer, craftsman, poet and socialist, William Morris studied at Exeter College, Oxford, where in 1853 he met Burne-Jones. He was articled to the architect G.E. Street with Philip Webb in 1856 and began painting under the influence of Rossetti. In 1861, he established the firm of Morris, Marshall, Faulkner and Co. for which he designed embroideries, wallpapers, printed and woven textiles, carpets and tapestries. His own particular contribution to design was in the field of flat pattern making, and almost all designers of the late nineteenth century, both in this country and abroad, came under his influence. The Kelmscott Press was his chief concern in the last decade of his life (see Cat.197).

Shortly after meeting Wilde for the first time, Morris wrote to his wife Jane on 31 March 1881: 'Did the babes tell you how I met Oscar Wilde at the Richmonds'? I must admit that the devil is painted blacker than he is, so it fares with O.W. Not but what he is an ass: but he certainly is clever too.' (LL/TS)

111

108 *Foliage Tapestry*, c.1887
　　Wool weft on a cotton with appliqué wool
　　embroidery, 76 x 115 cm
　　Trustees of the Watts Gallery,
　　Compton, Guildford

Morris gave a lecture on Carpet and Tapestry Weaving in 1888 on the occasion of the Arts and Crafts Exhibition at the New Gallery. Reporting the lecture in *The Pall Mall Gazette* (2 November, 1888), Wilde quoted Morris: 'Commercialism, with its vile god cheapness, its callous indifference to the worker, its innate vulgarity of temper, is our enemy. To gain anything good we must sacrifice something of our luxury — must think more of others, more of the State, the commonwealth'. This view was shared by Wilde in his essay of 1891 'The Soul of Man under Socialism'.

Gustave Adolphe Mossa
1883–1971

Born in Nice, Gustave Mossa was the son of the painter Alexis Mossa. In his native Nice, he became a professor at the Ecole des Art Décoratifs and the curator of the Nice Museum.

He painted mostly in watercolours, only occasionally using oils. In the early years of the twentieth century, he painted an extraordinary series of Symbolist pictures, frequently cruel and even horrifying in a lushly sensual manner (Cat.109). At the outbreak of the war in 1914, he began painting landscapes, still-lives and figures; was appointed Curator of the Jules Chéret Museum in Nice (now the Museum of Modern Art); and designed many spectacular floats for the annual Carnival in Nice. He also illustrated many books. A large proportion of his Symbolist works is on permanent exhibition at the Nice Museum, to which he willed them. (VA)

109 *Salomé kissing the head of St. John the Baptist*,
early 1900s
Pen and ink and watercolour on paper, 45 x 25 cm
Signed b.l.
Inscribed b.l.: 'SALOME'
Victor and Gretha Arwas, London

Cat.109

Cat.111

Alphonse Maria Mucha
1860–1939

One of the chief exponents of Art Nouveau, Mucha was born in a Moravian town, Ivancice. He came to Paris in 1887, where he studied at the Académie Julian under Jules Lefebvre and Jean-Paul Laurens. His fame was established with the poster *Gismonda* (1894) for Sarah Bernhardt (p.94) and for the next six years he was to grace the golden period of this great actress with posters such as *La Dame aux camélias* (1896) and *Hamlet* (1899). He also did many commercial advertisements and illustrations as well as designs for furniture, jewellery and stained glass. Posing languidly, with flowing hair in curvilinear flourishes, Mucha's nymph-like women became *fin-de-siècle* icons, along with Wilde and Beardsley's Salome (Cats 15, 19), who would represent an alternative aspect of womanhood.

Like his fellow Central Europeans, Mucha was a passionate believer of the political independence of his native Czech land, which had been under the Habsburg Empire. His vision of free Slav states was to be expressed later, in his native Prague, in a cycle of twenty vast canvases, *The Slav Epic* (1911–26). With this scheme in mind, he visited America frequently between 1904 and 1913. There he painted portraits, taught at the Chicago Art Institute and eventually found a sponsor for his epic paintings in Charles Crane.

A noted patriot in Prague, Mucha was among the first to be interrogated by the Nazis in 1939, when the German troops marched into the city. He died a few months later. (TS)

110 *Sarah Bernhardt*, 1896
Lithograph, tinted with watercolour, 62.5 x 40 cm
Signed b.l.
Victor and Gretha Arwas, London

111 *Salome*, 1897
Page from the magazine *L'Estampe moderne*
Colour lithograph, 41 x 31 cm
Signed b.l.
Mucha Trust, London

William Nicholson
1872–1949

Nicholson is perhaps best remembered as a poster artist, collaborating with his brother-in-law James Pryde under the name 'the Beggarstaff Brothers'. He also painted sensitive and deeply memorable still life compositions of such objects as jugs and boots. (LL)

112 *H. M. The Queen Victoria*, 1897
As published in Nicholson's *Twelve Portraits*, 1899
Woodcut, hand-coloured on Japanese paper,
22.9 x 24.1 cm
Syndics of the Fitzwilliam Museum, Cambridge.

When it first appeared in the *New Review* in 1897, this likeness of Queen Victoria was described as 'The Animated Tea-Cosy' and enjoyed a *succés de scandale*. Wilde hung it at his chalet at Berneval and wrote to Robert Ross to express his delight at the portrait. 'Every poet should gaze at the portrait of his Queen, all day long.' In 1899, Wilde is recorded as saying 'The three women I have most admired are Queen Victoria, Sarah Bernhardt, and Lillie Langtry. I would have married any one of them with pleasure.'

=+=+=+=+=+=+=+=+=+=+=+=+=+=+=+=+=+

William Orpen
1878–1931

Born at Stillorgan in County Dublin, Orpen studied at the Metropolitan School of Art in Dublin for seven years before going to London. In 1897–9, he trained at the Slade School with his friend and rival Augustus John (pp.108–9). His technical brilliance was founded on an understanding of Dutch seventeenth-century masters, such as Pieter de Hooch and Jan Vermeer. He also responded to Whistler (pp.132–3) and Impressionist paintings, and in 1900 became a member of the New English Art Club. From 1902, he was Co-Principal of the Chelsea Art School with Augustus John.

Orpen was successful as a portrait painter and he co-founded the National Portrait Society in 1911, with John Lavery and Ambrose McEvoy.

A fellow Irishman from Dublin and close to Wilde's friends Charles Conder (p.98) and William Rothenstein (pp.119–20), Orpen must have been familiar with countless Wildean episodes told by them. Cat. 113 was made for a proposed edition of Wilde's fairytales to be published by Gerald Duckworth. (TS)

113 *The Happy Prince*, 1913
  Ink and watercolour on paper, 46.4 x 36.8 cm
  Inscribed and dated t.r.
  Mark Samuels Lasner, Washington, D. C.

=+=+=+=+=+=+=+=+=+=+=+=+=+=+=+=+=+

Bernard Partridge
1861–1945

After a short and successful acting career, Du Maurier (pp. 68–9) persuaded Partridge to join *Punch* in 1891, and ten years later, in 1901, he succeeded Linley Sambourne as chief cartoonist. During his long and distinguished service on the magazine, Partridge caricatured every political figure from the Kaiser to Hitler and all the major personalities of the inter-war years. (LL)

114 *Portrait of James McNeill Whistler*, c.1890
  Watercolour on paper, 28.6 x 13 cm
  Signed b.r.
  Board of Trustees of the National Portrait Gallery, London, (Reg.no.3541)

=+=+=+=+=+=+=+=+=+=+=+=+=+=+=+=+=+

Walter Pater
1839–94

A Fellow of Brasenose College, Oxford, his apparently quiet and uneventful daily routine concealed an inner mental life which was to have a profound influence on the emergent Aesthetic Movement. For Oscar Wilde, the concluding words of Pater's *Studies in the History of the Renaissance* – 'to burn always with this hard gem-like flame, to maintain this ecstasy, is success in life' – had the authority of the holy writ of Beauty. The volume (Cat. 115) contains essays on the then neglected Botticelli (cf. Cat. 151) and his celebrated evocation of the *Mona Lisa*. Pater's theories such as that 'all art consistently aspires to the condition of music' provided a welcome respite from the moral rigour of Ruskin's teachings (p.121). (LL)

115 *Studies in the History of the Renaissance*
  Published in London, Macmillan and Co., 1873
  First edition, with the suppressed 'Conclusion'
  Book, dark blue-green cloth, 20.6 x 13.3 cm
  Stephen Calloway, Brighton

=+=+=+=+=+=+=+=+=+=+=+=+=+=+=+=+=+

Edward Poynter
1836–1919

After studying in Italy where he met Leighton (p.110) and Paris where he met Whistler (p.132–3) and Du Maurier (pp.68–9), Poynter scored a great success with *Israel in Egypt*, 1867 (Guildhall Art Gallery, London). He became one of the most popular artists of his time, painting both portraits and classical themes, the studies for which reveal his great powers as a draughtsman. In later years, he increasingly devoted himself to art administration, becoming Director of the National Gallery and President of the Royal Academy. (LL)

116 *Portrait of Lillie Langtry*, 1878
  Oil on canvas, 76 x 66 cm
  The Jersey Heritage Trust

Lillie Langtry (1853–1929), often known as the 'Jersey Lily', was one of the great society beauties of her day, the protégé of Oscar Wilde and mistress of the Prince of Wales. She made 'the little black dress' unadorned by jewellery one of the great fashion statements of all time. For Wilde, her beauty was a form of genius. Lillie later recalled: 'he always made a point of bringing me flowers, but he was not in the circumstances to afford great posies, so, in coming to call, he would drop into Covent Garden flower market, buy me a single gorgeous amaryllis (all his slender purse would allow) and stroll down Piccadilly carefully carrying the solitary flower.'

=+=+=+=+=+=+=+=+=+=+=+=+=+=+=+=+=+

Guido Reni
1575–1642

Reni was the leading painter of the Bolognese school in the seventeenth century. According to his biographer Malvasia, 'it was generally thought that he was a virgin... When observing the many lovely young girls who served as his models, he was like marble.' For Reynolds, 'his idea of Beauty... is acknowledged superior to that of any other painter', while Winckelmann compared him to Praxiteles. However, by the nineteenth century his fame was on the wane, and his work subject to scornful attacks by John Ruskin (p.121). This was due in part to the imitation of his work by legions of, often insipid, copyists.

Nevertheless, Oscar Wilde, Ruskin's young follower, had different views. In 1877, Wilde visited the Palazzo Rossi in Genoa to see Guido Reni's painting *St. Sebastian.* Some weeks later, while standing next to Keats's grave in Rome (Cat.156), Wilde recalled the painting:

'As I stood beside the mean grave of this divine boy I thought of him as a Priest of Beauty slain before his time; and the vision of Guido's San Sebastian came before my eyes as I saw him at Genoa, a lovely brown boy, with crisp, clustering hair and red lips, bound by his evil enemies to a tree, and, though pierced by arrows, raising his eyes with divine, impassioned gaze towards the Eternal Beauty of the opening Heavens.'

In his review of the Grosvenor Gallery exhibition of 1877, Wilde again mentions Reni's painting in a panegyric of the type of boys as beautiful as the Charmides of Plato. Wilde's attachment to this image can be linked to the fact that he took 'Sebastian' as the Christian name for his alias when he was living in France after release from gaol.

In Reni's time, St Sebastian was one of the few

113

images of the male nude that were allowed by the Christian Church, following a ruling passed at the Council of Trent in 1563 that had forbidden the depiction of the male nude. Cat. 117 is one of three copies made of Reni's *St Sebastian* in the seventeenth century. (LL/LV)

117 Anonymous, after Guido Reni
   St. Sebastian, 17th century
   Oil on canvas, 133 x 96.5 cm
   Cheltenham Art Gallery and Museum

=+=+=+=+=+=+=+=+=+=+=+=+=+=+=+=+=+

Charles Ricketts
1866–1931

Ricketts was a painter, designer, sculptor and art critic, as well as a passionate collector of art. When a student, he met his lifelong partner Charles Shannon (p.123). He trained as an illustrator and in 1889 founded a private printing press – the Vale Press (Cat.118) – for which he designed fonts, initials, borders and illustrations. Ricketts and Shannon became 'almost official artists' to Oscar Wilde, who dubbed them 'Orchid' and 'Marigold'. Their house (which had belonged to Whistler) in a Chelsea cul-de-sac called The Vale was praised by Wilde as 'the one house in London where you will never be bored'.

Jointly, Ricketts and Shannon designed and decorated Wilde's *The House of Pomegranates* (Cat.120) in 1891. A critical review enabled Wilde to defend the book's appearance with the retort, 'there are only two people in the world whom it is absolutely necessary that the cover should please. One is Mr Ricketts, who designed it, the other is myself whose book it binds. We both admire it immensely!' Wilde appreciated Rickett's wit and his artistry, and recommended him as a book designer to John Lane (p.109) at the Bodley Head. They used him to design virtually all Wilde's books. (LL)

118 Edited, designs and illustrations by Charles
   Ricketts and Charles Shannon
   The Dial, volume I
   Published in London, The Vale Press, 1889
   Magazine, 32.5 x 25.5 cm
   Contributors include John Gray, Michael Field
   and Sturge Moore
   Mark Samuels Lasner, Washington, D. C.

Cat.121

119 Oscar Wilde
   Designed by Charles Ricketts
   The Picture of Dorian Gray
   Published in London, Unicorn Press, 1945:
   a replica of the first edition published by Ward,
   Lock & Co.,1891
   Book, cream cloth cover, spine and grey boards
   blocked in gold, 19.5 x 13.5 cm
   Simon Wilson, London

120 Oscar Wilde
   Designed by Charles Ricketts and
   Charles Shannon
   A House of Pomegranates
   Published in London, James R. Osgood,
   McIlvaine and Co., 1891 (one of 1,000 copies)
   Book, green cloth spine with cream cloth boards
   blocked in gold and orange,
   21.6 x 17.2 cm
   Stephen Calloway, Brighton

121 *Oedipus and the Sphinx*, 1891
Pen and ink, 23.2 x 20.7 cm
Tullie House Museum and Art Gallery, Carlisle
(Acc.no.1949.125.74)

Although this subject had been used previously by
Ingres, the legend of the Sphinx was to become one
of the most potent Symbolist themes, especially for
Gustave Moreau (pp.110–11), an artist whom
Ricketts idealised. The Sphinx was a monster who
ravaged Thebes, devouring all who failed to answer
her riddle. Oedipus answered it correctly, causing
the Sphinx to perish, and was rewarded with the
hand of the widowed Queen Jocasta, thus
innocently marrying his own mother.

Cat. 121 was commissioned for £5 in 1891
by Lord Leighton (p.110). He was delighted with
the result and found it 'full of imagination and a
weird charm … a marvellous piece of penmanship'.
It was later bought back by Ricketts, who
considered it his finest early drawing. Although
made three years before the publication of Oscar
Wilde's book *The Sphinx* (Cat.125), it may well
have played a part in the gestation of that work,
which had begun while he was still at Oxford.

122 Oscar Wilde
Designed by Charles Ricketts
Poems
Published in London, Elkin Matthews and
John Lane, 1892 (No. 217 of 220 copies)
'Iris' cloth blocked in gold, 19 x 13.5 cm
Signed by the author
Simon Wilson, London

123 *Album of Drawings*, c.1890s
57 pages, with drawings in pen and ink,
watercolour and bodycolour, some on
tracing paper
Cover size: 40 x 28 cm
Contains drawings for *The Sphinx* by
Oscar Wilde
Tullie House Museum and Art Gallery,
Carlisle (Acc.no.1949–125)

124 *Christ Crucified* c.1893
Pen and ink on pink paper, 17.1 x 14 cm
Manchester City Art Galleries (Inv.no.1925.419)

A drawing of the crucifixion for Oscar Wilde's
The Sphinx (Cat.125) which illustrates the lines:

'Whose pallid burden, sick with pain,
watches the world with wearied eyes,
And weeps for every soul that dies,
and weeps for every soul in vain.'

125 Oscar Wilde
Illustrated by Charles Ricketts
The Sphinx
Published in London, Elkin Mathews and
John Lane, 1894 (one of 200 copies)
Book, vellum, blocked in gold to a design
by Ricketts, 22.3 x 16.9 cm
Stephen Calloway, Brighton

126 Oscar Wilde
Designed by Charles Ricketts
Intentions
Published in London, James R. Osgood,
McIlvane and Co., 1894
Second edition (first in the same format in 1891)

Book, light green cloth blocked with lettering by
Ricketts, 19.4 x 12.7 cm (one of 1,000 copies)
Containing the four essays: 'The Decay of Lying',
'Pen, Pencil and Poison', 'The Critic as Artist'
and 'The Truth of Masks'
Stephen Calloway, Brighton

127 ***Miniature Portrait of Edith Emma Cooper
or 'Henry'***, 1901
Card, set in 'The Pegasus Locket', made of
gold with white and green enamel, set with
pearls, garnets and rubies (made by Giuliano
to Rickett's design)
Portrait: (Diam) 3.4 cm; inscribed with the
monogram 'MF' ('Michael Field') and with
twinned rings.
Locket: 10 x 5 cm
Syndics of the Fitzwilliam Museum, Cambridge
(M.3-1914)

Miss Edith Emma Cooper and her aunt Katherine
Bradley wrote poems and plays together under the
pseudonym 'Michael Field'. They were in many ways
a feminine version of their close friends Ricketts
and Shannon, who decorated a number of their
volumes for the Vale Press. To their inner circle,
Edith was known as 'Henry' and Katherine as

Cat.124

Cat.127

'Michael'. The 'Pegasus' pendant shown here, with its splendid use of Baroque pearls, must in this exhibition stand for another pastiche made by Ricketts for Oscar Wilde. In the autumn of 1889, Wilde asked Ricketts to paint 'a small Elizabethan picture' of Willie Hughes, 'quite in Clouet's style', which was to act as a frontispiece to an enlarged edition of *The Portrait of Mr W.H.* which never appeared. Rickett's pastiche was greeted with delight by Wilde, who wrote: 'it is not a forgery at all – it is an authentic Clouet of the highest artistic value. It is absurd of you and Shannon to try and take me in – as if I did not know the master's touch or was no judge of frames.' It was knocked down for a guinea at the sale of Wilde's goods during his trial in April 1895.

128 ***Design for Salomé by Oscar Wilde,*** *as produced*
for a private performance at the King's Hall, Covent
Garden in 1906, c.1906
Watercolour on paper, 34.5 x 47 cm
Board of Trustees of the Victoria and Albert
Museum, London (E956-1933)

Wilde had initially discussed the staging of *Salomé* in 1892 with Charles Ricketts and W. Graham Robertson, fantasising about an all-yellow set with scented clouds of perfume, but the production never took place owing to censorship. In June 1906, the Literary Theatre Society staged a private performance of *Salomé* for which this is a design.

129 ***Stage Setting for Wilde's Salomé planned for Tokyo,***
1919
Watercolour and bodycolour, 21.1 x 40 cm
Syndics of the Fitzwilliam Museum, Cambridge.
(No. 1646)

130 ***The Death of Orpheus,*** 1929
Pen, ink and Chinese white on paper,
22.2 x 16.2 cm
Tullie House Museum and Art Gallery, Carlisle
(Acc.no.1949.125.71)

131 ***Judas Iscariot,*** 1929
An illustration for Rickett's book
Beyond the Threshold (1929)
Pen and ink on paper, 21.2 x 15.1 cm
Tullie House Museum and Art Gallery, Carlisle
(Acc.no.1949.125.340)

Cat.128

132 ***Oscar Wilde; Recollections by Jean Paul Raymond***
and Charles Ricketts
Published in London, Bloomsbury, The Nonesuch
Press, 1932 (one of 800 copies)
Ivory cloth blocked in gold with a design by
Ricketts based on the 1894 cover for *The Sphinx,*
26 x 16.4 cm
Stephen Calloway, Brighton

=+=+=+=+=+=+=+=+=+=+=+=+=+=+=+=+=+=+=+

Auguste Rodin
1840–1917
The most influential sculptor of the late nineteenth century, Rodin was a late starter. Born in Paris, he received an initial art training at the Ecole Spéciale de Dessin et de Mathématiques. Failing the entrance to the Ecole des Beaux-Arts, he worked as a craftsman in porcelain factories and workshops until the early 1880s. Determined to be a sculptor, he supplemented his technical training by studying in museums and became interested in Puget and Michelangelo. In 1874–5, he visited Italy, where he was strongly affected by the spiritual intensity and the powerful modelling of Michaelangelo's work.

Its impact was demonstrated in his *Age of Bronze,* which led to his first showing at the Paris Salon in 1877. However, the lifelike quality of his figure provoked accusations of him having used life-casts, and the work received no genuine recognition until it was shown in London in 1884.

In 1880, Rodin began his most ambitious project, *The Gate of Hell,* which was commissioned as a doorway for the Ecole des Arts Décoratifs. At his death in 1917, it was still unfinished, but its numerous figures provided him with a vast stock of ideas, which he would develop separately into independent works, such as *The Thinker* (1880) and *The Kiss* (1886). Cat. 133 is a variation of the head used in the upper right side of *The Gate.*

Wilde was a great admirer of Rodin. He was in a minority in praising Rodin's controversial portrait of Balzac in 1891–8 (Cat. 135): 'The head is gorgeous, the dressing-gown is an entirely unshaped cone of white plaster. People howl with rage over it' (Butler: p.317). In the last year of his life, Wilde visited Rodin's pavilion at the Exposition Universelle. Shown round the exhibition by Rodin himself, Wilde was entranced by 'all his great dreams in marble' and described the sculptor as 'the greatest poet in France' (Montgomery-Hyde: pp.461–2).

Rodin had close contacts with the English art world: he was Whistler's friend and was represented by William Rothenstein (pp.119–20) and Robert Ross's Carfax Gallery in London. His last important monument commission was that for Whistler (pp.132–3), which was planned to be erected at the Chelsea Embankment near the former Whistler house. It never materialised as a monument, but a small-scale study (Cat.134) shows Rodin's idea of a 'muse' for the Whistler monument. The model was Gwen John, the elder sister of Augustus John's (see pp.108–9) and Rodin's mistress. Briefly, John had also been Whistler's student in Paris. (TS)

133 *The Head of St. John the Baptist on the Plate*, 1887
    Bronze, 21 x 41 x 27 cm
    Signed on back
    Musée Rodin, Paris (Inv. S.771)

134 *Study for 'La Muse Whistler'*, 1905–6
    Bronze, 65.5 x 33 x 34 cm
    Signed r. side of base
    Musée Rodin, Paris (Inv. S.761)

135 Eduard Steichen
    Memorial to Balzac by Rodin at Jardin de Meudon, facing three-quarter right, 1908
    Photograph, 49 x 36 cm
    Musée Rodin, Paris (Inv. Ph233)

=+=+=+=+=+=+=+=+=+=+=+=+=+=+=+=+=+=+=+

Frederick William Rolfe [also known as 'Baron Corvo']
1860–1913

A convert to Catholicism, Rolfe failed to become a priest, but in his most famous novel, *Hadrian the Seventh*, he fantasises about becoming Pope. He alienated all his friends by his constant paranoia and requests for financial support, and was described by W.H. Auden as one 'of the great masters of vituperation'. In Venice, where he died, he lived out sexual fantasies with gondoliers on the lagoon, and wrote haunting accounts of the beauty of Venice, published posthumously in 1934 in his novel *The Desire and Pursuit of the Whole: a romance of Modern Venice*. His life inspired the classic biography *The Quest for Corvo*, 1934, by A.J.A. Symons.

136 *St. Sebastian*, c. 1893
    Modern copy print
    Courtesy Bodleian Library, University of Oxford

137 *St. Sebastian*, c. 1893
    Modern copy print
    Courtesy Bodleian Library, University of Oxford

138 *Boy nude resting*, c. 1893
    Modern copy print
    Courtesy Bodleian Library, University of Oxford

139 *Two Boys in the Lake*, c. 1893
    Modern copy print
    Courtesy Bodleian Library, University of Oxford

=+=+=+=+=+=+=+=+=+=+=+=+=+=+=+=+=+=+=+

Félicien Rops
1833–98

Born in Namur, Rops received his initial art training at the town's Academy of Fine Arts from 1849. He moved to Brussels in 1853 to study law at the Free University of Brussels. While there, he joined the Atelier Saint-Luc, where he met the sculptor Constantin Meunier and the painter Charles de Groux; he also became a member of the Société des Joyeux, founded by the writer Charles de Coster. In 1856, Rops founded a weekly 'magazine of artistic and literary frolics', *Uylenspiegel*.

In 1862, Rops left for Paris to study with Bracquemond (pp.95–6) and Jacquemard, and he divided his time between Brussels and Paris until he finally settled in Paris in 1874. While he continued to paint, especially landscapes of Flanders in *plein-air*, he turned increasingly to engraving, making illustrations for periodicals and literary works, through which his name was to be known abroad. In 1864, he met Charles Baudelaire, the renowned author of *Les Fleurs du Mal* (1857), who came to Brussels to lecture on Théophile Gautier. The meeting had a profound impact on Rops' vision of the world and his choice of subject matter. His satirical views on politics and middle-class society were replaced by frightening visions of women (e.g. Cats 140, 141) – frivolous, corrupted, cruel and destructive – who would dominate the dark side of society, with Death and the Devil. In the context of the changing views of women during the late nineteenth century, Rops' response to 'new women' is

Cat.131

Cat.130

comparable with Wilde and Beardsley's images of Salome (see pp.67–8, 71).

Rops was a highly successful artist in his lifetime. Close to the Symbolist circle (Cat.142), he was praised by the Goncourt Brothers (Cat.41), Baudelaire, Huysmans (Cat.182) and the Sâr Péladan. (TS)

118

140 *'Le Calvaire' from Les Sataniques series*, 1882
Pencil and crayon, heightened with red,
20.7 x 14,5 cm
Victor and Gretha Arwas, London

141 *L'Intimation sentimentale*, c.1887
Etching, drypoint, 16.5 x 11.5 cm
Signed t.l.
Inscribed bottom:
'DIABOLI/VIRTUS/IN/LOMBIS!…/
(St Augustin)
Victor and Gretha Arwas, London

142 *The Great Lyre,* 1887
Frontispiece for Stéphane Mallarmé's *Poesies*,
published in La Revue indépendante, Paris, 1887
Heliogravure, 21.7 x 14.7 cm
Musée Félicien Rops, Province de Namur

William Rothenstein
1872–1945

Son of a German Jewish wool industrialist, Rothenstein was born in Bradford. After a brief training at the Slade School in 1888–9 under Alfonse Legros (p.110), he left for Paris in 1889 to study at the Académie Julian. At the Académie he met Charles Conder (p.98 and Cat.144) in 1890, and they briefly shared a studio on Montmartre. There he also formed friendships with Toulouse-Lautrec (pp.128–9 and Cat.145), Louis Anquetin (p.89) and Emile Bernard, and together they enjoyed Parisian bohemian life. Rothenstein first met Wilde in 1891 at his Montmartre studio, and immediately they became friendly. Wilde admired Rothenstein's pastels and Rothenstein was fascinated by Wilde's art of talking. In his *Men and Memories*, Rothenstein wrote: 'Wilde talked as others painted or wrote; talking was his art'.

In March 1892, Rothenstein and Conder showed their works at Père Thomas's gallery, arranged by Lautrec. A prestigious Parisian venue, the exhibition attracted considerable critical attention. Highly praising Cat. 143, which was among the exhibits,

Cat.147

Degas sent a message of invitation to Rothenstein, which led to their long-lasting friendship. The same year, Conder, a born stylist, was portrayed in Cat. 144, the first and only painting Rothenstein showed at the Salon du Champ de Mars. Wearing a long black overcoat and tall hat, with a sidelong glance, Conder was depicted as a *fatale*, a romantic dandy.

In 1894, Rothenstein became a member of the New English Art Club, and he came back to London. Throughout this period, portraits became the principal part of his work: he had been publishing a series of lithographic portraits since 1893 (Cats 146, 147, 148 and 149). From 1899, he was involved in the artistic management of the avant-garde Carfax Gallery, which was joined later by Robert Ross as Director. Between 1920 and 1935 he was the Principal of the Royal College of Art. (TS)

143. **Parting at Morning**, 1891
Pastel, chalk and bronze paint on paper on board, 129.5 x 50.8 cm
Signed, dated and inscribed b.l.: 'Will Rothenstein to Arthur H. Studd/Paris-November 1891'
Inscribed b.r.:
'Round the cliff on [sic] a sudden came the sea / And the sun looked over the mountain's rim / And straight was a path of gold for him / And the need of a world of men for me
Robert Browning'
Board of Trustees of the Tate Gallery, London (T 07283)

144 **L'homme qui sort: the Painter Charles Conder**, 1892
Oil on canvas, 120.3 x 55.2 cm
Signed and dated b.l.
The Toledo Museum of Art;
Purchased with funds from the Libbey Endowment, Gift of Edward Drummond Libbey (Acc. no.52.86)

145 **Portrait of Toulouse-Lautrec**, early 1890s
Pencil and white chalk on brown paper, 31.4 x 17.9 cm
Collection Barry Humphries, London

146 **Portrait of Aubrey Beardsley**, 1897
Lithograph, 34 x 25.5 cm
Stephen Calloway, Brighton

Cat.150

147 **Charles Ricketts and Charles Shannon**, 1897
Lithograph, 34.3 x 21.6 cm
Signed and dated b.l.
Mark Samuels Lasner, Washington, D. C.

148 **Portrait of George Bernard Shaw**, 1897
Lithograph, 32.4 x 22.9 cm
Signed and dated b.r.
Mark Samuels Lasner, Washington, D. C.

149 **Portrait of Max Beerbohm**, 1898
Lithograph, 34.3 x 16.5 cm
Signed and dated b.l.
Board of Trustees of the Victoria and Albert Museum, London (E2143-1920)

150 **Portrait of Augustus John**, 1899
Oil on canvas, 77 x 56.2 cm
Walker Art Gallery, Liverpool
(Board of Trustees of the National Museums and Galleries on Merseyside)

120

Cat.143

Will Rothenstein found in an old sketch book of the early nineties

Cat.145

John Ruskin
1819–1900

The critical champion of Turner, the Pre-Raphaelites and the Gothic style, Ruskin was himself a fine artist. He studied watercolour painting, and illustrated his own *The Seven Lamps of Architecture* (1849) and *The Stones of Venice* (1851–3). He was made to pay a farthing's damages in 1878 for libelling Whistler (pp.132–3) by accusing him of 'throwing a pot of paint in the public's face' when he exhibited his *Nocturne in Black and Gold – The Falling Rocket* (Fig.3). Increasing mental health problems subsequently led to the slow deterioration of one of the most remarkable critical minds of the nineteenth century. In 1888, Wilde wrote a valedictory letter to his old mentor, 'the dearest memories of my Oxford days are my walks and talks with you, and from you I learnt nothing but what was good … There is in you something of prophet, of priest, and of poet, and to you the gods gave eloquence such as they have given to none other…' (LL)

151 After Sandro Botticelli (c.1445–1510)
   Study of Zipporah, 1874
   Pencil, watercolour and gouache on paper,
   155 x 66 cm
   Ruskin Foundation
   (Ruskin Library, University of Lancaster)

This figure appears in one of the paintings by Botticelli in the Sistine Chapel at Rome, painted between 1481 and 1482. The work illustrates *The Trials of Moses* and represents Zipporah, the daughter of Jethro of Midian. (Midian was where Moses fled after slaying an Egyptian, and Zipporah later became Moses's wife.) This copy by Ruskin is one of his largest copies after an Italian old master. Botticelli as an artist was very much the discovery of Pater and Swinburne in the 1860s, but Ruskin soon became interested and visited Rome to study his work. The figure of Zipporah also inspired the character Odette in Marcel Proust's *A la recherche du temps perdu*. In a lighter vein, Botticelli features in W.S. Gilbert's description of the 'Heavy Dragoons' when they become aesthetes in *Patience*. Their aesthetic sweethearts exclaim, 'How Botticellian! How Fra Angelico! O Art we thank thee for this boon!'

152 *Amateur navvies at Oxford – Undergraduates making a road as suggested by Mr Ruskin, Oxford,* 1874
   Double page spread from *Graphic* magazine,
   29.7 x 50 cm
   Ruskin Foundation (Ruskin Library, University of Lancaster)

Ruskin extolled the value of physical exercise, and this contemporary illustration (Cat.152) shows Oxford undergraduates working on Ruskin's road building project across a swamp in Ferry Hinksey, just outside Oxford. According to a fellow undergraduate, 'Wilde was one of the most regular navvies … specially invited to fill the great man's barrow, and help him trundle it down the plank.'

=+

John Singer Sargent
1856–1925

An American expatriate, Sargent was educated in Italy, France and Germany. He studied in 1874 with Carolus Duran in Paris, and travelled in Spain and Morocco in 1880. While in Madrid, he was much impressed by the Velazquez and Goya paintings. A friend of Monet and the Impressionists, Sargent exhibited mostly portraits at both the Paris Salon and the Royal Academy, and also painted some vivid landscapes. He was a war artist, and his large painting *Gassed* is one of the great masterpieces inspired by the First World War. (LL)

153 ***Ellen Terry as Lady Macbeth***, 1889
   Oil on canvas, 221 x 114.3 cm
   Board of Trustees of the Tate Gallery, London
   (N 02053)

W. Graham Robertson recalled in *Time Was*:
   'As Lady Macbeth her appearance was magnificent: long plaits of deep red hair fell from under a purple veil over a robe of green upon which iridescent wings of beetles glittered like emeralds, and a great wine coloured cloak, gold embroidered, swept from her shoulders. The effect was barbaric and exactly right, though whence the wife of an ancient Scottish chieftain obtained so many oriental beetles wings was not explained. I remember Oscar Wilde remarking "Lady Macbeth seems an economical housekeeper and evidently

patronises local industries for her husband's clothes but she takes care to do her own shopping in Byzantium."'

=+

Raymond Savage
fl. 1894

Savage contributed several illustrations to *The Dial* (Cat.118), but little else is known about him. (LL)

154 ***Portrait of John Gray***, 1890s
   Lithograph, 25.4 x21 cms
   Board of Trustees of the National Portrait Gallery, London (reg. no. 3844)

In 1889, Wilde met the young poet John Gray (1866–1934), who became his constant companion. Although there was no evidence, he was generally thought to be the model for *The Picture of Dorian Gray*. In 1893, Wilde paid for the costs of the publication and design by Ricketts of a volume of Gray's poems, entitled *Silverpoints*, in an edition of only 275 copies. The friendship waned after Wilde met Douglas and Gray met André Raffalovich (1864–1934), a rich Russian, of whom Wilde cruelly remarked, 'he came to London to found a *salon* and only succeeded in founding a saloon'. Gray became a Catholic priest at the age of thirty five and lived in Edinburgh near the church of St Peter's, which Raffalovich built for him.

121

=+

William Bell Scott
1811–90

William was the brother of the painter David Scott. After exhibiting at the Royal Scottish Academy, he moved to London in 1837 and got to know William Powell Frith (p.106), Augustus Egg and Richard Dadd. The following year, he published his first volume of poems. His murals at Wallington Hall, Northumberland depicting Northumbrian history are among his most important works. (LL)

155 *Portrait of Algernon Charles Swinburne*, 1860
    Oil on canvas, 45.7 x 33 cm
    Inscribed, signed and dated: 'A.C.S. [Jan.y. Oct]
    1860 W.B.SCott'
    Master and Fellows of Balliol College, Oxford

In 1859, Scott and Swinburne had visited the Longstone lighthouse on the Northumberland coast so that Scott could study the background for the fresco of Grace Darling at Wallington Hall. Swinburne's lifelong love of the sea must surely have suggested the background for this memorable portrait. 'No seagull likes to have his wings clipped,' wrote Swinburne in his early novel *Lesbia Brandon*, which describes the 'spring weather sea... grey and green ... swelling and quivering under clouds and sunbeams ... like the tired tossing limbs of a goddess.' As the leading poet of the Aesthetic Movement, Swinburne returned to such themes throughout his career. Always highly strung, his health, weakened by excessive drinking, gave way in 1879, and for the rest of his life he was always to be supervised by his friend Theodore Watts-Dunton.

156 *Keats's Grave in the New Protestant Cemetery,*
    Rome, 1873
    Oil on canvas, 48 x 33 cm
    Visitors of the Ashmolean Museum, Oxford
    (A 263)

Wilde first visited the Protestant Cemetery in Rome (Cats 156, 157) in 1877. When standing by the poet's grave, Wilde thought of Keats as 'a Prince of Beauty killed before his time, a lovely Sebastian killed by the arrows of a lying and unjust tongue', sentiments expressed in a sonnet entitled *Keats's Grave*. He disliked the bas-relief of Keats erected a year earlier, which he deemed *extremely ugly*, and tried to raise funds for 'a tinted bust of Keats' in its place – fortunately without success. Years later, Keats's grave remained for Wilde 'the holiest place in Rome', and while in prison he tried to obtain a copy of Keats's poems. Wilde also admired Scott's portrayal of Shelley's grave (Cat.157), and sent a print of it to a friend.

157 *Shelley's Grave in the New Protestant Cemetery, Rome*, 1873
Oil on canvas, 48 x 33 cm
Visitors of the Ashmolean Museum, Oxford
(A 264)

=+=+=+=+=+=+=+=+=+=+=+=+=+=+=+=+=+

Charles Haslewood Shannon
1863–1937

Shannon was the lifelong partner of Charles Ricketts (pp.114–6). The two met as students at Lambeth School of Art, and from then on they began working together. Shannon is praised for the quality of his lithography, a technique that he used with rare sensitivity. The work of Ricketts and Shannon was reproduced in *The Pageant* and the sporadically issued periodical *The Dial* (Cat.118). In 1929, Shannon fell while hanging a picture and never fully recovered health or sense. (LL)

158 *The Wood Engraver, Charles Ricketts*, 1894
Lithograph, 17.0 x 17.5 cm
Signed b.l.
Inscribed b.l.: 'R28 The Wood Engraver'
Tullie House Museum and Art Gallery, Carlisle
(Acc.no.1949.125.113)

Just as Rickett's excelled at the process of wood engraving, so did Shannon at lithography. It is interesting to note the oil lamp and water-filled globe used to focus the light on the wood block.

cat.155

cat.158

159 *Signboard for the Vale Press Office, Warwick Street, London*, 1894–6
Oil on panel, 85.8 x 48.8 cm
Inscribed t.l.: 'HACON ET RICKETTS. THE. SIGN. OF. THE DIAL'
Aberdeen Art Gallery and Museums

The design represents the Dial and Captive Pegasus. The aim of the Vale Press (1894–1903) was to give the classics of English literature a new and beautiful form.

160 *Bathers*, late 1890s
Oil on panel, 46.5 x 37.5 cm
Trustees of the Watts Gallery, Compton, Guildford

161 *Tibullus in the House of Delia*, 1900–5
Oil on canvas, 89 x 89 cm
Nottingham Castle Museum and Art Gallery

The life of the elegiac Roman poet Albius Tibullus (c.48–19 BC) made a most suitable subject for Shannon. There are earlier versions of this composition as a lithograph (1895) and as an oil sketch (1898). The figures to the immediate left and right of Delia are Ricketts and Shannon respectively.

123

cat.160

124

Walter Richard Sickert
1860–1942

Sickert was born in Munich, the son of a Danish artist father and Anglo-Irish mother. From the age of eight, he lived in England and attended the Slade School of Art (1877–81). He studied briefly with Whistler (pp.132–3), before leaving for Paris, where he became a disciple of Degas. Sickert's personality dominated a generation of British artists, particularly through his association with the New English Art Club and his foundation of the Camden Town Group, named after a London location that he favoured, alongside Dieppe and Venice. His paintings and etchings of music halls, statues and streets are low in tone, controlled and fastidious, and match the wit of his prose criticism. (LL)

162 *Portrait of Aubrey Beardsley*, 1894
    Oil on canvas, 76.2 x 31.1 cm
    Signed b.l.
    Board of Trustees of the Tate Gallery, London
    (N 04655)

On 16 July 1894, a memorial bust to the poet John Keats (Cat.156), who had died aged twenty five in 1821, was unveiled in Hampstead Church. Beardsley (pp.90–91), himself suffering from the same consumption that had killed Keats, identified with the poet, remarking to a friend, 'I shall not live longer than did Keats.' After the ceremony, Beardsley was observed walking off through the churchyard, occasionally tripping over the gravestones or mounds of earth. Sickert's poignant image has captured this moment, creating the immediacy recalled by a music-hall song of the period entitled, 'I've only a moment to linger with you'.

163 *Café des Arcades, Dieppe* (or 'The Café Suisse'),
    1914
    Oil on canvas, 53.3 x 38.1 cm
    Leeds City Art Galleries

This was a favourite café of Sickert's in Dieppe, and it still exists today. It was while seated at the café that Oscar Wilde, a frequent visitor, wrote one of his most delightful letters to Douglas, in which he recounted his enjoyment of the celebrations of Queen Victoria's Jubilee (see Cat.81).

Leonard Smithers
1861–1909

Born in Sheffield, Smithers first worked there as a solicitor. His first contact with Wilde in July 1888 arose when he wrote to congratulate him on the appearance of *The Happy Prince*. (see Cat.57) Smithers became a specialist publisher of erotica, avant-garde poetry and the works of Aubrey Beardsley (pp.90–91). He also came to feature greatly in Wilde's life in exile, a relationship which had its ups and downs. Wilde describes his appearance in Dieppe as follows: he wore 'a blue tie fastened with a diamond brooch of the impurest water – or perhaps wine, as he never touches water: it goes to his head at once. His face, clean shaven as befits a priest who serves at the altar whose God is Literature, is wasted and pale – not with poetry, but with poets, who, he says have wrecked his life by publishing with him. He loves first editions, especially of women: little girls are his passion. He is the most learned erotomaniac in Europe. He is also a delightful companion, and a dear fellow, very kind to me.' Their friendship broke down after Smither's bankruptcy in 1900. (See also Cats 17, 18) (LL)

164 Oscar Wilde
  Phrases and Philosophies for the Use of the Young
  'Privately Printed for Presentation, MDCCCXCIV' in London, 1894
  (Probably a slightly later pirated reprint by Leonard Smithers)
  Booklet, brown paper wrappers (one of 75 copies), 19.8 x 12.8 cm
  Stephen Calloway, Brighton

165 *Wilde versus Whistler; Being an Acrimonious Correspondence on Art*
  'Privately Printed, MCMVI' in London, Leonard Smithers, 1906
  Booklet, paper wrappers (one of 400 copies), 19.7 x 14.6 cm
  Stephen Calloway, Brighton

Simeon Solomon
1840–1905

Solomon was born in the East End of London, a member of an artistic Jewish family, (his elder brother Abraham and sister Rebecca were also painters). His early paintings use Old Testament themes and are in a style deeply infused with Hebraic feeling. But, after contact with the Pre-Raphaelites, Swinburne (Cat.155), Robert Browning and Walter Pater (p.113 and Cat.170), he developed a distinctive Symbolist style, with which he depicted Hellenic, androgynous and ritualistic subject matter. After imprisonment for a homosexual scandal in 1873, while living in a workhouse, he painted a number of sensual, mystical works. These paintings often feature disembodied heads, an image derived from his prose poem in 1871 *A Vision of Love Revealed in Sleep* (Cat. 169). He died in St Giles workhouse in August 1905 of heart failure, aggravated by bronchitis and alcoholism. His career and disgrace in some respects anticipates that of Wilde, who was an admirer of Solomon's work. When writing to Douglas in *De Profundis*, Wilde regretted the loss of his Solomon drawings. (LL)

166 *The Bride, Bridegroom and Sad Love*, 1865
  Pencil, pen and ink, 24.8 x 17.1 cm
  Board of Trustees of the Victoria and Albert Museum, London (E 1367-1919)

cat.166

This is one of the earliest of Solomon's drawings to manifest a homoerotic quality. A quality that Douglas would later describe with the memorable phrase, 'the Love that dare not speak its name'. Solomon gave a drawing, similar in composition but with clothed figures, to his friend Walter Pater.

167 *Dawn*, 1870–71
  Watercolour on paper, 35.3 x 50.7 cm
  Birmingham Museums and Art Gallery

This work is closely related to the lines in Solomon's Prose poem *A Vision of Love Revealed in Sleep* (Cat.169), which describes the moments 'Until the Day Breaks and the Shadows pass away,' from the Song of Songs, 'Upon the waning of the night, at that time when the stars are pale, and when dreams wrap us about…'

168 *Love Dreaming by the Sea*, 1871
  Watercolour on paper, 37.5 x 27.5 cm
  Signed (monogram) and dated
  (on wood panel) b.r.
  The University of Wales, Aberystwyth

This is one of many drawings that play on the symbolic themes that fascinated Solomon at this time – themes that he also developed verbally in *A Vision of Love Revealed in Sleep* (Cat.169). Wilde admired this prose poem by Solomon, and once regretted that there were no works by 'the author of that strange vision of love on view in the Grosvenor Gallery exhibition'.

169 *A Vision of Love Revealed in Sleep*, 1871
  Printed by F.S. Ellis, London
  Book, 37pp., demi-octavo, cloth boards, 26 x 20.5 cm
  Lionel Lambourne, London

170 *Portrait of Walter Pater*, 1872
  Pencil on paper, 17.1 x 9.5 cm
  Gabinetto Desegni e Stampe degli Uffizi, Firenze (n. 5967)

This drawing has caught something of Pater's reticent, introspective personality, a man described as a 'Caliban of Letters'. Pater is said to have once remarked, 'I would give ten years of my life to be handsome.'

cat.167

=+

126

Walter Spindler (French School)
fl.1895

Little is known of Walter Spindler, a portrait painter and watercolourist, apart from the fact that he painted portraits of Sarah Bernhardt on several occasions, which may well provide a link with the sitter on this occasion.

171 *Portrait of Lord Alfred Douglas*,
    November 1895
    Pencil on paper, 25.5 x 16 cm
    Signed and dated b.l.
    Sheila Colman, Lancing
    (The Lord Alfred Douglas Literary Estate)

=+

'Spy' [pseudonym of Leslie Ward]
1851–1922

In 1873, Ward began to work for the society magazine *Vanity Fair*, which published a weekly caricature of a celebrity. Over the next forty years, 'Spy' contributed nearly half of its 2,400 caricatures. (LL)

172 *'Patience' – W.S. Gilbert*, 1881
    Published in *Vanity Fair*, 21 May 1881
    Colour lithograph 28.2 x 18.4 cm
    Catherine Haill, London

Sir William Schwenk Gilbert (1836–1911) will always be remembered for his fruitful but stormy collaboration with Sir Arthur Sullivan (Cat.8), which resulted in several operettas, notably *Patience* in 1881. In *Patience*, the character of Bunthorne, although probably intended to represent Rossetti, was regarded by the public as a notable satire of Wilde. A combative wit and master of repartee, Gilbert once claimed that 'all humour properly so called is based upon a grave and quasi-respectful treatment of the ludicrous'.

173 *Richard D'Oyly Carte*, 1891
    Published in *Vanity Fair*, 14 February 1891
    Colour lithograph, 28.2 x 18.4 cm
    Catherine Haill, London

The great impresario Richard D'Oyly Carte (1841–1901) combined knowledge of art with outstanding organisational ability. His lifelong friendship with Sullivan (Cat.8) and ability to gain the respect of the touchy Gilbert (Cat.172) enabled him to form one of the greatest partnerships in the history of musical entertainment. He also organised lecture tours, and instigated Wilde's triumphant tour of America in 1882.

=+

Sydney Starr
1857–1925

A brilliant pastelist, Starr was born in Hull, and studied at the Slade under Poynter (p.113) and Legros (p.110). In 1882, with seven other committed followers of Whistler (pp.132–3), he decided to rent a joint studio at Baker Street. A studio stamp was devised showing a steam engine advancing with a red light: 'a danger signal to the Philistines to warn them that reformers were on their track'. In December 1889, Sickert (p.124), and a group of friends sympathetic to Impressionism, including Wilson Steer, Sidney Starr and Théodore Roussel nailed their colours to the mast and opened an independent exhibition at the Goupil Gallery called 'The London Impressionists'. (LL)

174 With James McNeill Whistler
    Portrait of James McNeill Whistler, 1890
    Pen and ink on paper, 22.2 x 19.1 cm
    Signed b.l. with Whistler's 'butterfly'
    Dated t.r.
    Mark Samuels Lasner, Washington, D. C.

The drawing was started by Starr but it was worked on and signed by Whistler. The portrait was intended for publication in *The Whirlpool*.

=+

John Melhuish Strudwick
1849–1935

Strudwick studied at the Royal Academy and worked as a studio assistant to Spencer Stanhope, uncle to Evelyn De Morgan (p.100), and Burne-Jones (p.96). The influence of both painters can be seen in Strudwick's work, in which he favoured rich deep colours, complex drapery and figures that resembled those by Burne-Jones.

Cat. 175 takes its subject from a poem by Keats, entitled 'Isabella; or a Pot of Basil', (from Boccacio), which is a tragic love story between Isabella and

Lorenzo. In Oscar Wilde's review of the work in the 1879 Grosvenor Gallery exhibition, he draws on this connection, feeling that in some measure Strudwick has managed to realise the pathos of Keats's poem.

In 1877, whilst in Rome, Wilde paid humble respects to Keats's grave (Cat.156). And in his poem 'The Grave of Keats', Wilde blended Reni's image of *San Sebastian* (Cat. 117) with that of Keats.

'The youngest of the martyrs here is lain
Fair as Sebastian, and as early slain'.
(LV)

175 *Isabella and the Pot of Basil*, 1879
Tempera on canvas, 99 x 58 cm
The De Morgan Foundation, London

=+=+=+=+=+=+=+=+=+=+=+=+=+=+=+=+=+

George Tinworth
1843–1913

An English potter employed from 1866 to 1913 at Doulton's Lambeth Factory, Tinworth made terracotta panels of religious subjects, including *Gethsemane*, *The Foot of the Cross* and *The Descent from the Cross* (1874), as well as a reredos for York Minster. As a member of the Plymouth Brethren, these religious groups have a moral directness that is quite different from other artists of the time. As well as his religious subjects, he also modelled small figures of mouse chessmen, frogs going to the Derby and mice musicians. When tackling the theme of Herod and Salome, like Armitage (cf. Cat.9), Tinworth avoided any reference to Salome's request for the head of John the Baptist, the aspect of the story that so appealed to European artists of the time. (LL)

176 *Herod's Birthday Feast*, 1880s
Terracotta relief, 13.2 x 30 cm
Signed
Inscribed: 'Herod's Birthday Feast' with Biblical text
Private Collection

cat.174

cat.176

cat.175

128

Henri de Toulouse-Lautrec
1864–1901

Born into an eminent aristocratic family in Albi, Toulouse-Lautrec was a fragile child. While suffering from pains in his legs from an early age, a falling accident at the age of thirteen damaged his legs permanently and arrested his full physical growth. In 1872, he moved to Paris, accompanied by his mother, to start studying at the Lycée Fontanes (later Condorcet).

Following informal lessons from the horse painter René Princeteau, Lautrec joined Léon Bonnat's atelier briefly in 1882, and then that of Fernand Cormon, where he met Emile Bernard, Van Gogh and Louis Anquetin (p.89). In 1884, he moved into a studio on Montmartre and from 1885 began to frequent Aristide Bruant's café-cabaret Le Mirliton (Cat.177), where his works were exhibited on a permanent basis. From this period onwards, the subjects of his paintings and lithographs were drawn from local café scenes, dancers and prostitutes. From 1888, Lautrec began exhibiting with Les XX and by the beginning of the 1890s had become a leading figure among the young and independent Parisian artists.

Lautrec was a great friend of William Rothenstein (pp.119–20) and Charles Conder (p.98). They first met, probably in 1890, at Le Rat Mort, a Monmartre restaurant, which was also a lesbian centre by night. To Rothenstein's eye, Lautrec was 'a frank … brutal cynic … endowed with a keen intellect' (Rothenstein I, p.64). In the company of his young English friends, Lautrec explored the Montmartre nights. During this period, while Lautrec influenced Conder's paintings, such as *The Moulin Rouge*, 1890 (Manchester City Art Galleries), Conder appeared in many of Lautrec's works.

There is no record of Wilde's first meeting with Lautrec but it was probably during 1891. At the time, Wilde was exploring the Paris art world in the company of his friends, who included Conder and Rothenstein. At Le Mirliton, Lautrec's familiar spot, Wilde was presented a book by Aristide Bruant, with the inscription: 'Pour Oscar Wilde le joyeux fantaisiste anglais.' (Ellmann: p.330) Lautrec produced many portraits of Wilde: one painted in London in 1895 during the Wilde trials (see Cat.179) and drawings for Félix Fénéon's *La Revue blanche*, of which Lautrec was a close associate (Cat.178). Furthermore, Wilde's link with the Parisian avant-garde culture was epitomised in Lautrec's large panel, one of a pair produced for La Goulue's booth in 1895 (Fig.20). In effect, it was a group portrait of his friends: in the centre La Goulue dancing to exotic musicians, surrounded by a crowd, including distinctive figures of Wilde, the dancer Jane Avril and Fénéon in the foreground. (TS)

177 *Aristide Bruant at Le Mirliton*, 1893
　　Lithograph, 79 x 59.8 cm
　　Signed (with monogram) b.r.
　　Suntory Museum, Osaka

178 *Poster for 'La Revue blanche'*, 1895
　　Lithograph, 128.1 x 93.3 cm
　　Signed (with monogram) and dated b.l.
　　Suntory Museum, Osaka

179 *Oscar Wilde and Romain Coolus*, 1896
　　Programme for the double bill, Wilde's *Salomé* and Coolus's *Raphaël* at the Théâtre de l'Oeuvre, Paris, 1896
　　Lithograph, 30.3 x 49 cm
　　Julia Rosenthal, Oxford

=+=+=+=+=+=+=+=+=+=+=+=+=+=+=+=+=+=+

Louis Abel Truchet
1857–1918

Truchet studied at the Académie Julian and from 1891 exhibited at the Autumn Salon and the Society of Humourists, of which he was the Founder and Treasurer. He was a genre painter who specialised in views of Paris, notably Montmartre, but Truchet also painted landscapes throughout France using Impressionist techniques. His works include views of circuses, *Parisians at the Folies Bergère*, *The Arrival of Edward the Seventh in Paris*, and *Quadrilles at the Moulin Rouge*. (LL)

180 *The Quadrille at the Bal Tabarin*, 1890s
　　Oil on canvas, 81 x 65 cm
　　Signed b.l.
　　Musée Carnavalet, Paris (Inv. P.1920)

cat.181

129

=+=+=+=+=+=+=+=+=+=+=+=+=+=+=+=+=+

Henry Scott Tuke
1858–1929

Tuke studied in London at the Slade and later – in Paris and Florence, specialising in capturing the effect of sunlight on naked flesh. He settled briefly in Newlyn before returning to his childhood home at Falmouth, where he painted marine and figurative subjects, often combined in sensuous paintings of nude boys in boats. In *The Studio* (Cat.14) in 1895 he wrote,

　'I always return to my first option, the truth and beauty of flesh in sunlight by the sea.'

　Tuke's paintings became known through reproduction in *The Studio*, which also published photographs of nude Sicilian and Italian boys by the German Baron von Gloeden (p.130), and Frederick Rolfe (1860–1913), the self-styled 'Baron Corvo' (p.117), who much admired Tuke's work. Rolfe wrote from Venice:

　'a painter like Tuke would have a free field here: for there is not a single painter of young Venetians poised on lofty poops, out on the wide lagoon, at white dawn, when the whole world gleams with the candid iridescence of mother-of-pearl, glowing white flesh with green blue eyes and shining hair … Tuke is the only man alive who can do such paintings; and he has not seen them …' (LL)

181 *Ruby, Gold and Malachite*, 1902
　　Oil on canvas, 116.8 x 157.5 cm
　　Guildhall Art Gallery
　　(The Corporation of London)

The exotic title refers to the colour of the sweater, the sunlit bodies and the green sea. It also unconsciously recalls the language of the Book of Revelations (Ch 21 V.19- 22) and Wilde's list of gemstones in *Salomé* (Cats 15, 95).

=+=+=+=+=+=+=+=+=+=+=+=+=+=+=+=+=+=+

Félix Vallotton
1865–1925

Born in Lausanne, Valotton moved to Paris in 1882, where he studied at the Ecole des Beaux-Arts and the Académie Julian. During this period, his painting style was sombre and realistic. By the early 1890s, he had begun radically simplified woodcuts and lithographs under the influences of Japanese prints, Van Gogh and Toulouse-Lautrec (pp.128–9). Accordingly, he also developed a new painting style with a strong outline and form and sombre flat colours.

In 1892, he participated in the first exhibition of the Salon de la Rose + Croix with fourteen woodcuts, which were highly praised by Félix Fénéon. Also, sharing an anarchist view with Fénéon, Valotton was invited to contribute to *La Revue blanche* magazine (cf. Cat.178), for which he provided a long series of portrait vignettes. Portraying the renowned author of *A Rebours* (1884) and *La-Bas* (1891), Cat. 182 shows his gift for catching the essentials of personality in a simplified scheme of black and white. A close associate of the Nabis, Valotton was also deeply influenced by their theories of design, and participated in their exhibitions at Le Barc de Boutteville, at Siegfried Bing's Maison Art Nouveau and in Brussels. (TS)

182 *Portrait of Joris Karl Huysmans*, 1896
Pen and ink on paper, 12.8 x 10.3 cm
Musée Cantonal des Beaux-Arts, Lausanne

=+=+=+=+=+=+=+=+=+=+=+=+=+=+=+=+=+=+=+

Baron Wilhelm von Gloeden
1856–1931

Von Gloeden's studies of Sicilian Boys (e.g. Cats 183, 184) have enjoyed a perennial popularity among aesthetes, falling within a traditional view of the ancient world that stretches back, via Pater, at least as far as Winckelmann in the eighteenth century. His photographs of Sicilian youths posed 'noble and nude and antique' in the guise of Theocritan goatherds appealed to Wilde, who sent the photographer a copy of *The Ballad of Reading Gaol*. (LL)

183 *Two Boys with Urns*, 1904
Silver albumen print, 26 x 37 cm
The Royal Photographic Society, Bath
(RPS 8234)

184 *Boy adorned with Lilies*, 1904
Modern copy print, 16 x 22 cm
The Royal Photographic Society, Bath
(RPS 8235)

cat.185 (detail)

=+=+=+=+=+=+=+=+=+=+=+=+=+=+=+=+=+=+=+

Theodor von Holst
1810–44

Holst was considered by Rossetti to be a significant link between the Romantic Movement and the Pre-Raphaelites. He was a pupil of Fuselli and was the first artist to illustrate Mary Shelley's *Frankenstein*. In the 1830s, he became a friend of Thomas Griffiths Wainewright (1794–1847). (LL)

185 *Sketch Portrait of Thomas Griffiths Wainewright*,
c.1825–30
Pen and ink on paper, 15.2 x 20.3 cm
Paul Grinke, London

Wilde was fascinated by the life of Thomas Griffiths Wainewright, whom he discussed in the brilliant essay 'Pen, Pencil and Poison: A Study in Green' (first published 1889). Wainewright's life fell into two halves, public and private. As a young artist, he was taught by Thomas Phillips and John Linnel, and was friendly with William Blake, Henry Fuseli, John Keats (Cat.156), William Hazlitt, John Clare and Thomas de Quincey. Privately his criminal activities included the almost certain poisoning of three close relatives in an insurance scam. When finally brought to justice, he was convicted not of murder but forgery, and transported for life to Van Diemens Land (Tasmania). (LL)

=+=+=+=+=+=+=+=+=+=+=+=+=+=+=+=+=+=+=+

George Frederic Watts
1817–1904

In 1843, Watts won a prize in the competition to design murals in the new Houses of Parliament. He used the money to visit Italy, where he studied the works of the old masters. This pursuit conditioned Watts to think in terms of allegory and exalted idealism. He returned to England in 1847 and was soon recognised as a major painter in aesthetic circles, before achieving popular fame in 1880. Thereafter, he became a revered figure in the English art establishment. His style was influenced by Etty, the Elgin marbles, Titian and Michelangelo. (LL)

186 *Portrait of William Morris*, 1870
Oil on canvas, 64.8 x 52.1 cm
Board of Trustees of the National Portrait Gallery,
London (Reg.no. 1078)

187 *The Daughter of Herodias (Salome)*, c.1870–80
Oil on canvas, 109.2 x 83.8 cm
Private Collection

According to the notes by Mrs Watts (Watts Gallery archives), Salome's action of holding up the ring of Herod indicates that responsibility for the death of St John the Baptist is not hers but the King's.

188 *Love and Death*, 1875
Oil on canvas, 151 x 75 cm
Signed b.r.
Bristol Museums and Art Gallery

Watts' thoughts were almost invariably expressed in such allegorical terms as *Love and Death*. Oscar Wilde reviewed the first version of this work (Whitworth Art Gallery, Manchester) in the exhibition at the Grosvenor Gallery in 1877. In his notice, he described the work as:
'a large painting, representing a marble doorway, all overgrown with white-starred jasmine and sweet briar rose. Death a giant form, veiled in grey draperies, is passing in with inevitable and mysterious power, breaking through all the flowers. One foot is already on the threshold, and one relentless hand is extended, while Love, a beautiful boy with lithe brown limbs and rainbow coloured wings, all shrinking like a crumpled leaf, is trying,

with vain hands, to bar the entrance. A little dove, undisturbed by the agony of the terrible conflict, waits patiently at the foot of the steps for her playmate; but will wait in vain, for though the face of death is hidden from us, yet we can see from the terror in the boy's eyes and quivering lips, that Medusa-like, this grey phantom turns all it looks upon to stone; and the wings of love are rent and crushed.'

He compares Watts' work with Michelangelo's Sistine Chapel. Continuing in the same vein two years later, Wilde considered Watts the 'most powerful of all our living English artists'.

189 *The Genius of Greek Poetry* c.1878
Oil on canvas, 66 x 53.3 cm
Trustees of the Watts Gallery, Compton, Guildford

The inspiration for this painting dates from Watts' travels around the Greek islands in 1856. For Wilde, as for Watts, early visits to Greece and a love of Greek poetry were to be of great inspirational importance. When rusticated for truancy for being late back from a trip to Greece, Wilde claimed later that he was sent down 'for being the first undergraduate to visit Olympia'. In the 'Critic as Artist' (1890), Wilde wrote of his strong conviction that Aristotle, unlike Plato, offered a theory of art 'from the purely aesthetic point of view' and a sense of beauty realised through the passions of pity and awe'. Wilde was to give his own highly personal spin to the whole concept of Hellenism, writing, in a characteristic aphorism: 'To be Greek one should have no clothes: to be mediaeval one should have no body: to be modern one should have no soul.'

cat.190

cat.187

190 *The Genius of Greek Poetry*, c.1878/1947
Bronze, 21.3 x 23 x 15.2 cm
Trustees of the Watts Gallery, Compton, Guildford

During the evolution of the composition of the painting (Cat.189), Watts made wax models after the pose of Phidias's Theseus from the Parthenon pediment, which was the artist's major source of inspiration for the central reclining figure in the composition. Cat.190 is a bronze cast made in 1947 from Watt's original model.

191 *The Dean's Daughter – A Portrait of Mrs Langtry*, 1879–80
Oil on canvas, 74.9 x 52.1 cm
Trustees of the Watts Gallery, Compton, Guildford

Lillie Langtry sat for Watts on many occasions, and left amusing accounts of her visits to his studio. On one visit, he decided to depict her in 'a quaint little poke bonnet from which he ruthlessly tore the opulent ostrich feather which I regarded at the time as the glory of my head gear'.

cat.192

=+=+=+=+=+=+=+=+=+=+=+=+=+=+=+=+=+=+=+

James Abbott McNeill Whistler
1834–1903

Born in Lowell, Massachusetts, Whistler's early years were passed in St Petersburg, where his father was a railway engineer. In 1851, he attended the Military Academy at West Point, but decided that he wanted to pursue an artistic career. In 1856, he went to Paris and entered the studio of Gleyre, where Degas and Fantin-Latour were fellow students. He was greatly influenced by Japanese prints, which were then newly discovered in Europe.

In 1859, he settled in London, where his flamboyant personality and mordant wit made him a conspicuous figure, although his work was little understood. In 1877, his attempt to sue Ruskin (p.121) for libel resulted in an award of just a farthing's damages, while the cost of the case led to Whistler's bankruptcy. In the 1890s he lived chiefly in Paris, but returned to Chelsea to die by the river Thames, which he had so memorably painted in his Nocturnes.

192 **Old Putney Bridge**, 1878
   Etching, 20.1 x 29.8 cm
   Signed with the 'butterfly' b.c.
   Mark Samuels Lasner, Washington, D. C.

193 **Mr Whistler's 'Ten O'Clock'**
   Published in London, Chatto and Windus, 1888
   Book, brown paper wrappers, preserved in green cloth binding lettered with title.
   The first published edition, preceded by a very small privately printed issue
   19.1 x 14.3 cm
   Stephen Calloway, Brighton

In his review of the lecture, Wilde was full of praise for Whistler's eloquence, but demurred at the personal attack on his own views: 'An Artist is not an isolated fact ... [he] can no more be born of a nation that is devoid of any sense of beauty than a fig can grow from a thorn ... The poet is the supreme artist, for he is the master of colour and form, and the real musician besides, and is Lord over all life and all arts.'

194 *The Gentle Art of Making Enemies*
Published in London, William Heineman, 1890
(the first edition)
Book, yellow cloth spine and brown paper-covered
boards, 21 x 15.9 cm
Stephen Calloway, Brighton

The book contains reprints of written exchanges
and old quarrels with art critics and former friends.
Its format may have influenced a book by another
controversial figure, Jacob Epstein (pp.103–5),
in the creation of his *Let there be Sculpture*, 1913.

195 *Nocturnes, Marines and Chevalet Pieces*
Published in London, by the artist, 1891
Book, brown paper wrappers, 19.7 x 14.9 cm
Stephen Calloway, Brighton

196 *Portrait of Stéphane Mallarmé*, 1892
Lithograph, 20 x 14.8 cm
Signed with the 'butterfly' monogram b.r.
Inscribed: 'Au Maitre Rodin son admirateur SM'
Musée Rodin, Paris (Inv. Gr.9355)

Mallarmé (1842–98), who translated Whistler's
'Ten O'Clock Lecture' into French in 1888, paid
tribute to Whistler's 'unique and solitary genius' and
was active in persuading the French government to
acquire the portrait of Whistler's mother. Mallarmé
was also on friendly terms with Wilde and was
impressed by *The Picture of Dorian Gray*. By 1891,
Whistler's dislike of Wilde, whom he constantly
accused of plagiarism, was manic. This caused
difficulties at Mallarmé's famous Tuesday evening
soirées, although the two protagonists narrowly
escaped meeting each other.

=+=+=+=+=+=+=+=+=+=+=+=+=+=+=+=+=+

Lady Jane Francesca Wilde [or 'Speranza']
1821–96
Wilde's tall and strikingly attractive mother was a
talented linguist, poet, and Irish patriot, who had
written six books and translated others. Her best-
known work is a translation of Meinhold's *Sidonia the
Sorceress*. Lady Wilde's nom de plume, Speranza (the
Italian for 'Hope') came from her advocacy of the
cause of Irish freedom.

In 1879, following the death of her husband,
Lady Wilde left Dublin for London, where she
was a central figure of the circle of Irish writers,
including George Bernard Shaw (Cat.148) and
William Butler Yeats (Cat.93). She contributed
her poems and articles to periodicals, including
The Woman's World, of which Oscar Wilde was the
editor in 1887–9. Under his editorship, he raised
its status (formerly called *The Lady's World*) from
a fashion magazine for society ladies to a culture
magazine for new, independent women.

During the Wilde trials in 1895, while many of
Wilde's friends persuaded him to leave the country,
it was Lady Wilde who insisted that he should stay
and stand trial: 'If you stay, even if you go to
prison, you will always be my son. It will make no
difference to my affection. But if you go, I will
never speak to you again.' After Wilde's conviction,
however, her health declined rapidly in her despair
and sorrow for 'dear Oscar'. She died in February
1896. Learning that she would not be able to see
him again on her deathbed, she said, 'may the
prison help him'. (Ellmann: p.467) (TS/LL)

197 Wilhelm Johann Meinhold
Translated by Lady Wilde
Sidonia the Sorceress
Published in London, Kelmscott Press, 1893
Book, 30.5 x 22.2 cm
Wiliam Morris Gallery
(London Borough of Waltham Forest)

As discussed in the entry for Cat. 42, *Sidonia the
Sorceress*, a historical romance by Wilhelm Johann
Meinhold (1797–1851), was first published in
Germany in 1847 and two years later appeared
in an English translation by Lady Wilde, Oscar
Wilde's mother. Extremely popular in Pre-
Raphaelite circles, Burne-Jones (p.96) painted
two scenes from it in 1860. When William Morris
(p.111) republished it in 1893 in Kelmscott Press
edition, he wrote to Oscar Wilde for his mother's
address, in order to ask for her permission to
republish her translation. At the time, Aubrey
Beardsley (pp.90–91) was suggested as a possible
illustrator, but his rough drawings were rejected
by Morris, although he praised Beardsley's 'feeling
for draperies'.

SELECTION OF EPHEMERA associated with
Oscar Wilde

198 *'Oscar The Apostle. Puck's "Wilde" Dream of an
Aesthetic Future for America'*, c.1882
A page from *Puck* magazine, 11 January 1882
25 x 33.5 cm
Paul Jeromack and Robert Tuggle, New York

199 *Seven 'Aesthetic' Caricature Cards*:
'National Aesthetics', early 1880s
Colour lithographs
Paul Jeromack and Robert Tuggle, New York

   a. 'Isè gwine to worship dat lily/Kase it sembles
      me'
   b. 'No Likee to callee me Charlie/Callee me Oscar'
   c. 'I vas Aesthetic/aint it'
   d. 'Mon Dieu!/I feel utterly too too'
   e. 'For Sale'
   f. 'Begorra/and I belave/I am/Oscar/Himself'
   g. 'Take me back to home and Mother'

200 *Twelve 'Aesthetic' Advertisements*, early 1880s
Colour lithographs
Paul Jeromack and Robert Tuggle, New York

   a. Marie Fontaine's Moth & Freckle cure
   b. J. & H. Phillips, Oil Cloths and Rubber Goods
   c. Hegan Bros. Wall Papers: 'People are going
      "Wilde"…'
   d. Hegan Bros. Wall Papers: 'A Japanese young
      man …'
   e. Warner Bros. Caroline Corsets: 'The Latest
      Aesthetic Craze'
   f. Straiton and Storms New Cigars
   g. Compliments of Erlick Bros.
   h. Clark's Spool Cotton – Jumbo Aesthetic
   i. Clarence Brooks & Co. Fine Coach Varnishes
   j. Strike me with a Sun Flower
   k. Use Garland Stoves & Ranges
   l. Use Garland Stoves & Ranges (variation)

CHRONology

OSCAR WILDE + HIS TIMES

COMPILED BY LOUISE VAUGHAN

DATE	OSCAR WILDE'S LIFE	Artistic + Cultural Events	Political and Social Events
1854	16 Oct., born Dublin, second legitimate son of William Robert Wilde, physician and surgeon and Jane Elgee, Irish nationalist poet, known as Speranza. Christened, in Protestant ritual, Oscar Fingal O'Flahertie Wills Wilde	Working Men's College in London founded by Rev F.D. Maurice; Rossetti, Ruskin, Brown and Morris all later taught there. Exposition Universelle, Paris.	Declaration of war by England and France on Russia, beginning of Crimean War (1854–1856).
1855	The Wilde family moves to fashionable Merrion Square, Dublin, where Lady Wilde starts a salon.	Bracquemond discovers Hukuski's *Manga*.	Lord Palmerston (PM). Australian colonies become self-governing.
1857	Birth of sister, Isola.	South Kensington (now Victoria and Albert) Museum opened on present site. National Portrait Gallery opens. PRB exhibition organised by Brown in Bloomsbury. Rossetti, Burne-Jones, Hughes, Prinsep and Morris decorate debating chamber of the Oxford Union with frescoes.	Uprising against British Rule in India. Albert created Prince Consort. Divorce Courts established by Matrimonial Cause Act. Women given right to their property after a legal separation.
1858		National Gallery of Scotland opens.	Earl of Derby (PM). *Englishwoman's Journal* launched to debate issues of women's work, legal rights, suffrage and education.
1859		Charles Darwin, *On the Origin of Species by Natural Selection*.	The Second Empire (Napoleon III) 1859–1870.
1861		Morris, Marshall, Faulkner & Company founded. George Eliot, *Silas Marner*. Première of Wagner's *Tannhaüser* in Paris.	Death of Prince Albert in December. Queen Victoria's withdrawal from public duties.
1862		George Gilbert Scott designs Albert Memorial. Sarah Bernhardt makes her début at the Comédie Français. Hugo, *Les Misérables*.	Homosexual act of sodomy no longer a capital offence. Start of American Civil War. Russia abolishes serfdom.
1863		Ruskin writes *Sesame and Lilies*, on social issues (published in 1865). Baudelaire's *Le Peintre de la vie moderne*. Salon des Refusés founded by Napoleon III. Whistler settles in London. Death of Delacroix.	Opening of first underground railway in London.
1864	Father knighted. Oscar and his older brother Willie sent to Portora Royal School, Enniskillen.	Julia Margaret Cameron, *Portrait of Ellen Terry*.	Pasteur develops germ theory of disease.
1865		Tolstoy, *War and Peace*. Carroll, *Alice in Wonderland*. Wagner, *Tristan and Isolde*.	Poor Law Bill introduced to improve workhouse conditions. 13th Amendment abolishes slavery in America.
1866		Zola writes *Mon Salon* dedicated to Cézanne. Swinburne, *Poems and Ballads*.	Barbara Bodichon forms first Women's Suffrage Committee. Nobel invents dynamite.
1867	Isola, Wilde's much loved sister dies.	Paris Universal Exhibition.	Fenian disturbances including bomb attacks.

134

OSCAR WILDE'S LIFE	Artistic + Cultural Events	Political and Social Events
	Zola's second edition of *Thérèse Raquin* published, with his manifesto for Naturalism. Death of Baudelaire and Ingres.	on Clerkenwell prison make Gladstone aware of the urgency of the Irish issue of Home Rule.
1868		
	RA moves to Burlington House, Piccadilly.	Disraeli (PM). Meeting in Manchester of first Trade Union Congress. Resignation of Disraeli; William Gladstone (PM and Chancellor of the Exchequer).
1869		
		Opening of Suez Canal. Vote in local elections given to women ratepayers. 1869–70 France declares war on Prussia. Capture of Napoleon at Sedan; defeat of France; Alsace and Lorraine ceded; Proclamation of the Third Republic.
1870		
Wins Carpenter Prize for Greek Testament studies.	Monet, Pissarro, Tissot and Alma-Tadema arrive in London, fugitives from events in France.	Bankruptcy Act comes into force. Education Act provides elementary education for girls as well as boys.
1871		
10 Nov., Enters Trinity College, Dublin.	Sisley arrives in London. Eliot, *Middlemarch*.	The Paris Commune. Proclamation of German Reich.
1872		
	Carroll, *Through the Looking Glass*. Schliemann's excavations of Troy.	London School of Medicine for Women opened.
1873		
Awarded a Trinity College, Dublin Foundation Scholarship.	Walter Pater, *Studies in the History of the Renaissance* (Cat. 115). Solomon imprisoned for a homosexual scandal. New Salon des Refusés, Paris. Tolstoy, *Anna Karenina*.	Home Rule League founded in Dublin. Custody of Infants Act extends access to children to all women in the event of separation or divorce. Death of Napoleon III. German troops leave France. 1873–79 MacMahon President; fails in his aim to restore the French monarchy.
1874		
Wins Berkeley Gold Medal for Greek; takes scholarship examination for Magdalen College, Oxford and wins Demyship. Oct., goes up to Oxford; attends Ruskin's lectures and joined in his road-building activities at Hinksey (Cat.152).	First Exhibition of Société Anonyme des Artistes, *Peintres, Sculpteurs, et Graveurs* (later called Impressionists), at Nadar's, Paris.	Disraeli (PM). Factory Act introduces maximum 56-hour working week.
1875		
Joins a Masonic Lodge; comes close to conversion to Roman Catholicism. Travels to Italy during his vacation.	Watts, *Love and Death* (Cat. 188). Degas, Monet, Pissarro, Renoir and Sisley exhibit in London.	Republican Constitution agreed, France.
1876		
Death of Sir William Wilde. Gains First Class in Honours in Moderations (second year examinations).	Moreau's Salome *The Apparition* (Cat.106) exhibited in Salon. Whistler begins painting the *Peacock Room* in London.	Bell invents telephone.
1877		
Prolonged vacation in Greece with Professor Mahaffy of T.C.D., returning via Rome. Visits the Palazzo Rossi, Genoa to see Guido Reni's painting *St. Sebastian*. (Cat. 117). Rusticated for six months because of late arrival back in Oxford. Spends 10 days in London, reviews the Grosvenor Gallery then returns to Dublin. July, first article published, 'The Grosvenor Gallery', in *Dublin University Magazine*. Meeting with Walter Pater, on return to Oxford. Works on long poem, *The Sphinx*, begun in 1874.	Grosvenor Gallery founded in London; the opening exhibition includes Whistler's *Nocturne – The Falling Rocket*, which leads to the Whistler-Ruskin trial (1878). Monet's, *Gare St-Lazare*. Rodin, *Age of Bronze*, first showing at the Paris Salon. Edison invents phonograph.	Republican victory in French legislative elections.

OSCAR WILDE'S LIFE	Artistic + Cultural Events	Political and Social Events
1878		
His poem *Ravenna* won the Newdigate Prize. Gains a First in Greats (Final examination).	Paris Universal Exhibition. Muybridge publishes multi-exposure photographs for the first time.	Women admitted to University of London Congress of Berlin.
1879		
Failing to get a Classical Fellowship at Oxford, Wilde concentrates on London's intellectual and political society, developing a friendship with Lillie Langtry (Cats 116, 191) and getting to know Ellen Terry (Cat. 153), Sarah Bernhardt (Cats 17, 36, 37a–c, 38, 47, 110), and other leading actresses. Shares bachelor quarters with Frank Miles in Salisbury Street, Strand. Lady Wilde moves to London.	Redon's first album of lithographs *The Dream* published. Edison invents electric light bulb.	Call for fair rents, fixity of tenure and free sale in Ireland. Opening of Lady Margaret Hall and Somerville College, Oxford. 1879–1885. Jules Ferry leads the attack on Catholic Church's control of education, France.
1880		
With Miles moves to the more fashionable address of Tite Street, Chelsea, which had been redesigned by E.W. Godwin (Cat. 86). Sept., sends Ellen Terry a copy of his first play *Vera*.	Zola's *Le Naturalisme*. Rodin begins *The Gates of Hell*.	Parnell becomes the new leader of the Home Rulers, Ireland. Assembly moves from Versailles to Paris.
1881		
Satirized as Reginald Bunthorne in Gilbert and Sullivan's comic opera (Cats 8, 172, 173). First volume of *Poems* published in England and America. Rehearsals of *Vera* cancelled because of politically sensitive situation.	Frith, *The Private View of the Royal Academy, 1881* (Cat.84).	Gladstone introduces a new Land Act conceding many of the basic demands of the Land League. Death of Disraeli.
1882		
Jan – Dec., lecture tour of Great Britain and Canada. (Lectures on 'The England Renaissance', 'The House Beautiful' and 'The Decorative Arts'.)	Toulouse-Lautrec meets Bernard, Van Gogh and Anquetin. Courbet retrospective, Ecole des Beaux-Arts. Manet, *A Bar at the Folies-Bergères*.	National League founded by Parnell, closely linked to Irish parliamentary party. Married Women's Property Act allows women to own and administer their property. Italy joins Austro-German Alliance.
1883		
Feb. – May, went to Paris, where he met painters, writers and actors in a crowded social life and writes *The Duchess of Padua*. Aug., production of *Vera* in USA. Sept., begins lecture tour of USA. Nov., engaged to Constance Lloyd while lecturing in Dublin.	Khnopff (Cat. 94) becomes a founding member of Société des Vingt (Les XX). Huysman's *L'Art moderne*. Publication of *A Problem in Greek Ethics* by John Addington Symonds which increases awareness of homosexuality in classical world. Death of Manet.	Orient Express train introduced.
1884		
29 May, marriage to Constance Lloyd. Honeymoon in Paris. Wilde reads Huysman's *A Rebours* on its first appearance.	First exhibition of Les XX, Brussels. Retrospective Manet exhibition at the Ecole des Beaux-Arts, Paris. Huysman's *A Rebours*. Art Workers Guild founded, Britain. Rodin, *Burghers of Calais*.	Married Women's Property Act makes a woman no longer a 'chattel' but an independent and separate person. The French upper House of the Assembly make the object of popular election a democratic step within French politics.
1885		
The couple settles in a house in Tite Street, decorated by E.W. Godwin. 20 Feb., Whistler's *Ten O'Clock Lecture*, (Cat. 193) attacking Wilde, who replies in two articles in *The Pall Mall Gazette*. 5 June, birth of Cyril Wilde.	Symbolist periodical *Revue Wagnérienne* appears in Paris. Nietzsche completes *Also sprach Zarathustra*. American painter Sargent settles in London. Gilbert & Sullivan's successful operetta, *The Mikado*.	Labouchère amendment to Criminal Law Amendment Act makes homosexual acts between consenting male adults illegal. First internal combustion engine.
1886		
Meets Robert Ross, then 17, in Oxford. According to Ross, this was Wilde's first homosexual affair. 3 Nov., birth of Vyvyan Wilde.	Eighth and last Impressionist Exhibition. Retrospective of Whistler exhibition at the Petit Palais, Paris. Van Gogh arrives in Paris. Gauguin paints at Pont-Aven. Jean Moréas manifesto for Symbolism appears in *Le Figaro*.	1886–89. The Boulanger Affair.

	OSCAR WILDE'S LIFE	Artistic + Cultural Events	Political and Social Events
		Rimbaud's poems *Illuminations*. The New English Art Club founded in London.	
1887			
	Nov., assumes editorship of *The Lady's World*, changing the journal's title to *The Woman's World* and raising its quality. Writes many reviews.	Gauguin visits Martinique. Van Gogh organises an exhibition of Japanese prints at the café Le Tambourin. Goodwin invents celluloid film.	Queen Victoria's Golden Jubilee.
1888			
	Attends meetings of socialist Fabian Society. May, publishes *The Happy Prince and Other Tales* (Cat.57).	Mallarmé translates poems of Poe. First Arts and Crafts exhibition, London. The Nabis formed in Paris. Gauguin visits van Gogh in Arles. Sargent visits Monet in Giverny.	Match girls' strike. Wilhelm II becomes Emperor of Germany.
1889			
	Meets W.B. Yeats. (Cats 29, 93) Jan., 'Pen, Pencil and Poison' appears in *Fortnightly Review* and 'The Decay of Lying' in *The Nineteenth Century*. Gives up editorship of *The Woman's World*.	Paris International Exhibition. John Singer Sargent, *Ellen Terry as Lady Macbeth* (Cat. 153). Symbolist periodicals *La Revue blanche* and *La Plume* founded. Moulin Rouge opens at Montmartre, Paris. Impressionists Exhibition at the Goupil Gallery; the catalogue preface written by Sickert. Ricketts's and Shannon's Symbolist magazine *The Dial* founded in London (Cat. 118).	Cleveland Street scandal exposes male brothel. Gustave Eiffel designs the Eiffel Tower. Eastman's Kodak camera comes into production using photographic film.
1890			
	July and Sept., 'The Critic as Artist' published in *The Nineteenth Century*. June, *The Picture of Dorian Gray* published in *Lippincott's Magazine*	Whistler's *The Gentle Art of Making Enemies* published (Cat.194). Exhibition of over 900 Ukiyo-e prints, Ecole des Beaux-Arts. Death of Van Gogh.	1890s. French Trade Unions became legal. Growing power of socialists and Trade Unions in France. Kaiser Wilhelm II dismisses Bismarck.
1891			
	The Duchess of Padua presented in USA, under the title *Guido Ferranti*, without an author's name. Visits Paris, meets Mallarmé (Cat. 196), as well as Rothenstein and Conder. Publishes two volumes of stories, a book of critical essays *Intentions*, *The Picture of Dorian Gray* (in expanded book form), (Cat. 119) and 'The Soul of Man under Socialism' in the *Fortnightly Review*. Writes *Lady Windermere's Fan* and much of *Salomé* (in French) (Cat.95). Late June, introduced to Lord Alfred Douglas by Lionel Johnson. July, first meeting with Aubrey Beardsley Oct.–Dec., visits Paris.	Moreau appointed Professor at the Ecole des Beaux-Arts, Paris. First exhibiton of the Nabis. Gauguin sails for Tahiti. Toulouse-Lautrec designs his first posters. France buys Whistler's *Study in Grey and Black*. Death of Seurat.	Triple Alliance (Italy, Germany, Austria) renewed. Construction of Trans-Siberian Railway.
1892			
	Production of *Lady Windermere's Fan*. *Salomé* banned from public performance in England.	Rothenstein and Conder show their work at Père Thomas's gallery, arranged by Lautrec. Salon de la Rose + Croix opens, Paris.	Cholera epidemic in France.
1893			
	Production of *A Woman of No Importance*.	The *Studio* magazine published in London. Vollard opens gallery, Paris.	Franco-Russian Alliance.
1894			
	An Ideal Husband finishes. *A Florentine Tragedy* and most of *La Sainte Courtisane* written. *The Sphinx* published, illustrated by Ricketts (Cat.125). Aug.–Oct., writing *The Importance of Being Earnest* while at Worthing with Constance and their sons. Some of Wilde's letters to Lord Alfred Douglas come into the hands of Douglas's father, the Marquess of Queensberry. Sept., publication of Robert Hichens's	Rothenstein becomes member of the New English Art Club and returned to London. Sickert, *Portrait of Aubrey Beardsley* (Cat.162). Mucha establishes fame with the poster *Gismonda* for Sarah Bernhardt.(Cat.110). Puvis de Chavannes visits America. Debussy's *L'Après-midi d'un faune*, inspired by Mallarmé's poem, first performed in Paris. Beardsley's art magazine *The Yellow Book* founded in London (Cats 16a & 16b). Lumière Brothers make first films. Edison invents motion pictures.	Women eligible to vote for parochial councils. Dreyfus Affair.

OSCAR WILDE'S LIFE	Artistic + Cultural Events	Political and Social Events

1895

scandalous novel, *The Green Carnation*, based on the Wilde circle (Cat. 89).

3 Jan., production of *An Ideal Husband* opens. 14 Feb., Queensberry's plans demonstration against Wilde, at the first performance of *The Importance of Being Earnest*, foiled by the actor-manager, George Alexander. 28 Feb., insulting note from Queensberry found by Wilde at the Albemarle Club. 1 Mar., urged on by 'Bosie' (Lord Alfred Douglas), Wilde brings a libel charge against Queenberry. 3 Apr., libel case opens at the Old Bailey. 5 Apr., Queensberry acquitted; warrant issued for the arrest of Wilde. His name is subsequently removed from advertisement hoardings outside the theatres where his plays are being performed. 24 Apr., Bailiff's sale of Wilde's possessions at Tite Street. 26 Apr., the trial opens. 25 May, sentenced to two years' imprisonment with hard labour. Taken to Newgate, thence to Wandsworth, where he injures his ear in a fall. 8 Sept., Constance decides against a divorce. 21 Nov., transferred to Reading Gaol.	Lautrec produces several portraits of Wilde, including one in London during the trial and drawings for *La Revue blanche* (Cat.178). First major exhibition of Cézanne's works organized by Vollard in Paris. S. Bing's Galerie Art Nouveau, opens, Paris. Death of Morisot.	Resignation of Liberal government, general election returns Conservatives. Roentgen discovers X-ray. First public presentation of projected film.

1896

11 Feb., Lugné-Poë presents *Salomé* at Théâtre de l'Oeuvre in Paris. 19 Feb., Constance visits her husband, bringing news of Lady Wilde's death on 3 Feb. July, appointment of a new, more humane governor at Reading. Oscar is allowed writing materials. He begins to write *De Profundis* in the form of a long letter to Alfred Douglas.	Morris's Kelmscott Press publishes the *Works of Geoffrey Chaucer* with woodcuts by Burne-Jones. Charles Ricketts founds a private printing press – the Vale Press. Puccini, *La Bohème*. Aubrey Beardsley (as Art Editor) involved in another magazine *The Savoy* (Cat.17). Death of Morris.	Marconi demonstrates wireless telegraphy.

1897

19 May released from prison. 20 May, travels to Dieppe, where he hands Robert Ross the manuscript of *De Profundis* for copying and begins life as Sebastian Melmoth with £800 raised by Ross from subscriptions. May–Oct., writes and revises *The Ballad of Reading Gaol* (later expanded). Sept.–Dec., with Alfred Douglas in Naples.	Tate Gallery, London opens. Sezession group, Vienna founded. Charles Rennie MacIntosh begins Glasgow School of Art. Kollwitz begins Weavers' Revolt etchings. Chekhov, *Uncle Vanya*. Bram Stoker, *Dracula*. Wells, *Invisible Man*. Rostand, *Cyrano de Bergerac*.	Queen Victoria's Diamond Jubilee (Cat. 81). Foundation of National Union of Women's Suffrage Societies under the presidency of Mrs Millicent Fawcett.

1898

13 Feb., Leonard Smithers publishes *The Ballad of Reading Gaol*, which goes into many reprints. Apr., Constance dies, following an operation on her spine. (She and the boys had adopted the surname Holland).	Rodin, *Balzac*. Max Beerbohm succeeds Bernard Shaw as drama critic for the Saturday Review. Wells, *War of the Worlds*. Death of Beardsley, Moreau, Burne-Jones, Puvis de Chavannes and Mallarmé.	Irish Socialist Republic Party founded. Paris Métro opens.

1899

Wilde meets Augustus John whilst in Paris (Cat. 92). Publications of *The Importance of Being Earnest* and *An Ideal Husband*.	Rothenstein involved in the artistic management of the avant-garde Carfax Gallery, joined later by Robert Ross as Director. Vollard publishes Redon's lithographs *The Apocalypse of St John*.	Dreyfus given a pardon. Second Boer War. A.J. Evans begins excavations of Minoan culture, Crete.

1900

1 Jan., Queensberry dies, leaving £20,000 to Alfred Douglas, who refuses financial help to Wilde. Some months later, George	Exposition Universelle, Paris. Death of Ruskin.	1900–1914. Increased pace of social reforms in France.

OSCAR WILDE'S LIFE	Artistic + Cultural Events	Political and Social Events
Alexander offers to make voluntary payments on performances of Wilde's plays and to bequeathe the copyright to Wilde's sons. Visits Rodin's pavilion at the Exposition Universelle. 30 Nov., Oscar Wilde dies in Paris, having been baptised into the Catholic Church. Alfred Douglas pays for his funeral. Buried at Bagneux Cemetery, Paris		
1901	Death of Toulouse-Lautrec.	Death of Queen Victoria; accession of Edward VII. Marconi transmits first transatlantic telegraph message.
1902	Death of Émile Zola.	Sinn Fein ('ourselves alone') founded by Arthur Griffith.
1903	Salon d'Automne founded in Paris. Large memorial exhibition of work by Gauguin. Death of Pissarro, Gauguin and Whistler.	Women's Social and Political Union (WSPU) founded by Emmeline Pankhurst in Manchester. First powered flight by Wright brothers. Lenin establishes Bolshevik wing of Russian Social-Democratic Workers Party.
1904	Abbey Theatre opens in Dublin.	Negotiations between government and Irish Nationalists for a scheme for devolution. Entente Cordiale between Britain and France.
1905 **Ross publishes *De Profundis* in abridged form.**	First Fauve exhibition in Paris. Die Brücke group formed in Dresden. Strauss's opera *Salomé* written after Wilde's French play, first performed in Dresden. Einstein's Special Theory of Relativity.	Revolution in Russia. Dreyfus Affair – Conviction set aside. Dreyfus restored to full military honours.
1906 **Through Ross's efforts, the Wilde estate discharged from bankruptcy.**	Symbolist periodical *The Golden Fleece* appears in Moscow. Salon Russe first important presentation of Symbolist art of Moscow in the West.	
1907	Retrospective Cézanne exhibition *Salon d'Automne*, Paris. Puccini attempts to turn *A Florentine Tragedy* into an opera.	Sinn Fein League organised for 'the re-establishment of the independence of Ireland'. Triple Entente (Great Britain, France and Russia) formed to balance Triple Alliance.
1909 **Wilde's remains moved to Père Lachaise. *De Profundis* presented by Ross to the British Museum.**	Marinetti's Futurist Manifesto appears in *Le Figaro*. Diaghilev brings the Ballet Russe to Paris. Picasso, *Portrait of Ambroise Vollard*.	First hunger strike in protest at treatment of suffragettes in prison. Blériot flies the English Channel.
1910	Periodical *Der Sturm* appears in Berlin. Die Brücke moves to Berlin. *Manet and the Post-Impressionists exhibition* organised by Roger Fry at the Grafton Gallery, London. Technical Manifesto of the Futurist Painters published.	Death of King George V, succeeded by Edward VII.
1912 **A monument by Epstein erected at his grave (Cats 76, 77, 78 & 80)**	Italian Futurist Exhibition in Paris. First major Blaue Reiter exhibition and publication of the Blaue Reiter almanac. Mann, *Death in Venice*.	Nationwide hunger strike by suffragette prisoners. New paper the Suffragette, launched. Militancy at a new peak. Titanic sinks on maiden voyage.

BIBLIOGRAPHY

Books and Articles

Amor, Ann Clark
*Mrs Oscar Wilde: A Woman
of Some Importance*
(London, 1983)

Arwas, Victor
Alastair: Illustrator of Decadence
(London, 1979)

Aslin, Elizabeth
*The Aesthetic Movement: Prelude to
Art Nouveau* (London, 1969)

Baily, Leslie
The Gilbert and Sullivan Book
(London, 1952)

Bartlett, Neil
*Who was that Man? A Present for
Mr Oscar Wilde*
(London, 1988)

Beatty, Laura
*Lillie Langtry: Manners,
Masks and Morals*
(London, 1999)

Beckson, Karl
Aesthetes and Decadents of the 1890s
(New York, London, 1966)

Beckson, Karl
London in the 1890s: A Cultural History
(New York, 1990)

Beerbohm, Max
Rossetti and his Circle
(London, 1922)

Benkovitz, Miriam
J. Aubrey Beardsley
(London, 1981)

Borland, Maureen
*Wilde's Devoted Friend: A Life of
Robert Ross 1869-1918*
(Oxford Lennard, 1990)

Butler, Ruth
Rodin: The Shape of Genius
(New Haven and London, 1993)

Calloway, Stephen
*Charles Ricketts: Subtle and
Fantastick Decorator*
(London, 1979)

Carr, Mrs J. Comyns
Reminiscences
(London, n.d. c.1920)

Cohen, Ed.
Talk on the Wilde Side
(New York, 1992)

Cook, Clarence
The House Beautiful
(New York, 1878)

Darracott, Joseph
The World of Charles Ricketts
(London, 1980)

Delaney, Paul
'Charles Ricketts: The Decisive
Friendship of Oscar Wilde',
Antiquarian Book Monthly Review,
vol. v, no.7
(London, July 1978), pp.290–3

Douglas, Alfred
Oscar Wilde: A Summing Up
(London, 1940)

Du Maurier, Daphne
The Young George Du Maurier
(London, 1951)

Ellmann, Richard
Oscar Wilde: A Collection of Critical Essays
(New Jersey, 1969)

Ellmann, Richard
Oscar Wilde (London, 1987)

Eltis, Sos
*Revising Wilde: Society and Subversion in
the Plays of Oscar Wilde*
(Oxford, 1996)

Farr, Dennis
English Art 1870-1940
(paperback edition: Oxford, 1984)

Fletcher, Ian *Walter Pater*
(London, 1959)

Fletcher, Ian
Decadence and the 1890s
(Stratford-upon-Avon Studies 17:
London, 1979)

Fryer, Jonathan
*André and Oscar: Gide, Wilde and the Gay
Art of Living* (London, 1997)

Gardiner, Juliet
*Oscar Wilde: A Life in Letters,
Writings and Wit*
(London, 1995)

Gardiner, Stephen
Epstein: Artist against the Establishment
(London, 1992)

Gaunt, William
The Pre-Raphaelite Tragedy
(London, 1942)

Gaunt, William
The Aesthetic Adventure
(London, 1945)

Gaunt, William
Victorian Olympus
(London, 1949)

Gold, Arthur and Fizdale, Robert
The Divine Sarah: A Life of Sarah Bernhardt
(London, 1991)

Goldwater, Robert *Symbolism*
(London, 1979)

Hamilton, Walter
The Aesthetic Movement in England
(London, 1882)

Harbron, Dudley
*The Conscious Stone: The Life of
Edward William Godwin*
(London, 1949)

Harper Collins
Collins Complete Works of Oscar Wilde
(Centenary edition: Glasgow, 1999)

Harris, Frank
Oscar Wilde: His Life and Confessions
(New York, 1916)

Hart-Davis, Rupert (ed)
The Letters of Oscar Wilde
(London, 1962)

Hart-Davis, Rupert (ed)
More Letters of Oscar Wilde
(London, 1985)

Hichens, Robert
The Green Carnation
(ed. with an introduction by Stanley
Weintraub: Lincoln, 1970)

Hoare, Philip
*Oscar Wilde's Last Stand: Decadence,
Conspiracy, and the most Outrageous
Trial of the Century*
(New York, 1998)

Holland, Merlin
The Wilde Album
(London, 1997)

Holland, Vyvyan
Son of Oscar Wilde
(London, 1954)

Huysmans, Joris-Karl
Against Nature [A Rebours]
(trans. by Robert Baldick:
London, 1959)

Hyde, H. Montgomery
'Oscar Wilde and his Architect,
Edward Godwin',
Architectural Review
(London, March 1951),
pp.175–6

Hyde, H. Montgomery
The Trials of Oscar Wilde
(new paperback edition:
New York, 1973)

Hyde, H. Montgomery
Oscar Wilde
(paperback edition: London, 1977)

Jackson, Holbrook
*The Eighteen Nineties: A Review of Art and
Ideas at the Close of the Nineteenth Century*
(new illustrated edition with an
introduction by Christophe
Campos: Dublin, 1976)

James, Henry (ed. Leon Edel)
Letters
(4 vols, Cambridge, Mass.,
1974–80)

Kaplan, Joel H. and Stowell, Sheila
*Theatre and Fashion: Oscar Wilde
to the Suffragettes*
(Cambridge, 1994)

Kermode, Frank
The Romantic Image
(London, 1957)

Kohl, Norbert
*Oscar Wilde: The Works
of a Conformist Rebel*
(Cambridge, 1989)

Knox, Melissa
Oscar Wilde: A Long and Lovely Suicide
(Yale University, 1994)

Lambourne, Lionel
The Aesthetic Movement
(London, 1996)

Le Gallienne, Richard
The Romantic '90s
(New York, 1925)

Levy, Michael
The Case of Walter Pater
(London, 1978)

Lewis, L and Smith, H.J. *Oscar Wilde
Discovers America 1882*
(New York, 1936)

Maas, Duncan and Good (ed)
The Letters of Aubrey Beardsley
(London, 1971)

Matthieseb, F.O. and Murdoch, K.B.(ed.)
Notebooks of Henry James
(New York and Oxford, 1947)

McCormack, Jerusha (ed)
Wilde: The Irishman
(New Haven and London, 1998)

Merril, Linda
*A Pot of Paint: Aesthetics on Trial
in Whistler v. Ruskin*
(Washington, D.C. and London,
1992)

Milner, John
Symbolists and Decadents
(Studio Vista London, 1971)

Milner, John
The Studios of Paris
(Yale University, 1988)

Moers, Ellen
The Dandy: Brummell to Beerbohm
(Lincoln and London, 1978)

Morgan, Margery (comp.)
File on Wilde (comp.)
(Methuen Drama: London, 1990)

Ormonde, Leonee
George Du Maurier
(London, 1969)

Pearse, Joseph
The Unmasking of Oscar Wilde
(London, 2000)

Pearson, Hesketh
Gilbert and Sullivan
(London, 1935)

Pennell, Elizabeth and Joseph
The Life of James McNeill Whistler,
2 vols
(London and Philadelphia, 1908)

Pennington, Michael
*An Angel for a Martyr: Jacob Epstein's
Tomb for Oscar Wilde*
(Reading, 1987)

Penny, Nicholas
*Ruskin's Drawings in the
Ashmolean Museum*
(Oxford, 1988)

Perruchot, Henri
Toulouse-Lautrec
(tr. by Humphrey Hare:
London, 1994)

Peters, Robert L.
*The Crowns of Apollo:
Swinburne's Art Criticism*
(Detroit, 1965)

Pevsner, Nikolaus
*Studies in Art, Architecture and Design,
Vol.II: Victorian and After*
(London, 1968)

Powell, Kerry
Oscar Wilde and the Theatre of the 1890s
(Cambridge, 1990)

Quennell, Peter (ed)
*Marcel Proust 1871-1922
A Centenary Volume*
(London, 1971)

Raby, Peter (ed)
The Cambridge Companion to Oscar Wilde
(Cambridge, 1997)

Reade, Brian
Aubrey Beardsley
(London, 1967)

Reade, Brian
Sexual Heretics
(London, 1970)

Ricketts, Charles
Recollections of Oscar Wilde
(London, 1932)

Riesald, J.G.
Beerbohm's Literary Caricatures
(London, 1977)

Robertson, W. Graham
Time Was
(London, 1931)

Ross, Margery
Robert Ross: Friend of Friends
(London, 1919)

Rothenstein, John
The Life and Death of Charles Conder
(London, 1938)

Rothenstein, William
Men and Memories
(London, 1931)

Sansom, William
Proust
(London, 1973)

Schmidgall, Gary
The Stranger Wilde
(London, 1994)

Schroeder, Horst
*Additions and Corrections to
Richard Ellmann's 'Oscar Wilde'*
(privately printed, Braunschweig,
1989)

Sherard, Robert Harborough
The Real Oscar Wilde
(London, 1906)

Sherard, Robert Harborough
The Life of Oscar Wilde
(London, 1917)

Showalter, Elaine
*Sexual Anarchy: Gender and Culture
at the Fin de Siècle*
(New York, 1990)

Silverman, Debora L.
*Art Nouveau in Fin-de- Siècle France:
Politics, Psychology, and Style*
(Berkeley, Los Angeles,
London, 1989)

Small, Ian
*Oscar Wilde Revalued: An Essay on New
Materials and Methods of Research*
(Greensboro, 1993)

Spencer, Isobel
Walter Crane
(London, 1975)

Spencer, Robin
The Aesthetic Movement
(London, 1972)

Sutton, Denys
*Nocturne: The Art of
James McNeill Whistler*
(London, 1963)

Sweetman, David
Toulouse-Lautrec and the Fin de Siècle
(London, 1999)

Whistler, James McNeill Whistler
The Gentle Art of Making Enemies
(London, 1890; reprinted
New York, 1967)

Wilson, Simon
'A Newly Discovered Sketch by
Jacob Epstein for the Tomb of
Oscar Wilde',
Burlington Magazine, Vol. CXVII,
No.872 (Nov.1975), pp.726–9.

Worth, Katharine
Oscar Wilde
(Macmillan Modern Dramatists:
London: 1983)

Young, McLaren, Macdonald,
Spencer and Miles
The Paintings of James McNeill Whistler,
2 vols.
(New Haven and London, 1980)

Exhibition and Catalogue Collections

Arwas, Victor *Félicien Rops*
(Arts Council Touring
Exhibition, 1976-7)

Bowness, Engert, Jullian and Lacambre
French Symbolist Painters (London:
Hayward Gallery and Liverpool:
Walker Art
Gallery, 1972)

Bowness, Berresford, Gore, Gruetzner,
House, Rosenthal and Stevens, *Post-
Impressionism*
(Royal Academy of Arts, London,
1979–80)

Casteras, Suzan and Denney, Colleen
*The Grosvenor Gallery: A Palace of Art
in Victorian England*
(New Haven: Yale Centre for the
Studies of British Art, 1996)

Christian, John
The Last Romantics
(London: Barbican Art
Gallery, 1989)

Dorment, R. and MacDonald M.F.
James McNeill Whistler
(London: Tate Gallery, 1994)

Lacambre, Geneviève et al
Gustave Moreau 1826-1898
(Paris: Galeries nationales du
Grand Palais, 1999)

Lambourne, Lionel &
Calloway, Stephen
*The Studio - High Art and Low Life:
The Studio and The fin de siècle*
(London, 1993)

Le Normand-Romain, Antoinette
Rodin, Whiatler et la Muse
(Paris: Musée Rodin, 1995)

McConkey, Kenneth
Impressionism in Britain
(London: Barbican Art Gallery,
1995)

Pétry, Claude et al. *Jacques-Emile Blanche,
peintre (1861–1942)*
(Rouen: Musée des Beaux-Arts,
1997)

Robins, Anna Gruetzner
Modern Art in Britain 1910-1914
(London: Barbican Art
Gallery, 1997)

Soros, Suzan Weber
E.W. Godwin
(New York, 1999)

Stevens, MaryAnne and Hoozee, Robert
*Impressionism to Symbolism: The Belgian
Avant-Garde 1880-1900*
(London: Royal Academy
of Arts, 1994)

Tadié, Jean-Yves and Callu, Florence
Marcel Proust: l'écriture et les arts
(Paris: Bibliothèque nationale
de France, 1999)

Thomson, Richard
Toulouse-Lautrec (London: Hayward
Gallery, 1991)

Willett, John, Bowness, Sophie and
Robins, Anna Gruezner
*The Dieppe Connection: The Town and its
Artists from Turner to Braque*
(Brighton: The Royal Pavilion, Art
Gallery and Museum, 1992)

This index covers the catalogue section only, and artists/personalities are indicated by CATALOGUE NUMBER

✠ ACKNOWLEDGMENTS ✠

Editors' Acknowledgements

In researching the exhibition and compiling this book, we have been helped by a number of colleagues in the art world. Our first thanks are to Merlin Holland, who has advised us and worked closely with throughout. In particular, he performed as the interviewer in the sound installation, which forms an important part of the exhibition display, and he also graced this book with an essay that provides a new perspective on the position of his grandfather in late nineteenth-century art. We also thank Michael Barker, Declan Kiberd and Jonathan Fryer for their contribution of essays to this book. In the early stage of the organisation of the exhibition, we were inspired by the late David Rogers. We hope he would approve of the final result.

While we are greatly indebted to all the lenders for the realisation of this project, we are especially grateful for the kindness and patience of the following individuals, both in their public and private capacity, in providing invaluable information and helping the process of selection and loan process:

Victor and Gretha Arwas, Stephen Calloway, Sheila Colman, Anthony d'Offay, Patricia Evans, Dr Peter Funnell, Melanie Gardner, Catherine Haill, Barry Humphries, Richard Jefferies, Kyoko Jimbo, Christina Kennedy, Geneviève Lacambre, Mark Samuels Lasner, Christophe Leribault, Rupert Maas, Donald Mead, Andrew McIntosh Patrick, Hélène Pinet, Evelyne Posséme, Jane Roberts, Antoinette Romain, Peyton Skipwith, Peter Vernier, Norma Watt and Simon Wilson.

We are also grateful to our Barbican Art Galleries colleagues, especially John Hoole, who coined the title of the exhibition and with whom we have developed the concept; Louise Vaughan who has so reliably supported our research work and compilation of the catalogue, in addition to her share of loan administration; and Sophie Persson for her efficient assistance to the organisation of the exhibition.

In producing this book, we would like to thank Cangy Venables and Anne Jackson at Philip Wilson Publishers as well as the editor Mike Ellis; and Jonathan Barnbrook and his colleagues Jason Beard and Manuela Wyss for the innovative design.

Finally, we would like to thank our respective families Gos, Nicola and Christopher; and Maureen and Patrick, for their understanding and patience as well as for their moral and practical supports.

TS & LL

Photographic Credits

Barbican Art Galleries would like to thank all those lenders to the exhibition who have kindly supplied photographic material for the book. We extend particular thanks to the following:

ADAGP, Paris, p.83 (Fig.25), p.85 (Cat.39), p.95 (Cat.40); Bibliothèque Nationale de France, Paris p.56 (Fig.15); Max Beerbohm Estate p.41 (Cat.29), p.86 (Cat.25), p.93 (Cat.33); Bridgeman Art Library, London pp. 34-5 (Cat.84), p.35, p.45 (Cat.148), p.54 (Cat.149), p.80 (Cat.144), p.100 (Cat.63), p.101 (Cat.62), p.108 (Cats 92, 93), p.129 (Cat.181), p.119 (Cats 147, 150), p.120 (Cats 143, 145), p.128 (Cat.175); The British Library, London p.39 (Fig.8), p.51 (Fig.12); Courtauld Institute of Art, London p.100 (Cat.100), p.127 (Cat.176); DACS, London p.76 (Cat.163), p.83 (Fig.25), p.85 (Cat.39), p.95 (Cat.40), p.124 (Cat.162); The Detroit Institute of Arts p.17 (Fig.3); The Estate of Jacob Epstein p.104 (Cats 77, 78), p.105 (Cat.76); Mary Evans Picture Library, London p.10 (Fig.1), p.26 (Fig.4), p.33 (Fig.6), p.40 (Fig. 9), p.46 (Fig.11), p.52 (Fig.13), p.56 (Fig.16), p.71 (Fig.22), p.72 (Fig.23), p.77 (Fig.24), p.83 (Fig.25); The Estate of Augustus John p.108 (Cat.92) Jonathan Morris-Ebbs p.30 (Cat.38), p.31 (Cat.200d), p.31 (Cats 200 e, j, k, l); Musée d'Orsay, Paris p.59 (Fig.18), p.69 (Fig.20); The Estate of William Rothenstein p.45 (Cat.148), p.54 (Cat.149), p.80 (Cat.144), p.119 (Cats 147, 150), p.120 (Cats 143, 145); The Estate of Charles Ricketts p.114 (Cat.121), p.115 (Cats 124, 127), p.116 (Cat.128), Cat.117 (Cats 130, 131); Musée des Beaux-Arts, Rouen p.83 (Fig.25); The Estate of Charles Shannon p.128 (Cats 158, 160); V&A Picture Library, London p.29 (Cat.72), p.36 (Cat.46), P.111 (Cat.107), 116 (Cat.128); Wandsworth Museum (Wandsworth Council, London) p.42 (Fig.10)

143

BARBICAN CENTRE WOULD LIKE TO THANK ITS PARTNERS AND PATRONS FOR THEIR CONTINUED SUPPORT:-
KPMG, Linklaters, Clifford Chance, Merrill Lynch, Bloomberg, BP Amoco, Flemings, Christian Salvesen, Shelton Fleming

Works added to
*The Wilde Years: Oscar Wilde and the Art
of His Time*
Barbican Gallery, Barbican Centre
5 October 2000 – 14 January 2001

=+=+=+=+=+=+=+=+=+=+=+=+=+=+=+=+=+=+=+

Whistler's Venetian Etchings

It is often forgotten that Wilde as well as Ruskin
wrote an adverse review of Whistler's *Nocturne in Black
and Gold: The Falling Rocket*, c.1875 (Fig.3), commenting
that it was only worthwhile looking at for about the
same time that one looks at a real rocket – a quarter of
a second. Rather surprisingly, Whistler never castigated
Wilde for this criticism, and beyond the exchange of
a few cheery insults by telegram their lives in the early
1880s were spent in different parts of the world,
Wilde in America, Whistler in Venice.

Whistler began to practice etching in 1858, four
years before he first settled in London. There he found
inspiration in recording the river Thames, its shipping
and its tides, and the effect of light on water. This
work, requiring careful and meticulous notation,
was the ideal preparation for the creation of his
controversial 'Nocturnes'.

After the libel case and his bankruptcy, Whistler
was pursued by creditors. He continued to create
etchings to raise money, an interesting example being
Old Putney Bridge, 1878 (Cat.192), in which his study
of Japanese prints is apparent. With remarkable even-
handedness the Fine Art Society, which had organised
a subscription for the payment of Ruskin's legal costs,
now also gave Whistler a helping hand, commissioning
him to create a dozen etchings of Venice. At first
Whistler tried to meet the Christmas deadline set by
the Gallery for completion of the commission, despite
bitterly cold weather: 'I rashly thought I might hasten
matters by standing in the snow with an etching plate
in my hand and an icicle on the end of my nose.' But
the process would take far longer, as he remained in
Venice for fourteen months producing fifty etchings, a
hundred pastels and seven or eight paintings. In those
months Whistler came to know a Venice that other
artists seem never to have perceived, a city unknown
to the eyes of Ruskin or Turner, a city of elaborately
carved Renaissance façades in an advanced stage
of dereliction, palaces with crumbling walls as in

The Garden, scenes of human life and activities such as the gondoliers waiting for passengers seen in *The Traghetto*, or the dramatic scene in *Nocturne: Furnace*, probably inspired by the glare of a burning furnace at a glass works in Murano. In this composition, doorway and window form abstract shapes which frame the most dramatic visual element of the image.

Nocturnes continued to capture his imagination, such as *Nocturne: Salute* and *Nocturne: Palaces*, one of the most remarkable of his etched works, a plate to which he would return again and again, creating fascinating variations of effect by the varied tinting of the plate with ink of paler or warmer brown. The tonal values were created by wiping away the ink, a technique which ensured that practically every impression printed from these plates was an original work of art. By using such elaborate and daring techniques, Whistler could create etching of the utmost simplicity such as *The Littler Lagoon*, one of the most delicate of the Venetian etchings. It is a peaceful view captured with extraordinary economies of means, reminiscent in its minimal visual shorthand of the bold economy of the Japonist style of which Whistler was perhaps the greatest exponent.

On Whistler's return to London in November, 1880 to supervise the installation of the exhibition at the Fine Arts Society, he once more found a home in Tite Street, Chelsea and became a neighbour of Frank Miles and Oscar Wilde. At first the two wits got on really well, together often meeting with their mutual friend, the designer E.W. Godwin (p.107), who has left us a useful description of Whistler's exhibition, a subtle arrangement of gold and brown. The twelve Venetian etchings were criticised in some quarters as 'unfinished', but the pastels included in the same show sold well, Whistler netting 1,800 guineas from their sale. Entitled 'Arrangements in Yellow', the second exhibition in February 1883 saw the famous yellow and white installation carried out in the colour of flowers, pots, chairs, curtains, the assistants' neck-ties and even Whistler's socks at the Private View. (LL)

EX1
***The Little Lagoon**, 1879-80*
Second and final state (Kennedy 186; Lochnan 221), 22.5 x 15 cm
One of the 'Twelve Etchings' ('First Venice Set') exhibited at the Fine Art Society, December 1880
Private collection, London

EX2
***The Traghetto, No.2**, 1879-80*
Fourth state of six (Kennedy 191; Lochnan 187), 23.8 x 30 cm
One of the 'Twelve Etchings' ('First Venice Set') exhibited at the Fine Art Society, December 1880
Private collection, London

EX3
***Nocturne: Salute**, 1879-80*
Third state of five (Kennedy 226; Lochnan 218), 15.3 x 22.2 cm
Private collection, London

EX4
***Nocturne: Furnace**, c.1879-86*
Seventh and final state (Kennedy 213; Lochnan 225), 16.5 x 12.3 cm
One of the 'Twenty-six Etchings' ('Second Venice Set') published by Dowdeswell & Dowdeswell, 1886
Private collection, London

EX5
***The Garden**, c.1879-86*
Eighth and final state (Kennedy 210; Lochnan 201), 30 x 23 cm
One of the 'Twenty-six Etchings' ('Second Venice Set') published by Dowdeswell & Dowdeswell, 1886
Private collection, London

EX6
***Nocturne: Palaces**, c.1879-86*
Seventh and final state (Kennedy 202; Lochnan 201), 29 x 19.5 cm
One of the 'Twenty-six Etchings' ('Second Venice Set') published by Dowdeswell & Dowdeswell, 1886
Private collection, London

EX5